Cinema in the **Digital Age**

Cinema in the **Digital Age**

Nicholas Rombes

WALLFLOWER PRESS

LONDON & NEW YORK

First published in Great Britain in 2009 by
Wallflower Press
6 Market Place, London W1W 8AF
www.wallflowerpress.co.uk

A catalogue record for this book is available from the British Library

ISBN 978-1-905674-85-5 (pbk)
ISBN 978-1-905674-86-2 (hbk)

Book design by Elsa Mathern

Printed in India by Imprint Digital

Contents

'Assuredly, then, this world is a lie'
– Herman Melville, *Pierre*, 1852

'The Importance of Doing Things Badly'
– Essay by I. A. Williams, 1923

'By exchanging digital signals, zeros and ones, these life forms were able to manipulate more and more information. As a result, their survival rate went up. It was unmistakable: they'd acquired language.'
– Koji Suzuki, *Loop*, 1998

'Mistakism'
– term used by Harmony Korine, 2001

'I pressed Pause and enlarged the image again.'
– Bret Easton Ellis, *Lunar Park*, 2005

Acknowledgements

I am grateful to many people at the University of Detroit Mercy – faculty, students and administrators – whose support and intellectual curiosity have made the writing of this book possible. I am especially fortunate for my colleagues in the Department of English, as well as Stephen Manning in Political Science, who have helped in various ways. Our many conversations over the years have helped to shape and test the ideas in this book. Dean Charles Marske, of the College of Liberal Arts and Education, has been supportive of this project from the beginning. The students in my film classes have always been open to detecting the nearly invisible boundaries of ideology and I am thankful for their presence in my life. This project was partially supported by funding from the Mellon Funds for Humanistic Studies, University of Detroit Mercy, for which I am grateful.

There are several people whose writing has meant a lot to me over the years, including Marcel O'Gorman and Alejandro Adams. Deep gratitude goes to the many people at Wallflower Press, especially Yoram Allon and Jacqueline Downs, whose careful attention to the book undoubtedly made it stronger. I am also deeply grateful to Yoram for taking a chance on the non-traditional structure, and sometimes tone, of the book.

Most of all, I am grateful for the blessings of my family. My mom and dad provided a loving home where I was encouraged to ask the bigger questions. My children, Maddy and Niko: watching episodes of *Twin Peaks* with you at the end of our busy days· is something I will never forget. And to my wife, Lisa: you are my beautiful mystery.

Introduction

At the heart of the perfect digital image – coded by its clean binaries – is a secret desire for mistakes, for randomness, for what Dick Hebdige might call 'little disasters'. It is no coincidence that the Dogme 95 movement – with its preference for disorder, for shaky, degraded images, for imperfection – emerged at the dawn of the digital era, an era that promised precisely the opposite: clarity, high definition, a sort of hyper-clarified reality. The digital image threatens the fragility of the traditional logic of the image. Projection itself is disappearing; the old source of motion pictures as the light shot through a moving film was itself a sort of realism. Everyone knew what a projectionist did. They understood the source of the images. The shift from analogue to digital has occurred on two related levels: a symbolic one and a literal one. Literally, the differences between analogue and digital are complicated; frequently the word 'digital' is used as a kind of shorthand for a certain stance, a certain look betrayed by the image. But Leo Enticknap provides a good, basic definition of the terms:

> An easy way to imagine how analogue recording works is to think of it as an analogy: images or sounds are represented, or analogised, as continuously variable physical quantities which can be read and written by a machine which converts them to and from visible images and audible sounds…

> Digital media does not record a direct representation of a continuous process of chance. Instead, it represents that process as information, or data … That information takes the form of numbers, hence the word 'digital'…

> Representing recorded images and sounds digitally has one crucial advantage from which several others flow: digital data can be copied with 100 per cent accuracy, whereas an analogue recording cannot. (2005: 203)

Symbolically, the pristine, perfect, one-to-one replication promised by the digital haunts movies from the digital era (whether shot on digital cameras or not) such as *Fight Club* and *Doppelgänger*, which concern characters haunted by themselves or their virtual others. Tyler's/Jack's line in *Fight Club* – 'Everything is a copy, of a copy, of a copy' – spoken as he is making photocopies, is a secret recognition of the wonder and terror of the digital. As Enticknap notes, 'because the image or sound recording is represented as a series of numbers, it is only necessary to copy those numbers (the data) accurately ... in order to reproduce a "clone" or perfect reproduction of the original, totally free of any imperfections' (2005: 204).

In the digital era, the loop has become an indicator for the way information is stored, reproduced and recirculated with no generation loss. Digital media – ranging from music to video – can be copied with no weakening of the sound or image in a sort of reproducibility that, unlike human reproduction (at least for now) doesn't introduce errors or mistakes into the code. In Steven Hall's novel *The Raw Shark Texts* (2007), a character – Mycroft Ward – devises a method of immortality that allows his single self to inhabit more than one body. As part of the code that he writes to achieve this, he inserts an increased desire for self-preservation that results in unintended consequences: when, once a week, Ward 'synchronises' both his bodies, this preservation urge is looped back into his body:

> Every week, the system would deliver the preservation urge into Ward, who, with this urge in him increased, would amend the system accordingly, just slightly, in line with what he now thought to be a wise and suitable survival precaution. The now increased urge would feed back into him again the following week, making him increase its presence in the system again. Once it had begun, there was no way to stop the loop from gathering momentum. As the weeks passed, Ward became a slave to his own machine. (2007: 203)

One of the main claims of this book is that, haunted by the spectre of perfection, there is a tendency in digital media – and cinema especially – to reassert *imperfection*, flaws, an aura of human mistakes to counterbalance the logic of perfection that pervades the digital. It is no accident that the radical shrinking of the screen – down to a mere 2.5 inches with the video iPod – serves as a reminder of the screen's frailty, its smallness, its subjugation to human beings who can toss it casually on the couch or on a car seat. But it is not just on the small screen. What theorists miss in their laments about the cold reproducibility of the digital code is its degraded representation of reality, its habit of rendering cinematic images in a shaky, pixilated way. As Amy Taubin has noted regarding David Lynch's film *Inland Empire*, the 'PD-150 [a low-end digital camera] produces images that look like nothing but video. The visuals in *Inland Empire* look as if they're decomposing before your eyes' (2007: 57). This decomposition is akin to death, and it is the prospect of death that reminds you that you are living. There is something intimate and human in these decomposed images, something of a human signature within a technology that ostensibly offers perfect reproduction and that is, to return to Enticknap, 'totally free of any imperfections'.

The shift from analogue to digital became a widely discussed topic in the 1990s, with public figures like George Lucas and Roger Ebert respectively championing and declaiming the new technologies that were emerging not only in DV cameras, but in the very projection of film itself, with talk of digital theatres that don't project film at all, but rather digital information. Indeed, the very term 'film' remains as a sign of the uncertain transformation from analogue to digital. This book uses terms like 'films' and 'movies' even when describing 'movies' that are not shot on film, in part because no matter what technologies are used in the making, editing and projection of film, they are still haunted by the history and logic of cinema. This is not to say that the narrative and aesthetic dimensions of film – or any medium – are not shaped by the very technology and apparatus that gives them material form, but rather that change happens gradually and not always rationally. In any case, our language is always on one level a projection of our desires, in this case of my desire to keep in sight the profound ways that 'film' haunts the digital even in the face of rapid transformations. As novelist William Gibson once noted: 'Digital video reminds me of a new platform wrapped in the language and mythology of an old platform ... We call movies "film", but the celluloid's drying up' (1999: 2).

The key texts for digital cinema are not only movies, but books as well. It is in them that the digital imagination was born and still thrives. It is to Japan – the symbolic, if not literal, birthplace of the analogue – that we must turn for the clearest and most poetic articulation of the deeply alluring and unsettling threshold between digital and analogue. The novel *Ring* by Koji Suzuki, first published in Japan as *Ringu* in 1991, is a sustained and dark exploration of the viral nature of biological and image reproduction disguised as a horror novel. Although the Japanese film version (*Ringu*, 1998) and the American version (*The Ring*, 2002) differ in significant ways, they both remain true to the basic plot of the novel, which centres on a mysterious videotape that, once watched, results in the death of the viewer within days unless that viewer makes a copy of the tape and passes it on to others to watch. The dread of reproduction haunts the novel. Here is the narrator near the end of the book, confronted with the choice of dying or saving himself by forcing his wife and child to watch the tape:

> He couldn't help but wonder. *What effect is this going to have? With my wife's copy and my daughter's copy, this virus is going to be set free in two directions – how's it going to spread from there?* He could imagine people making copies and passing them on to people who'd already seen it before, trying to keep the thing contained within a limited circle so that it wouldn't spread. But that would be going against the virus's will to reproduce. There was no way of knowing yet how that function was incorporated into the video. (2003: 283; emphasis in original)

We could compare this to a passage in Chuck Palahniuk's novel *Lullaby* (2002) about a children's song that is lethal to anyone who hears it spoken:

> The culling song would be a plague unique to the Information Age. Imagine a world where people shun the television, the radio, movies, the Internet, magazines and newspapers. People have to wear earplugs the way they wear condoms and rubber gloves … Imagine a plague you catch through your ears. (2002: 41)

It is not, perhaps, the idea of replication that frightens today (after all, reproduction lies at the essence of who and how we are) but rather that we are continually haunted by images because they are so easily archived and dispersed. Surely there is no escape from the tyranny of images now. They literally do not go away, or disintegrate upon duplication. Efforts to disengage ourselves from them are met with accusations of bad faith or, worse, nostalgia. David Thomas – of the Cleveland proto-punk rock bands Rocket from the Tombs and Pere Ubu – has said the problem with music on the Internet is not only that it is disembodied, but that it is no longer fragile: 'The problem I have with [music on the Internet] is the lack of the object. I think the object is very important … Because the object, the fragility of the object lends weight to the art contained within it' (in Anon. 2005c: 2). If the original was gauged against the degradation of second- and third- and fourth-generation copies (and so on) of the analogue, then the digital leaves no obvious traces or clues about how far removed it is from the original. In Kazuo Ishiguro's *Never Let Me Go* (2005), a novel about people who are raised to serve, ultimately, as living organ donors for their counterparts, Kathy the narrator discusses the desire for the donors (not clones exactly, but humans created to provide harvested organs for their doubles) to meet their 'possibles': 'Since each of us was copied at some point from a normal person, there must be, for each of us, somewhere out there, a model getting on with his or her life. This meant, at least in theory, you'd be able to find the person you were modelled from' (2005: 139). The interplay between models and originals becomes a sort of shell game; at some point what does it matter, since they are both the same, anyway?

As optics teaches us, sometimes we need to look not directly at an object, but rather slightly askance at it, for it to register fully in our vision. In this case, diverting our glance from digital cinema itself to a trilogy of books that are concerned (even obsessed) with the digital shift. The aforementioned *Ring*, along with *Spiral* (1995), and *Loop* (1998) by Japanese author Koji Suzuki constitute a trilogy that explores links between the reproduction of images on a videotape and the reproduction of a deadly virus in human beings. At the heart of these novels is a larger, darker philosophical question that also haunts *Cinema in the Digital Age*: does the mass reproduction of the same images threaten to exterminate diversity, in the same way that the mass reproduction of a single virus might threaten to exterminate the diversity of life on earth? Suzuki uses the horror genre to look at questions that haunt our digital era. How can one determine, the novels wonder, the difference between what is 'real' and what is 'abstract' in our age of pristine digital reproduction? For instance, one thread of the novels concerns deciphering the images on a mysterious tape that prompts its viewers to die seven days after viewing it. The tape is so disturbing because the source of many of its images are impossible to trace; they seem to have no 'original'. In *Spiral*, we are reminded how Ryuji – a character from *Ring* – attempted to categorise the tape's images: 'For example, the volcanic eruption and the man's face were clearly things that had really been seen, while the firefly-like light in the darkness at the beginning of the tape looked like something conjured up by the mind – like something out of a dream. So Ryuji called the two groups "real" and "abstract", for comparison's sake' (2003: 122). These distinctions between realism and abstract, or avant-garde, are the foundations upon which film itself has been divided. But in the digital era, such categories are confounded, as so-called reality (for example, a shot of a forest, a speeding car or even a human face) can now be rendered artificially so that all vestiges of the real disappear, leaving only the appearance of reality. Indeed, a child today in a movie theatre is more likely to lean over and ask her father, *are they real?*, regarding leaves blowing in the wind rather than regarding some spectacular special effect. Reality is today's special effect.

In the trilogy's final novel *Loop* – published in Japan a year prior to the release of *The Matrix* – we learn that possibly everything that has happened in the prior two books occurred within a virtual reality loop created by scientists to test theories of evolution. In the virtual world of the loop – a world that mirrors our own – we see that the deadly virus being advanced by the videotape has indeed spread and is now being transmitted by something else: a book called *Ring*: '*Ring* would be a book, then a movie, a video game, an Internet site – it would saturate the world through every branch of the media', we learn (2006b: 191). The virus has become the first book in the trilogy, and then its movie adaptations. If readers are familiar with a novel or a film called *Ring*, does that mean they are themselves trapped in the loop, or have the works jumped from the loop into the 'real world'?

Similarly, the work of Japanese artist Nagi Noda – especially in her video for the pop star Yuki's song 'Sentimental Journey' – speaks to the beauty of imperfection in the digital era, when technologies push ever-forward into realms of greater and greater high definition and perfection. The film is one long take (approximately three minutes) that follows Yuki through a series of events. Yuki, however, never moves: what we see instead are dozens of live body doubles (and a few mannequins), each one frozen in position.

Rather than relying on CGI, Noda used real people. We see them trying to hold perfectly still as the camera slowly tracks past them from left to right, in the manner of *manga*. But inevitably they blink or sway slightly. And it is heartbreakingly human. In fact, it is almost thrilling to see this unfold, and we are shocked that in this digital era of flawless special effects there are 'mistakes' in the video – that the people are real and not digitally reproduced. 'It was shot all in-camera, in one big shot', Noda has said. 'Computers can create nice images, but if you are using [CGI] you must decide on all

The beauty of imperfection: real time in Nagi Noda's 'Sentimental Journey' video

of the details in advance. I really like to work in more of a live fashion, shooting in my eyes and treating the whole scene as an experiment' (in Hunter 2005: 44). The video tells a story, as well as a story about the story. That is, through a sort of 'slow' technique (the deliberate, steady tracking of the camera) and through the 'mistakes' of the blinking, moving versions of Yuki, we see not only the story the video is telling, but a story about how the film was made.

To suggest that popular, genre-driven books like the *Ring* trilogy offer a form of media theory more potent and provocative than many film and media theory books written today is, perhaps, obvious. As writers like Stephen Johnson have noted, popular television shows like *24* or *The Sopranos* offered complex narrative webs that involve 'multiple threading' (see 2005: 65–72) and that make demands on an active, rather than passive, audience. And a series like R. Kelly's hip-hop soap opera 'Trapped in the Closet' (the first twelve parts debuted in 2005, with ten further instalments showing on IFC.com beginning in August 2007) scrambles the expectations (is it serious, ironic, self-mocking, or all of these?) of viewers. The series features playful and complicated narrative shifts; music and pop culture writers like Kelefa Sanneh have noted the drift from first-person narration in the early episodes, to third person in later episodes (see 2007: 2). That the show asks viewers to think about narration – the shifts are obvious and call attention to themselves – is itself a form of theory.

If media tends to theorise itself today – and that is a central premise of this book – then what is the role of the critic, of the academic? One strategy might be to come at the topic indirectly, from odd and unexpected angles, through a variety of objects and texts – some filmic and some not – whose characteristics speak to our new era, where theory comes not from the academics, but from the very objects of academic critique. Using this approach, the following panel by graphic novelist Chris Ware might serve as an illustration of the same cultural logic that informs increasingly complex DVD menus and database narratives generally.

Ware's diagrammatic approach – a flat, shadowless, expanded-time flowchart dissection of narrative movement – has many influences, as Ware has acknowledged, especially from the fields of music and architecture. But I think his diagrammatic approach is also influenced by digital interfaces, which allow for the freezing of information for purposes of navigation. Like Ware's diagrams, DVD scene or chapter selection

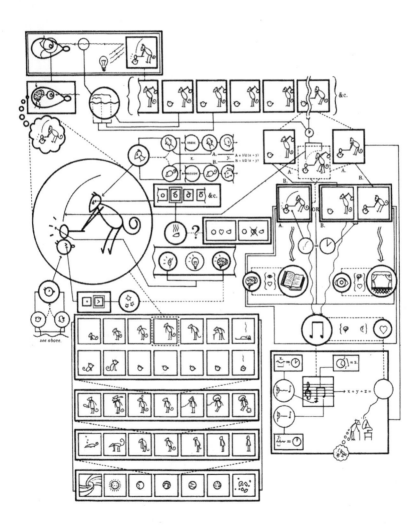

Navigating the interface in Chris Ware's *Quimby the Mouse*: a distant cousin of the DVD menu?

menus operate as a mixture of text and image that allows the viewer some choice in navigation, and also invites a more active readerly role. In Ware's illustration, one moment in time – the hitting on the head with a mallet – is surrounded by boxes and circles that provide various levels of context. In one, for instance, a dotted line connects the action to a square in a timeline showing that the mouse was in the middle of his life when he wielded the hammer, which leads to yet another time-line that shows the action happening during the middle part of the earth's lifespan, somewhere in between its creation and its destruction. It is a sort of vast archive of moments in time. We know there is a narrative there, but we are not sure how to fol-low it or what it means.

The benefits of such an approach are that it allows for a less predictable, even chance-based form of research, one that acknowledges the mistakist elements of digital cinema, and one that turns film scholarship away from the unfortunate social sciences model that still dominates it today. For, as this book argues, part of the allure of digital video lies not in its perfection, but rather its imperfection. 'The quality [of DV] is pretty terrible', David Lynch said in 2006, in advance of the release of *Inland Empire*, 'but I like that. It reminds me of the early days of 35mm, when there wasn't so much information in the frame or emulsion. But the human being is a beautiful creature; you act and react, and the medium starts talking to you. So I love working in digital video. High-def is a little bit too [much] information for me' (in Thill 2006: 4). If there is one idea that binds this book together, then hopefully it is this: that in the ruptures and gaps that have opened up as cinema transitions from the traditional analogue apparatus to the digital, there has been an unexpected resurgence of humanism – with all its mistakes, imperfections and flaws – that acts as a sort of countermeasure to the numerical clarity and disembodiment of the digital code. I am acutely aware of the tendency – still dominant, I would say – in cultural and cinema studies to 'debunk' every new innovation as just another tool to be co-opted by the dominant forces. While I am sensitive and in many ways sympathetic to such readings, I must confess that at the end of the day, my thinking has been deeply influenced by writers such as André Bazin, who maintained a critical distance from the films and styles he wrote about even as he recognised and opened himself up to the risk of falling under their deeper, almost magical power.

The 2007 'faux-Grindhouse' features by Quentin Tarantino and Robert Rodriguez are perhaps the clearest and most tortured mainstream expression of the conflicted shift from film (literal film) to digital. The movies, released theatrically in the US as a double feature (Rodriguez directed the zombie film *Planet Terror*; Tarantino directed the road-killer movie *Death Proof*) that also included fake trailers, were a widely commented on (though financially disappointing) homage to the 1970s B-cult grindhouse movies that were shown in notoriously imperfect conditions. The films included a host of built-in 'mistakes', such as scratches, unmotivated cuts, blurs, distracting sounds and announcements about missing reels. Rather than simply a cynical, postmodern pub-licity stunt (or perhaps in addition to that) the films are, as Rob Vaux has suggested,

The opening to *Death Proof*: nostalgia for analogue 'residual culture'

an 'understated experiment in cinematic theory' (2007: 2). *Planet Terror* was shot on digital video, while *Death Proof* was shot on film. Paradoxically, while Rodriguez used digital effects to make his digital film look like it was celluloid-based, the final, elaborate stunt sequence in *Death Proof* was shot using no CGI, no green screens, providing a level of danger that looks as if, ironically, it *must* have been shot using special effects. This is one of the strange side effects of the heightened realism of digital effects in cinema: it creates a nostalgia for the 'less realistic' special effects and stunts of analogue cinema, which look more impressive than ever today precisely because they were *not* digitally created. In the end, *Planet Terror* and *Death Proof* are about the experience of watching flawed movies whose creation and projection are marked by human error and the effects of time. A film that ages and that shows its age with missing frames, pops, hisses or graininess is a reminder of the history and material foundation of the film's creation. To strip away the visible signs of a film's history – to enhance it – is to cleanse it of its age, which perhaps tells us more about our own desires than anything about the film.

In the digital age, there is nostalgia for what Raymond Williams termed 'residual culture', which he defined as 'experiences, meanings and values . . . [which are] lived and practiced on the basis of the residue – cultural as well as social – of some previous social formation' (2001: 170). In cinema, this involves not only movies whose content hearkens back to the 1970s (such as *American Gangster*), but movies whose very texture is nostalgic for the golden era of analogue warmth and super saturated colours. *Planet Terror* and *Death Proof* reflect upon the physical *experience* of going to movies and the humanising elements of the 'mistakes' that characterised that experience. Of course nostalgia is a paradox, as the very elements longed for existed, at one point, in the present. Audiences viewing grindhouse movies in the 1970s were as likely to be frustrated by the imperfect viewing conditions, the pops and hisses on the screen, the scratchy prints. Nostalgia for these conditions emerges as digital technologies make it possible to 'scrub' away these imperfections, which betrayed traces of the human beings who made the films, owned the theatres, projected the movies, turned out the lights and swept the popcorn and candy wrappers up at the end of the night. The feeling that something has been lost goes deeper than nostalgia for a different kind of movie. Instead, it is a lament for the residue of, as Williams suggests, a 'social formation' such as the mundane qualities of everyday life included in the social experience of sitting in the dark with strangers laughing and complaining about the imperfections of the movie theatre experience.

Another theoretical approach made possible by the digital archive is something we might call the *theory of convergences*. This exploits the database archive to select images from separate times and places that seem haunted by each other. This method is adapted from Lawrence Weschler, whose book *Everything that Rises* (2006) juxtaposes seemingly unrelated images in ways that reveal secret correspondences. 'I have increasingly found myself', he writes, 'being visited by … uncanny moments of convergence, bizarre associations, eerie rhymes…' (2006: 1). Such a method recognises the potential for randomness in the cinema, and, even further, of the randomness that digital systems make possible. Lev Manovich has noted that 'Historically, the artist made a unique work of art within a particular medium. Therefore, the interface and the work were the same; in other words, the level of interface did not exist. With new media, the content of the work and the interface become separate' (1998: 5). One of the more radical consequences of this separation is that works of art – unmoored from the historical conditions of their production – are more easily exchangeable across time. The result is that old images and new are in play with one another, creating opportunities to see correspondences that may have remained buried previously.

The digital database – exemplified by the resurrection of older films that are restored, contextualised and made affordable and easily available – makes it possible to tune in to the echoes between film images across years. While there likely always will be a need for rationalist, formalist, methodical film criticism, what the digital database opens up is the possibility for a different approach, one that performs the randomness inherent in the digital system. The two women from *Man with a Movie Camera* and *The Ring* – separated by over seventy years and different continents – are united in the digital era. Once we see the stills side by side, we notice strange similarities:

Man with a Movie Camera	**The Ring**
• An avant-garde film	• A genre film hiding an avant-garde video inside it
• A woman edits the film we watch	• The video inside the film we watch edits us
• The film periodically stops or freezes	• The video inside the film is periodically stopped, or paused by those looking for clues to its meaning

Strange correspondences #1: editing the film we are watching in *Man with a Movie Camera*

Strange correspondences #2: watching the video-tape, looking for clues in *The Ring*

The digital archive – and the easy retrieval of images on DVDs, the Internet and other places – makes it possible to notice strange correspondences between film images, a sort of secret history. Imagine a history of cinema that traced these patterns, these hauntings, where images jump across time and suddenly reappear in the most unexpected of places, so that an experimental film like *Man with a Movie Camera* can exist in the same family tree as *The Ring*. In this form of investigation, terms like 'intention' and 'genre' need to be reinvented, for what links films together is not simply their plots, their styles, their directors, but something less coherent. Technology has stripped away a layer, and exposed uncanny associations that – thankfully – haven't been transformed yet by academics into a rigorous method for interpretation. Throughout this book, I have tried not only to articulate some possible avenues for film theory in the digital age, but to give shape to those theories on the page itself. Thus, *Cinema in the Digital Age* is arranged in such a way that corresponds, in spirit and metaphorically, to the database structures of the digital system.

I have been inspired by books such as Walter Benjamin's *The Arcades Project* (1927–40), Guy Debord's *The Society of the Spectacle* (1967), Raymond Williams' *Keywords* (1976), DJ Spooky's *Rhythm Science* (2002), Susan Sontag's 'Notes on "Camp"' (1964), George W. S. Trow's *Within the Context of No Context* (1981) and others, although I lay no claim to matching the insight and vitality of these projects. Instead, my modest hope is that the book takes shape in reaction to digital cinema in a way that both performs its logic, and resists it. Upon Jean Baudrillard's death, Arthur Kroker wrote that Baudrillard 'approached the delirium of contemporary reality with the delirious methods of art' (2007: 1). That delirious method was a risk that paid off, for at their best, Baudrillard's writings threatened the illusions of reality with equally compelling illusions.

In college, I had an English professor who, when asked about the formatting of a paper that was due soon, responded with something to the effect of, 'Let whatever you are writing about determine the format of your paper.' Of course, to follow his advice in any of my other classes would have amounted to academic suicide, and yet

I knew that his answer was the most honest I would ever receive. The delayed result of his advice is the book you are now holding in your hands, a book whose content is arranged not by chapter but by key words and phrases, listed alphabetically, with a bundled set of corresponding key words in brackets that serve as a sort of mini-index for the entry at hand. The reader is encouraged to read straight through, or to skip around and see where chance, and random access, takes her.

The Adorno Paradox
[Theodor Adorno]

In 1938, under the growing shadow of Nazism, the philosopher Theodor Adorno left Europe for the US, where he began an intense collaboration with Max Horkheimer. In his essay 'Culture and Administration' Adorno wrote: 'The film, above all, because of the scope of costs which can be met only through investment, is dependent upon a type of planning analogous to that of public administration' (1991a: 121). Writing from within an administered cultural apparatus that suppressed chance and spontaneity, Adorno recognised that the Hollywood film industry largely excluded 'arbitrariness in favour of an objectively regulated process ... But it is precisely art which gives voice to the seemingly individual and coincidental which is now to be the subject of total aesthetic prohibition' (1991a: 122). This arbitrariness, this chance, is the revenge of reality in the face of digital coding. And yet, paradoxically, Adorno's writing style appears highly ordered and consistent; there is almost a fatalism, a determinism that seems closed off to chance. In 'Transparencies on Film' he wrote that 'the consumers are made to remain what they are: consumers. That is why the culture industry is not the art of the consumer but rather the will of those in control onto their victims' (1991b: 185). There is a victory to those words that is both inspiring and defeating. Cinema, for Adorno, was not only a massively closed read-only system, but also the catalyst for his beautifully pessimistic writing. Without film's closed system, there would be no need for Adorno's assaultive writing. Hollywood cinema helped to make possible the very form of critique Adorno claimed was impossible. His writing proves the lie to the very claims it makes. It is paradoxical how completely the tables have turned: for now it is film theory which has become domesticated, safe and predictable, while digital cinema makes possible new and potentially radical ways of storytelling, and introduces interface systems that suggest a form of theory and critique. The challenge today is to write about digital cinema in ways that are as spontaneous and humanistic as cinema itself.

Against Method
[punk, Orson Welles]

In 1975, the year before punk broke, the philosopher Paul Feyerabend, in *Against Method*, wrote about how science needs and depends upon irrationality if it is to advance. Defending how science must in fact even return to older theories before the prevailing status quo can be overturned, he noted that 'This backward movement isn't just an accident; it has a definite function; it is essential if we want to overtake the status quo, for it gives us the time and the freedom that are needed for developing the main view in detail' (1988: 114). Both punk, in its 1970s incarnation, and early digital cinema, were 'primitive' in the sense that they rejected the very excesses that made them possible in the first place. How far is it from Feyerabend's 'against method' to Dogme 95's rejection of 'aesthetic considerations'? Well, twenty years, and the transformation of the punk aesthetic into a subversive mistakist shadow in the clean digital code. What Feyerabend recognised in 1975 – and what shortly thereafter was confirmed by punk and then later rearticulated by the early digital avant-gardists – was that 'mistakes' (in the form of playing instruments badly, or noise feedback, or shaky, hand-held camera shots, or irrationality in science) were preconditions for advancement. Simon Frith, in describing early punk rock, has noted that the 'punk vanguard turned such musical reference into artistic purpose: they queried the "naturalness" of musical language. Beginning with the assumption that all music is constructed, they sought to strip it down to its foundations' (1981: 162). The return to basics – a sort of primitivism – that was punk's early signature was also digital cinema's early signature, especially in the first films of the Dogme 95 movement, and in *The Blair Witch Project*, which offered a cinematic vision that was as incoherent and hysterical and shaky as its characters. In a sense, the do-it-yourself ethos of digital cinema and desktop moviemaking was a 'correction' to the overblown, overbudgeted movies of the 1980s and 1990s. But digital cinema differed from the indie film movement (that is, Steven Soderbergh's *sex, lies, and videotape*, the films of Jim Jarmusch and so forth) in its unmannerliness and its anti-art ethos. There is a raw ugliness to films like *The Idiots* or *julien donkey-boy* that is more akin to early punk than to the artful, well-intentioned indie movies associated with the Sundance Film Festival in the 1980s and 1990s.

My copy of *Against Method* is stamped 'From the Library of Angela & Johann Klaassen'. I have no idea who these people are, yet I hold a book that belonged to them in my hands. I read passages that they underlined. I try to decipher doodles. On the title page, someone has written, in beautiful lettering, KLAASSEN 525. Is this a numbering system, indicating # 525 in the family library? There is a sort of randomness at work that has lead to the printing of the name KLAASSEN in this book, *Cinema in the Digital Age*, that you are now holding in your hands. I will likely not ever correspond with or meet with them, any more than I will meet with you. And yet, here we are, together, briefly, the product of a momentary abandonment of the *methods* that have guided other parts of this book. And that personal touch, that almost sentimental humanism, is precisely what punk and what do-it-yourself digital cinema sought to re-establish: a personal connection achieved by stripping away the inherited artifice of generations.

For what was the classical era of film, other than an exercise in method, of which a film like *Citizen Kane* is but a point-by-point example, professional and flawless despite Welles' reputation as an unpredictable 'outsider'? The paradox is that the entire 'invisible editing' aesthetic of the classical era was, in fact, an elaborate method of the most visible sort. For the self-consciousness of films like *Citizen Kane* and *Sunset Blvd.* only served to highlight the supposed invisibility of other Hollywood studio films. And, as any good cynic would correctly point out, the 'return to basics' of digital movements like Dogme 95 was just as much a method. But there is a crucial difference: in foregrounding and publicising their 'method', the Dogme 95 directors (most notably Lars von Trier and Thomas Vinterberg) effectively rendered it pointless. Near the opening of *Festen* (*The Celebration*) as Christian is walking along a country road bordered by golden wheat, he says that 'I'm looking across the fields. At the land of my father. It's beautiful.' He could be talking, really, about his father's fields, or he could be talking (in secret code, to us) about the sort of beautiful film that was a staple of the classical era, that someone of his father's era would have made. This is a sorrowful recognition: that the degradation of the Dogme films is only possible against the beauty of the classical-era films of Welles, Douglas Sirk, William Wyler, Alfred Hitchcock and others who exploited the classical method to create surfaces so smooth they were positively disruptive, and signalled an invitation for future filmmakers. The gentle ironies of Sirk and Welles – the stylistic recognition in their films that their characters were just characters – was transformed in the Dogme films into a sort of brutal overexposure: in *The Celebration* and *The Idiots* the characters are so sincere that the only way to see them is through irony. And thus seeing them, you are complicit.

Analogue/Digital Splice

[*The Blair Witch Project*, The Dils, William Vollmann]

In *Within the Context of No Context*, the essayist George W. S. Trow wrote that the 'work of television is to establish false contexts and to chronicle the unravelling of existing contexts; finally, to establish the context of no-context and to chronicle it' (1981: 82). Rather than diminish in the face of digital media, television's basic interface dominates; the interrupted, click-through nature of television was an early form of web surfing. There is no context on the Internet, there is just the Internet. In a sense, this is true of all representation, and not that dissimilar to Walter Benjamin's insight that a work of art, reproduced, loses its aura. And yet, what if the context of television is television itself? For that matter, what if the context of any form of representation is representation? In this light, the disparate video clips – narrative, historical, animated, live-action, musical, amateur, professional and so forth – in places such as YouTube are not so much de-historicised postmodern surfaces as the fabric of a specific context: the context of YouTube. Television's 'heightened degree of self-consciousness in story-telling mechanics' (Mittell 2006: 39) noted by Jason Mittell, Steven Johnson and others is more than simply a shift towards complexity in storytelling. Rather, the mechanics of storytelling in the digital era have become the story itself.

Again, *The Blair Witch Project* – that pre-digital digital film – is a key document of the digital era. Because it is a genre film – and a horror film at that – it will probably never achieve the sort of critical respect given to less innovative but more artistically self-conscious so-called avant-garde films. Despite what we might think about the postmodern deconstruction of distinctions between High and Low cultural categories, film theory still tends to circle the wagons around supposedly avant-garde film in the face of mass, commercialised culture. During the 1970s punk era, distinctions in music between avant-garde (Karl Stockhausen) and pop (Velvet Underground, Ramones, Sex Pistols) were blurred, so that even popular press fanzines and newspapers included references to abstract art and music in their coverage of emerging pop bands. 'A Dils perfomance' wrote Greg McLean in a 1979 issue of the *New York Rocker*, 'is not a quirky artistic foray into the rock avant-garde, and it's not a safe, slick "new wave" act like the Police either' (1979: 19). The first wave of self-consciously digital films from the mid-1990s to the early 2000s, such as *The Blair Witch Project*, *The Celebration* and *julien donkey-boy* served as a reminder that genre and avant-garde films don't need to be mutually exclusive.

Shot on 16mm black-and-white film, and on a Hi-8mm consumer video camera bought from the retail store Circuit City, *The Blair Witch Project* itself acts as a splice between the analogue and digital eras. There is so much talk of the cameras throughout the film, especially early on, that by the time the most formally radical and experimental section unfolds, near the end, we see that the film literally runs out, and dies, with the characters. Near the beginning, conversations like this integrate the process of filmmaking into the movie itself:

Josh:	I'm checking my depth of field charts to see how bad…
Heather:	So you measure for metres? What? We're not in Europe!
Josh:	Yeah well the fucking lens has metres on it.
Heather:	It also has, it also has our system.
Josh:	Nah, it has metres on it.
Heather:	This is an American camera though.
Josh:	All those are metres.
Heather:	What about the brown ones?
Josh:	The brown ones are feet.

Exchanges like this about how to shoot the film that we are watching are more than empty, postmodern parlour tricks; they correspond to the very form and structure of the film itself, which is dual-narrated in the sense that part of it is shot from the perspective of two separate cameras. If *The Blair Witch Project* has any literary equivalent, it would be the fractured, time-bent aesthetics of the modernists, especially John Dos Passos, Virginia Woolf and James Joyce. The dual-narrated tempo of *The Blair Witch Project* – alternating between the 16mm and Hi-8 video perspectives – reaches its high point at the end of the film, when the shifts between these two points of view become more frequent. We are presented not only with alternating takes of the same events, but with alternating technological renderings of those events, as Heather (using the 16mm camera) and Mike (using the video camera) search an abandoned house for Josh, whose screams they think they hear. The sequence ends as Heather follows Mike into the basement, only to find him standing in the corner, facing the wall. She screams his name. Something violent happens to her, and her camera falls on the ground giving us a fixed, sideways view of the basement as the film jitters. The film ends, as does she.

The last images we see are from the analogue camera; then the screen goes black. *The Blair Witch Project* is a haunting film not only because of its ghosts, which remain forever off-screen, but because it foretells a transition into the digital, whose speed means that it doesn't need to be 'processed'. And of course there is an implied invisible hand at work behind the film and the fictional framing of its finding, as one or more people must have edited the 'found' footage into the movie we have watched. Yet this person or group remains invisible, their motives unknown, the footage they have excluded unavailable, and their role in the shaping of the narrative as mysterious as the fates of its protagonists.

The closest relative to the poetics of digital cinema might not be earlier cinematic movements (such as *cinéma vérité*, the French New Wave and so forth) but recent works of literature (with their own traditions) that have emerged out of the same cultural broth as digital cinema. William T. Vollmann's seven-volume 'moral calculus' of world violence – *Rising Up and Rising Down* – is an elaborate maze, part scholarly history, part autobiography, part documentary. Throughout the volumes, Vollmann periodically addresses the reader: 'I invite you to read each "theoretical" chapter with the moral calculus volume in hand, because it is there that the chapter in question has been boiled down to its own verbatim skeleton' (2003: 52). The volumes are filled with photos, illustrations, statistical tables, charts and graphs – including a 'Calculus of Righteousness' table. Very early on, we see that the project is about much more than its ostensible subject – violence – and that the book's performance of this subject is what commands our attention. What becomes clear is that Vollmann's project of concocting a moral calculus of violence is doomed to failure; but it is a beautiful failure, which is perhaps the point. Vollmann's book – like films including *Magnolia*, *Being John Malkovich*, *Fight Club*, *Memento*, *Mulholland Dr.*, *Ten*, *Inland Empire*, *Eternal Sunshine of the Spotless Mind* or *The Science of Sleep* – is really about the process of its own telling. Today, we can no longer simply dismiss these meta-textual digressions as 'postmodern parlour tricks' because these 'tricks' in fact constitute narrative itself. *Stories about the telling of stories have become a dominant narrative mode of our time.* As such, they constitute the splice between analogue and digital, realised most fully by films such as *The Blair Witch Project*.

And yet there is a paradox: for although we often think of early digital filmmaking such as *The Celebration* as being chaotic verging on anarchic, there is an element of control at work in the technology that minimises risk. Cinematographer John Bailey – who has worked on both analogue and digital films – has said that 'One thing that is terrifying but also very magic about [analogue] film is that it's an inexact science. It's analogue, it's unpredictable. You don't always know what you're going to see and things sometimes turn out differently than what you think' (in Roman 2001: 114–15). He contrasted this with digital video, which is 'like looking at your negative as you're exposing it' (in Roman 2001: 115). Digital video might be more spontaneous, but it is no more risky than analogue, which has traditionally required a leap of faith and delayed gratification: there is no immediate capture of reality in analogue, but rather captured images that need to be 'processed'.

Boredom and
Analogue Nostalgia

There is nostalgia today not only for the supposed aesthetic warmth of analogue cinema, but for the experience of actually, physically going to movies rather than having them come to you via home theatre systems, the Internet and mobile devices. Paradoxically, the home video era – which heralded the end of the classical cinematic experience – was also an era of boredom, memorialised in punk's anthems (the Ramones sang 'now I wanna have something to do' while the Sex Pistols sang 'oh we're so pretty/oh so pretty we're vacant'). In 1972, *National Lampoon* devoted an issue to boredom, featuring Bonnie Boredom on the cover, staring out at readers like a demented Betty Crocker, and wearing a badge that proclaimed 'I'M BORED'. In the opening editorial, George W. S. Trow considered the boredom of self-criticism sessions, Grateful Dead concerts, organic vitamins, Yoko Ono, Woodstock and 'your tedious Multi-Media in the Third World Studies program' (1972: 4). Later in the issue, a list of boring topics that included air-pollution statistics, cancer research, counterculture, cult murders, disarmament talks, economic sanctions, emerging nations, famines, gay liberation, generation gap, goodwill missions, holiday-death-toll predictions, juntas, labour unrest, nonviolent protest, nuclear holocaust, penal reform, police brutality, population explosion, poverty programmes, race riots, sexual revolution, skyjacking, Third World struggle, urban renewal, wage and price controls, and welfare cases. The sheer weight of 'issues' had become too much as cities in the UK and the US were faltering and crumbling in economic distress; the utopian idealism of the 1960s had been drained off, leaving a bitter residue of guilt, narcissism and boredom, a vacuum that punk filled. In 1976, the Buzzcocks wrote a song called 'Boredom': 'You know me – I'm acting dumb/you know the scene – very humdrum/ boredom – boredom'. These lines had the ringing endorsement of truth, and that was punk's solution: to transform boredom into a premise of modern life.

In the *SCUM Manifesto*, radical-feminist would-be-assassin of Andy Warhol, Valerie Solanas included an entry on Boredom that read: 'Life in a society made by and for creatures who, when they are not grim and depressing are utter bores, can only be, when not grim and depressing, an utter bore' (1968: 8). It was as if the Great Society had produced nothing so much as boredom, as the idealism of the 1960s deflated into real-isation that even though Nixon was on his way out and the Vietnam War was over, not that much had changed, after all. 'The Great American Soap Opera', declared the cover of the *Village Voice* in 1974, a week after Nixon resigned the Presidency on 9 August, the Fords replacing the Nixons. Alexander Cockburn wrote: 'Now we're talking here strictly about iconography: the new images, not the new political realities. And alas the new iconography is, at first sight, not encouraging. In the great American soap opera we've gone from grand guignol to family charades in a couple of days, from Key Biscayne and San Clemente to the boring good cheer of a Washington suburb' (1974: 8).

In that same issue, the *Village Voice* ran an advertisement for a Panasonic Concord half-inch videotape recorder that recorded and played back from 'any CCTV camera or monitor'. Although Sony's Betamax would not be introduced to markets until 1975, followed shortly thereafter by VHS, the dawn of affordable, compact home taping and viewing had arrived. The advertisement for the Concord, with its sleek, box-like struc-ture and tape reels that demystified the apparatus behind video images appeared alongside advertisements for *Serpico*, *The Conversation* and *Chinatown*, movies today associated with the Technicolor warmth and boldness of the New American Cinema. There is nostalgia not only for the content of these movies, but for their mediums, as well, which conjure boring, hot summer days of wandering around the city, taking in a movie to escape the heat in the dark. The boredom of the day, and the boredom of the long, slow takes in *The Conversation*, soon to be replaced by the fast-forward and rewind capabilities of the VCR, and then the instant-everywhere of digital, which leaves no space for boredom.

The Digital Spectacular
[Guy Debord, screen composition]

In 1967, in *The Society of the Spectacle*, Guy Debord wrote that 'Whatever lays claim to permanence in the spectacle is founded on change, and must change as that foundation changes' (1995: 46). To ask questions today about the ideological foundations of the digital imaginary smacks of bad faith, of the old academic retreat into the ivory tower matrix of uncomfortable and anachronistic language that suggests a power that is not there. What is the proper response – the proper theory – in the face of a global digital spectacular that is so busy evolving and changing that to write critically about it amounts to an act of nostalgia? The coming disembodiment of cinema in the digital era – films will arrive in public theatres via transmissions – means that their locations will always be the screen. They will have no source, so to speak. 'When the world, or reality, finds its artificial equivalent in the virtual, it becomes useless', Jean Baudrillard has written. 'When everything can be encoded digitally, language becomes a useless function' (2001: 40). The old cinematic syntax – crosscutting, montage, ellipses, dissolves, fade-ins and fade-outs, establishing shots – were responses not to a certain way of seeing images, but to a certain way of making them. They were expressions of technology, raised to the level of art and commerce. The ubiquity of digital motion picture technology today (even the cheapest digital still camera contains a digital video function) makes moving images more natural in the sense that they correspond more closely than ever before to our experience of everyday reality. The Dogme 95 'Vow of Chastity', with its rules about on-location shooting, natural lighting and hand-held camera movement is really a statement about film's ability to reflect back to us the reality that we already know. The camera must he hand-held because it *can* be hand-held. There must be no artificial light because the camera doesn't *need* any artificial light. In this regard, the Dogme rules are not rules at all, but rather statements of everyday fact about digital cameras. Many films in the digital era seem not overly concerned with elaborate framing and the poetics of *mise-en-scène*, not because filmmakers are lazy or lacking a strong visual sense but because the casual informality that marks our time marks our cinema, as well.

In the digital era, the frame replaces the screen as the dominant interface. The screen exists only insomuch as its frame brings it to life. If the size of the screen is more varied than ever before – and if users can exercise more control over its dimensions than previously – it is only because the frame is more available, more tenuous, more fragile. Movies on the big theatre screen. Movies on television. On computer screens. On cell phones. On iPods. And with each interface, a multitude of varieties, of dimensions. And on DVDs – and television sets – the ability to manipulate and select aspect ratios. As Anne Friedberg has noted: 'The window's metaphoric boundary is no longer the singular frame of perspective – as beholders of multiple-screen "windows", we now see the world in spatially and temporally fractured frames, through "virtual windows" that rely more on the multiple and simultaneous than on the singular and sequential' (1993: 243).

Today, almost anyone can make a film in the same way that almost anyone can write a story or a poem, or take a picture, or paint one. It is an obvious point, perhaps, but one worth making, because this was not always the case. Unavailable or mysterious technologies were always one of the elements that conferred an aura of mystery upon movies. Not only were they experienced in the dark, but audiences were largely in the dark about just how they were made. At the same time that theorists in the 1970s were busy demystifying the filmic 'apparatus' for students, the students were busy learning how to make their own movies on videotape. Learning how to use and manipulate the technology served a double purpose: in addition to teaching them the material conditions of ideology (thus weaning them from the need for theory), it also eroded the need for 'technique'. Without the elaborate process of setting up a shot during the classical era (lighting, sound, focus and so forth) the ready-made capabilities of digital cameras reconfigure what it means to 'frame' a shot. The careful *mise-en-scène* of Douglas Sirk, Roman Polanski or Stanley Kubrick gives way to a sort of first-person, subjective, shaky reality that is narcissistic, and thus tragically human. For it could be said that, rendered through the elaborate, expensive apparatus of classical cinema, human beings were, for the most part, configured as objects to be arranged in screen space. They were 'developed' in the same way that film stock was developed. The slow process of analogue moviemaking encouraged a deliberate and careful form of screen composition; they were aesthetic choices that arose out of specific technological limitations. As the studio system developed – and as the arrival of sound made it more practical to shoot indoors – screen space was carefully composed for many reasons, not least of which was because it was easier to move and rearrange the objects and people being filmed than to move the heavy camera. Today, when the dominant source of screen movement is the camera, camera mobility is no longer exceptional. In fact, movies like *Russian Ark*, *The Celebration*, *Ten* and *Timecode* are notorious not for their camera movement, but for moments when the camera is not moving.

Disposable Aesthetics

A style seemingly shorn of all calculation. Although it isn't new to the digital era, the technologies of the era make possible the replication and reproduction of the style across global markets. The style has its modern roots in the cinema of Italian neo-realism, although its key films are diverse:

Rome, Open City
Germany Year Zero
Faces
Pink Flamingos
The Foreigner
Gummo
The Blair Witch Project

One of the most striking characteristics of this disposable aesthetic style is in its treatment of the audience, which is invited to participate as a voyeur, watching experiences which mirror their own in terms of the shocking banality of everyday life. But it is more than that. For in their rejection of 'style', films in this tradition reject the distance of the gap between 'reality' and 'representation'. In her famous essay 'On Style', Susan Sontag wrote that all 'works of art are founded on a certain distance from the lived reality which is represented. This "distance" is, by definition, inhuman or impersonal to a certain degree; for in order to appear to us as art, the work must restrict sentimental intervention and emotional participation, which are functions of "closeness"' (1966a: 30). Today, that distance has all but closed up; real-time capabilities mean that the traces of the gap between reality and representation appear to have disappeared. I say *appeared* because, of course, even real-time video streaming is subject to someone's or some group's choices about framing what is being seen, and about selecting the point of view of the camera or cameras. Even real-time reality is a representation of that reality. But what we are talking about here is appearances, and artifacts in the disposable aesthetic tradition seem to have dispensed with formal style altogether, instead capturing reality 'as is', however shambling, chaotic and uneventfully ugly that reality may be. Elsewhere in this book I have argued that cinema in the digital era is deeply humanistic with its *détournement* of the cold logic of the digital code, with its pixilated blues and whites. This humanism is also marked by ugliness, prominent in *Gummo* and *The Blair Witch Project*, films that unfold as if style was something that reality itself imposed on film, rather than the traditional understanding of style as that which the artist consciously imposed to create art.

All films today are disposable in the sense that they end up piecemeal, fragments, in clips on the Internet, which levels high and low so radically and with such force that such distinctions are meaningless. Portions of the most serious 'art' films of Peter Greenaway are merely clicks away from videos so amateur that a new term of non-professionalism needs to be invented to describe them. It is no wonder that the logic of curiosity, boredom and disposability that governs web browsing would also emerge as a cinematic aesthetic, hinted at by earlier directors who strove to break free from the strictures of 'professionalism'. It isn't that the millions of video segments in places and on sites like YouTube are disposable in the sense of not being deliberate, unique or exceptionally memorable, but rather that, in this new context, they are experienced by solitary viewers, or in small groups, stripped of the traditional trappings of the theatre experience, which involved anticipation, the dark, the majesty of the big screen and the devotion of unbroken time to the viewing experience. This is precariously close to nostalgia, I know, as if the golden age of theatrical viewing was about to disappear, a fact to be lamented. Of course, the gap, the distance between the screen and the viewer shrunk decades ago, as television brought movies into homes. Today, reality seeps into screens from all sides, as they are immersed in everyday life, more disposable than ever before.

DV Humanism
[Mistakism, Harmony Korine, Long Takes, Archives, *Russian Ark*]

The hard-drive storage capabilities of digital and HD filmmaking make possible a virtual one-to-one correspondence between real time and represented time. The emergence of real-time screens can be traced to early military uses. According to Lev Manovich: 'What is new about such a screen [a radar screen] is that its image can change in real time, reflecting changes in the referent…' (2001: 99). And for Paul Virilio, with high definition images 'what gets decisively *resolved* is the reality of the object's real-time presence' (1994: 64; emphasis in original).

In this regard, the emblematic digital real-time film is Alexander Sokurov's *Russian Ark*, consisting of a single take that lasts approximately an hour-and-a-half and that could not have been shot on film. According to cinematographer and Steadicam operator Tilman Büttner, Sokurov's wish 'was to shoot in film but, technically, this was impossible. I proposed using the Sony HD 24p camera' (in Menasche 2003: 22). *Russian Ark* illustrates the fundamental paradox of real-time cinema: at the same time that the film seems more 'naturalistic' because it conforms to the rhythms and sequence of natural time, it also foregrounds the theatricality of performance. Watching *Russian Ark*, you are always aware of the intense choreography of the camera and the actors, the sheer hair-breadth escape from a mistake that would ruin the entire film just around the corner. It is a testament to how deeply we have absorbed the logic of montage and editing that watching a film like *Russian Ark* we perhaps think to ourselves, *here is where a where a cut would be*, or *the director has moved the camera into a darkened corner for a few moments to buy himself time – the momentary darkening of the screen substitutes for an edit.*

This paradox lies at the heart of digital cinema. For if modernism was about the radical rearranging of time and the destruction of linear chronology – as evidenced in the novels of William Faulkner, James Joyce and Virginia Woolf, the films of Sergei Eisenstein and Dziga Vertov, and the art of the surrealists – then contemporary digital cinema not only makes that violence against natural time easier than ever before, but also makes possible the resurrection of real time and the single take, which after all characterised the logic of the very first cinema: the work of the Lumière brothers. If their single takes were limited by the amount of film that could be loaded into the magazine – just as Hitchcock in directing *Rope* was limited to approximately twenty minutes per take – today's digital and HD filmmakers can look towards a not-to-distant future where cameras will have the ability to record not just hour-long but days-long unbroken takes. Mary Ann Doane has noted how:

> the sheer duration of filmic time allows for the random event, the surprise of the unexpected wave. This representation of time carries with it both the frisson and the threat/anxiety of the unexpected and is culturally tolerable only for a very brief period at the end of the century. In the classical cinema, the cut aborts the problem of an excess of the random, of chance in time. (2002: 157)

Obviously, this one-to-one correspondence to real time is, in fundamental ways, as mediated and representational as a heavily edited film, if for no other reason than the images we see are selected and framed. What appears within the screen's frame is edited in the sense that it offers but a selection of reality. As filmmaker Willard Van Dyke suggested nearly forty years ago, 'you never really capture reality with a camera, for reality is an illusion anyhow … As soon as you put up a motion picture camera and select a position, you alter reality' (quoted in Kevles 1965: 45). In a discussion that mirrors Manovich's notion that the database has become a dominant for how we think and tell stories, Clive Norris and Gary Armstrong, in *The Maximum Surveillance Society: The Rise of CCTV*, note that:

> What is crucial to understand is that the move from a mass surveillance society towards a maximum surveillance society is only partially dependent on the spread of the cameras. Cameras, or other sensing devices, are a necessary, but not a sufficient, condition in the move towards panopticanisation. It is the ability to store, sort, classify, retrieve, and match which is all important. (1999: 219)

I have a friend and colleague who dislikes 'postmodern' writers like Dave Eggers and the late David Foster Wallace because of their use of long – sometimes absurdly, comically long – digressions, footnotes and endnotes. 'If they were better writers, they wouldn't have to put all that stuff in footnotes,' he says. And yet, isn't this tendency to document relentlessly the multiple tributaries of thought that form the Main Idea – whether it be in digressive postmodern fiction, or in the ever-expanding bonus and supplementary features of DVDs, or in the replicating archive of YouTube – the practical outgrowth of postmodernism, which taught us that behind every story there was another story? We are living with the aesthetic consequences of deconstruction; these consequences are our new art. 'It is time for the destruction of error' states a line from W. H. Auden's poem 'It was Easter, as I walked in the public gardens' (1929).

The Dogme 95 movement and the related principle of what Harmony Korine has called 'mistakism' are testaments to the resurrection of errors and mistakes at a time when the hiss and feedback of degraded analogue copies are being replaced by the clean, pure, 'perfect copy' logic of the digital era. In the foreward to *Digital Babylon*, Korine proposes a 'mistakist manifesto':

> This is obviously for those of us who have made a dogme film or will one day. Although I had nothing to do with the vow of chastity authorship I would like to propose a less cosmetic attempt.
> 1. no plots. Only images. Stories are fine.
> 2. all edits affects in camera only.
> 3. 600 cameras / a wall of pictures / the Phil Spector of cine. (2001: viii)

In 1923, in an essay entitled 'The Importance of Doing Things Badly', I. A. Williams wrote that 'the world is full of things that are worth doing, but certainly not worth doing well'. And so, paradoxically, the 'pure' images of the digital have been put to use by those who would degrade them; for are there any more imperfect films than *Gummo, julien-donkey boy* or *The Celebration*? It turns out that the utopian apologists were right: digital cinema is, at its heart, democratic, at least for now. In these early stages, the messy, mistakist aesthetic of digital cinema stands against the pure, uncorrupted rigidity of fascism. The introduction of 'mistakes' into movies – which basically amounts to a human signature – is the most humanistic, the most tragic of things.

Indeed, the rough edges, the wavering cameras, the pixilated images of films like *The Celebration, The Idiots, Gummo, julien donkey-boy* or *Inland Empire* are more than just tricks or cover-ups for narrative vacuousness. Instead, they reveal and flaunt the seams that bind together reality and the representation of that reality; they assert a human presence in the face of smooth, invisible digital data. They offer a countermeasure – in the form of a human signature – to what information architect Adam Greenfield refers to as the 'imperceptibility' of digital systems. Greenfield notes that when it is invisible, 'technology's governing metaphors and assumptions have an easier time infiltrating the other decisions we make about the world. Their effects come to seem more normal, more natural, simply the way things are done' (2006: 136). The pixilated shakiness of early digital cinema responds by reminding us that the images on the screen are as frail and broken as we are. In his essay 'The Grain of the Voice', Roland Barthes wrote that 'the "grain" is the body in the voice as it sings, the hand as it writes, the limb as it performs' (1977b: 188). Such traces of humanness, in the era of digital cinema, are preserved in the imperfections – deliberate and accidental – that reveal themselves in the rough, spontaneous aesthetics of DV cinema.

Richard Linklater has said of his film *Tape* (2001) that 'we shot very spontaneously. We rehearsed in a few weeks and then shot it in one week … with two consumer-model Sony digital cameras' (2001). There is a warmth to *Tape* and to many other early period digital films, what we might call *DV humanism*, that puts a lie to the cold logic of the code, or to what Jean-Pierre Geuens has called the 'deep distrust of the everyday world' (2002: 22) inherent in digital cinema. This excess of humanism in such digital films as *Tape*, *The Celebration*, *Ten* and others suggests something quite unlike 'distrust'; for in these films we find a theatrical mode of investigative humanism. The metaphoric roundness of continuous analogue signal as opposed to the discrete sampling of the digital and its binary categories is thrown up to us on the screen as an answer to those who find dehumanisation in the digital.

The desire for human connection is something that motivates the work of Anthony Dod Mantle, whose pioneering work as director of photography on films including *The Celebration*, *julien donkey-boy* and *28 Days Later* suggests a visual degradation that has as much to do with life as with death. 'I felt that this image too, as an electronic image, had to be broken down and destroyed so that a new kind of organic emotional message could appear on the screen', Mantle has said with regards to his work on *julien donkey-boy* (in Macaulay 1999: 3). And that response – to break down and destroy the 'electronic image' – lies at the very heart of early digital cinema, and stands as a symbolic gesture of humanism in the face of digital technologies that seem evermore remote and complex, even as cameras become small enough to fit into the palms of our hands. Films that experimented with digital cameras around the turn of the millennium are an index not so much of changing technologies, but rather of how we have come to think of human beings in films. In a brief essay on Spike Lee's *Bamboozled* (2000), Zeinabu Irene Davis suggested that that film 'would be remembered by filmmakers as a hybrid film, one in which the veteran team of Spike Lee and Ellen Kuras combined traditional film stocks with digital video to create a unique look and mood' (2001: 16). In the end, *Bamboozled* is about the ideology – and sometimes the tyranny – of images. In a key scene, we see a series of clips from American television shows and movies of the past where 'blackness' is exaggerated and stereotyped. Of course, we become aware that we are watching a film that is also constructing – even while deconstructing – images of race on the screen. Most of all, *Bamboozled* reminds us that it is all there in the archive. These images live on today, accessible with just a few keystrokes at places like YouTube.

The archive in the digital era is so deep and potentially all-encompassing as to offer a continuous, real-time representation of at least one thread of reality. No longer stored in vast warehouses or libraries, data lives compressed in machines, symbolically in codes. In *Archive Fever*, Jacques Derrida wondered what sort of archive would have been left to us if Freud and his contemporaries had communicated with each other and generated their ideas through the ephemera of digital communication, such as e-mail. Indeed, Derrida suggests, the structure of a culture's archive shapes and conditions – in fact, it prepares us for – the sort of knowledge that we produce: 'the technical structure of the *archiving* archive also determines the structure of the *archivable* content even in its very coming into existence and in its relationship to the future. The archivisation produces as much as it records the event' (1996: 17; emphasis in original). And: 'What is no longer archived in the same way is no longer lived in the same way' (1996: 18). Film, in which mystique and aura were in some measure dependent on its fragility, on the fact that it decomposed, is no longer subject to the same threat of disappearance. To be sure, the digital archive is as unstable as any other; entire video-hosting services come and go on the Internet, files are purposefully or accidentally destroyed or corrupted, and so on. And yet, for all practical purposes, movies now inhabit a digital medium that archives and makes their accessibility and retrieval easier than ever. Just as films during the classical era, before television, were made with the knowledge that they would be displayed and then virtually disappear from the public view, films today are made with the knowledge that they can be duplicated and archived in ways that make them perpetually accessible.

The flattening of history – its dematerialisation – that for critics like Fredric Jameson was a sign of ahistorical postmodernity, has been realised even as history now abounds due to the digital archive. For while video sites like YouTube thrive on the current moment, these moments float atop an enormous and ever-growing database of the past. In this regard, such sites are deeply historical, even as they render history ironic through a random juxtaposition of video clips. Robert Ray has noted that the availability of television in the 1950s and 1960s gave rise to an increasingly ironic audience, who saw through the mythologies of American exceptionalism, in part, because of the intertextuality made possible by simply flipping through television channels: 'in the spring of 1963 ... a television viewer could watch as network videotapes of the Birmingham race riots led directly into "Cheyenne", "Laramie", "Mr. Ed", "Ozzie and Harriet", or "Wagon Train", depending on the network and the night. Inevitably, that viewer's attitude toward conventional versions of America's mythology became increasingly ironic' (1985: 266). Whereas in 1963 viewers' choices were limited to three or four channels, today there are hundreds of thousands – perhaps millions – of video choices available. The sheer mass and visibility of the historical archive (historical insofar as it is on videotape) means that footage like that used by Spike Lee in *Bamboozled* is more widely accessible than at any time before.

This was a future predicted in the early stages of videotape development, especially surrounding the work on electronic video recording systems being pioneered in the mid-1960s at CBS. In a column entitled 'Soon You'll Collect TV Reels, Like LP's' in the *New York Times* in 1967, Jack Gould wrote that 'by far the most interesting aspect of the innovation is its promise to introduce into the television medium the element of individual selectivity that up to now has been lacking' and that 'the individual set owner will not be at the mercy of what either a commercial or noncommercial broadcaster thinks might be best for him at a given hour' (1967: D13). And yet, the ability to time-shift introduced by recordable videotape simply meant that the viewer could rearrange the timing of a set constellation of choices; there was no possibility of altering content, only of shifting it around. But the rise of user-created media made possible by faster Internet connections and data transfer rates means that viewers' ironic consumption of media now extends to their production of it, as well. A 1928 advertisement for Eastman Kodak begins, 'Be Your Own Movie Director – Scenario Writer – Actor – All in One!' The demise of the aura of film was at work even as it was yet becoming the hegemony that well-intentioned film theorists sought to expose in the 1960s and 1970s. Another Eastman Kodak advert, from the previous year, pictured a salesman demonstrating a movie camera and projector to a potential client. 'Madam,' he says, 'anyone who can take an ordinary "snap-shot" can make a Ciné-Kodak Movie. It is simplicity itself!'

The cinematic turn to the long take made possible by DV and HD technologies, is, on one level, a radically democratic, yet contradictory, development. A film like *Russian Ark*, shot in one long take, allows for an entirely new level of viewer interaction, as all the formal 'edits' must be made by the spectator. As some theorists have noted, this had potentially profound implications for the montage system of editing, which deployed the aggressive use of cuts to construct narrative. Martin Roberts has written that the 'much longer takes that DV makes possible also remove the necessity of montage, or at least reduce it to a purely aesthetic consideration' (2003: 166). When the director of the avant-garde film-within-the-film *Timecode* comes to the executive meeting of Hollywood producers, she is met with open laughter and derision by some of them. Of course, the film she proposes to make is strikingly similar to the one we are watching: four films shot in one continuous take, with no edits, presented in four quadrants: 'My film,' she proclaims, 'has the necessity, the urge, to go beyond the paradigm of collage. Montage has created a fake reality. Technology has arrived. Digital video has arrived and is demanding new expressions, new sensations.' As viewers, it is unclear what our response to her lengthy speech – peppered with references to Eisenstein, Vertov and Guy Debord – is supposed to be. On the one hand, the project she describes sounds exciting, daring, even revolutionary. On the other hand, we perhaps share the response of some of the characters sitting around the conference table listening to her lecture: her project sounds dull and, worse, pretentious.

In some ways, you could say that we have broken free from the tyranny of meaning that is essential to traditional narrative, where viewers (or readers) are 'led to' follow the story through a form of editing that coerces certain interpretations. Long-take cinema – theoretically possible during the classical era and practically possible today – jettisons the spectator back into a semblance of everyday life, the experience of walking down the street, when the only 'edits' we perform are in the blinking of our eyes ('cuts') and in the selection of scenes we choose to look upon. And yet, of course, everything we see in a long-take film is already sanctioned by the parametres of the film itself. Bound by the screen, our eyes are free to roam as far as the borders of that screen. The paradox is that as so many have decried the digital/postmodern era as one of surfaces characterised by information overload that disrupts critical thinking, the deep storage, long-take possibilities of digital media cultivate a more active, sustained gaze.

Filmless Films
[channels, disintegration, invisibility]

What is cinema in the digital age? Is a film like Steven Soderbergh's *Bubble* – which was released in theatres and on DVD on the same day – still a 'movie' in the sense of a film that is released exclusively in the theatre? During the classical Hollywood era, 'cinema' was for the most part associated with projection for public audience. Even avant-garde films by the likes of Maya Deren, Stan Brakhage, Kenneth Anger, Andy Warhol and others achieved their status as projected images. Furthermore, cinema was exclusively associated with the materiality of celluloid – a film was, literally, a film. As television began showing 'films' that materiality became more confused. Was a movie that had a theatrical release but was now being rebroadcast on television still a 'movie'? With the advent of the VCR, and then DVD, this was complicated even further. In his 1947 book *From Caligari to Hitler*, Siegfried Kracauer noted a 'new realism' that gripped European film – especially that of G. W. Pabst – during the 1920s: 'This reality is post-war Europe in full disintegration. Its ghastliness unfolds in scenes which are unique not so much for their unhesitating frankness as for their insight into the symptoms of social morbidity' (2004: 176). Today, it isn't a question of whether or not our reality is in an advanced state of disintegration, but rather of how to compensate for the lack of material structure to film itself. In 1925 (or in 1935, 1945 or 1955) audiences could be sure that there was, in fact, a film in the dark, behind them, in the projection booth. Even if the film was hidden or off limits to the spectator, it could still be imagined.

The digital era inaugurates a new form of invisibility. Where is the film that you watch on YouTube? What shape does it take? What does it look like? In fact, no matter how abstract or avant-garde a film might have been during the analogue era, it was still linked to perceived reality by its materially identifiable and recognisable existence. It was a concrete *thing*. The source of the images on the screen came from a vaguely familiar place, a projector. The migration of film to videotape, and eventually DVD, involved the same thing, even if only on a symbolic level. Although one could not literally see images of a film on the smooth surface of a DVD, one could at least hold the object that was the DVD. The 'bodiless information' that Katherine Hayles writes of (1999: 22) in relation to virtual bodies is particularly resonant in cinema, which has always depended on illusion, even as the mechanisms of that illusion (a camera, film, a projector, a screen) have been generally understandable and knowable to audiences. Today, as the interface competes with film as a source of pleasure, the basic material-ity of film becomes unknown and invisible, a complex code known only to program-mers and engineers. In this regard, all film today is abstract.

In Don DeLillo's novel *The Body Artist*, the protagonist, Lauren, sits at night in front of her computer screen, transfixed by a real-time webcast of a remote road in Finland. The fact that nothing happens – but something might – fascinates her:

> She spent hours at the computer screen looking at a live-streaming video feed from the edge of a two-lane road in a city in Finland. It was the middle of the night in Kotka, in Finland, and she watched the screen. It was interesting to her because it was hap-pening now, as she sat here, and because it happened twenty-four hours a day, face-lessly, cars entering and leaving Kotka, or just the empty road in the dead times. The dead times were best. (2001: 40)

But where, in fact, do these images come from? Where are they stored? Who is 'direct-ing' the real-time feed? Who has made the choice to frame the shot as it has been framed? Is the webcast a work of art? A social statement? A hoax? A genuine effort at surveillance? Is the webcast, in fact, an experimental film: one long-take with no cuts that lasts for days, weeks, months, even years? The transmission of images in a continu-ous, unbroken fashion – which was not possible when, in the past, they needed to be stored or archived – means that we are approaching a method of representation that achieves a one-to-one correlation with what is being represented. A street in London can exist as a street in London, but also as an unbroken streaming image available to anyone with access to the web. The collective memory of a family, or an institution, or an art form, or even a culture, is strangely and almost overwhelmingly extended, as the digital archive (located someplace, but where?) not only remembers everything, but makes it all available. The *New York Times* has reported a new sort of problem as a consequence: people whose reputations are in danger because old stories about them – sometimes not accurate or corrected but not in the public record – threaten to come back to haunt them because of the easy access to old news articles on the Internet. Some editors 'say they recognise that because the Internet has opened to the world material once available only from microfilm or musty clippings in the news-paper's library, they have a new obligation to minimise harm' (Hoyt 2007: A17). The fact that the past is available within keystrokes and within seconds has consequences for the way we think about movies, too. For one thing, in the digital era of the archive, the decay wrought by time seems almost to disappear. For isn't memory, in a very real sense, always partial, corrupted, corroded, distorted? This is why the past is mythic: it doesn't exist any more, except in our imaginations. Perhaps we have all had the experience of fondly, and maybe indistinctly, remembering a movie from long ago, only to watch it again many years later and be disappointed, not so much in the movie, but in the bitter fact that it is we – not the movie – who have aged and changed.

At one point in David Lynch's DV film *Inland Empire,* Laura Dern comes upon two women who look vaguely familiar, and says, 'Hey, look at me. And tell me if you've known me before.' She is addressing them, and us as well, who have known her in this film and in other films. We will know her for a very long time, preserved as she is in the digital archive of movies that don't combust, don't corrode, don't fade, but instead remain clear and clean in their cool digital zeros and ones. The public preservation of film made possible by digital archives suggests the potential for a strange sort of continuity between past and present, when nothing ever really gets old. In some senses, this has always been true, as images and icons (such as the Virgin Mary, movie stars) remain forever young in the public domain and imagination. The important difference, though, lies in the continuity of technique from one historical era to another. 'Lost' films and film styles are no longer lost, but rather available for public consumption by whomever channels into them. This exchange, in William Gibson's novel *Spook Country*, describes a not-too-distant future (or already-present) when various manufactured realities will be available to whomever has the technology necessary to view them:

> He nodded. 'Each one [sites or servers] shows you a different world. Alberto's shows me River Phoenix dead on a sidewalk. Somebody else's shows me, I don't know, only good things. Only kittens, say. The world we walk around in would be channels.'
> She cocked her head at him. 'Channels'? (2007: 64)

Gibson describes a world where each person is wired to receive signals from a separate channel, signals that overlay the 'real' world with a slightly modified virtual one, designed to its user's desires and expectations. The seeds of this have been there, growing, for a long time in customisable media, ranging from video's time-shifting breakthrough in the 1970s, to multiple and extensive templates available to differentiate one user's Facebook site from another's.

Frame Dragging
[Laura Mulvey, mirror neurons, *The Ring*]

The importance of the database as a metaphor for digital culture, especially as expressed in the writings of Lev Manovich, has resonance with current theories of time and space. The notion that 'reality encompasses all of the events in spacetime' (Greene 2004: 139) rather than just the ones that are happening now, goes back at least to Einstein, who wrote that 'For we convinced physicists, the distinction between past, present, and future is only an illusion, however persistent' (quoted in Greene 2004: 139).

In 1918, physicists Joseph Lense and Hans Thirring used Einstein's theory of general relativity 'to show that just as a massive object warps time and space … so a rotating object drags space (and time) around it, like a spinning stone immersed in a bucket of syrup. This is known as frame dragging' (Greene 2004a: 416). And social neuroscience confirms another form of frame dragging, involving mirror neurons that, as Daniel Goleman suggests, 'actually act like neuro wi-fi in each person's brain. They attune two people during an interaction so that their physiology reflects the other's' (2006). Theorists suggest that mirror neurons connect us with others, tuning us into their frequencies and actually affecting our own physiologies.

There is a deep kind of symmetry at work in both of these discoveries, a symmetry that is also revealed in so many objects of our digital culture, where technologies make it easier to make art that investigates the invisible connections that underlie the seen world. In Gore Verbinski's *The Ring*, Rachel and Noah attempt to determine the 'signature' – or the source – for the tape Rachel has discovered in the cabin. When Rachel notices something in the upper corner of the screen ('Wait. Go back. There's something there. There's more picture', she says), Noah freezes the image and says 'Let me stretch the alignment.' The result of this stretching – of this frame dragging – is that the tape breaks, and Rachel hurts her finger.

In the novel upon which both the Japanese and American versions of *The Ring* were based – *Ringu*, by Koji Suzuki (1991) – one of the characters, Ryuji, interprets the

Stretching the alignment in *The Ring*: the pause button also pauses the viewer

mysterious videotape for his friend: "'Now, this falls into two broad categories: abstract scenes and real scenes.' Saying this, he pulled up the volcanic eruption and paused the tape on it. 'There, take that volcano. No matter how you look at it, that's real'" (2003: 103).

Both instances involve freezing the frame, or what passes for the frame in videotape. And preparing to write this section of the book, I used the pause button to freeze a frame of *The Ring* DVD. Unlike the paused tape in front of Rachel and Noah, there was no fluttering, no vibration, no movement, no breakage. And you, dear reader, may be paused right now, your eyes moving from these words to the still from *The Ring*, for the pause button is really an instruction to the user: pause, slow down, rest. Already in cinema and in contemporary literature, the 'paused video frame' has become a metaphor for the analogue flaws that we remember with a mixture of nostalgia and disdain. In Tom McCarthy's novel *Remainder* (2005), the narrator – who at one point cannot decide which direction to walk – keeps changing direction after a few steps. 'I realised that I was jerking back and forth like paused video images do on low-quality machines', he says (2007: 14). The in-between state of paused video images that were rendered on VCRs before they were supplanted by DVD players, creates a sort of liminal space, a threshold state between the cold, reproduced image on the screen and its living original. The imperfection of the paused video image on the television screen – with its distortion, its fuzziness, its wavy alignment – served as a reminder of the imperfect, human 'source' material. In contrast, the frozen digital image – which is much clearer and sharper – is part of larger social trends to reverse ageing, eliminate wrinkles and generally reverse-engineer ourselves back into youthfulness.

When the digital frame is paused, it becomes clear how much like a photograph it is, for without the blurriness of a paused videotape, the paused DVD reveals a very clear image, as if captured by a still camera. The frozen film image in the digital era allows for what Laura Mulvey describes as an 'unexpected, deferred meaning' (2006: 151) similar to what Roland Barthes called the 'third meaning' (1970). 'Now that films on DVD are indexed in chapters', Mulvey has written, 'the linearity associated with film projection begins to break down further' (2006: 150). The ability to move or to drag frames – literally to shift data from one database to another – has a profound impact not only on the way movies are made, but on the way they are experienced. Recombinant films of the digital era, such as *Go*, *Run Lola Run*, *Memento*, *Inland Empire*, or episodes of *24*, are the direct result of thinking made possible by digital technologies. Of course, films of this type – such as Maya Deren's *Meshes of the Afternoon* (directed with Alexander Hammid) and *At Land* – existed in the pre-digital era, where they were often considered as avant-garde, as gestures meant to subvert or defy dominant modes of cinematic storytelling. But today, it is the avant-garde itself which has been frame-dragged into the bright, eternal light of the mainstream.

The ability to pause a film and study its frames in detail may seem like a minor advancement, but it is in fact a major shift in the relationship between spectators and cinema. While it is true that spectators still have little or no real control over the content of a particular film (yet, at least), their control over the temporal unfolding of the film suggests that film's origination in the photographic image is being revisited in the digital era. In a way, the quietness of the stilled image is an oasis from the perpetual motion and fluidity of data in the digital era.

The loss of quality between copies of data is theoretically avoidable. That is, digital copies can be made with complete accuracy, provided they are not compressed or resampled, as opposed to analogue systems, which always introduced loss, even if minimally. Of course, such loss can in itself be a thing of beauty. In Elizabeth Hand's novel *Generation Loss*, the narrator reflects on the sad and fragile beauty of daguerreotypes: 'But then you tilt a daguerreotype just right, and the shadows and light fall into place, and what you're looking at becomes a 3-D image. It's an effect impossible to reproduce in a book or print, or even with computer imaging technology: the purest example of generation loss I can think of' (2007: 209). In the digital era, physics and cinema are exploring the new frontier that promises a sort of metaphoric immortality, for if images can be copied perfectly, with no degradation or loss, then they can, theoretically, reproduce forever, without the marks of age.

Already this is happening at the level of quantum physics. In 2007, Harvard physicist Lene Hau published work that demonstrated how she had trapped light, stopped it, converted it into matter and moved it, and then sent it on its way. In essence, she made a 'meta-copy' of the light – an exact duplicate of the original light pulse. This copying and exchanging of matter on the fundamental level, and in a way that involves no loss or degradation, is really the larger context for advances in digital cinema. On one level, it involves the displacement of the 'master' or source copy, as duplication in the digital era does not depend upon returning to the source as the best available copy. As Robert Dornsife has noted, once 'the role of time is revised as a result of its having no bearing on successive digital quality, other concepts will follow. Simultaneously, the terms "original" and "copy" will either need to be reconsidered or, it seems more probably to me, left for dead' (2006: 2).

The Ideology
of the Long Take
[Gilles Deleuze, blinking as editing]

The 'technical' aspects of digital cinema are, always, ideological. It could be said that, politically, the long take in the digital era has a double effect: it immerses us in the present, thus compromising the possibility of critique. Gilles Deleuze reminds us of Sergei Eisenstein's observation that parallel editing, especially in the films of D. W. Griffith, was an expression of ideology that ignored causes and looked only at effects:

> Eisenstein's strength thus lies in showing that the principal technical aspects of American montage since Griffith – the alternate parallel montage which makes up the situation, and the alternate concurrent montage which leads to the duel – relate back to this bourgeois historical conception (1986: 150).

Surveillance cameras and systems – with their endless gaze and deep storage capabilities – constitute an alternate cinema of the neo-liberal, post-9/11 age, when the extension of the market globally depends upon an unprecedented campaign of information awareness. HD cameras accompanied by ever-expanding hard drives that will allow for the storage of hundreds of hours of footage are as much products of a new sort of dread as they are of simple technology. If the classical style of crosscutting served to at least disrupt the gaze, then the emergence of the long take as a practical possibility suggests a sort of hard-eyed realism against reality itself, stripped of style. In her 1965 essay 'On Style', Susan Sontag wrote that '"Stylisation" in a work of art, as distinct from style, reflects an ambivalence (affectation contradicted by contempt, obsession contradicted by irony) toward the subject-matter' (1966a: 20). Our contemporary interest in realism, made possible by devices that allow for a long-take reproduction of so-called reality, signal a shift away from ambivalence, and an embrace of the abyss of the real.

David Lynch – whose *Inland Empire* was shot on a Sony PD 150 camera – and whose

Nostalgia for analogue warmth in David Lynch's digital movie *Inland Empire*

work had been so closely associated with the tactile, textural, even painterly qualities associated with film, was outspoken in his embrace of digital and rejection of film. Referring to *Inland Empire*, he noted that 'shooting digitally [with] lightweight, small cameras … seeing exactly what you're getting … You can move, you can be right in there, in the scene. You can turn around instantly. Forty-minute takes allow you to sink and sink and sink in there, and it's so good for the scenes' (2008). In *Inland Empire's* movie within the movie *On High in Blue Tomorrows*, Justin Theroux (Devon Berk/Billy Side) and Laura Dern (Nikki Grace/Susan Blue) talk and fall in love on a porch in the sun, and the warm glow of the scene unfolds as languorously as a scene from Alfred Hitchcock's *Vertigo*. This movie within *Inland Empire*, with its warm analogue qualities, is a ghost that haunts the film, a remainder from an earlier era.

The impact of digital video and HD goes far beyond the look and feel of the film; the long-take possibilities allow for the development of scenes that are, ironically, more organic than those made possible by the 'warmth' of film itself, which (in general) limited takes to around twenty minutes. Even in digital films that do not rely on extended or long takes, the deep-storage capabilities allow for longer takes on the set, encouraging a different kind of acting. Just as the cuts in classical cinema were motivated, in part, by the limits of how long filming could continue before the camera needed to be reloaded, the cuts in digital and HD cinema will evolve into a new grammar at least partially motivated by the fact that, literally, a film can be shot in one take with no cuts. The allure of simplicity associated with digital cinema – where directors simply point and shoot small, hand-held DV cameras – is in some ways a confirmation of cinema's earliest desires. An article – 'A Motion-Picture Camera and a Projector for Home Use' – from *Scientific American* in 1917 describes a home movie camera that measures '7 inches long, 5 inches high, and 2½ inches wide … Most important of all, however, is its simplicity; with a superficial knowledge of photography anyone can take motion pictures with this equipment' (Anon. 1917: 206). And, in an article from 1913 regarding a camera that was powered by compressed air ('A Cinematograph Hand Camera') the description of the viewfinder anticipates the camera mobility made possible by the LCD viewfinder on DV cameras: 'It [the camera] is also extremely useful for work in crowded thoroughfares. In this case a street procession or other incident may be taken without the operator's securing an elevated position to clear the heads of the people. He merely holds the aeroscope above his head with his two hands, and by means of a special view finder placed on the under side of the camera, he can follow the incidents and make the exposures' (Anon. 1913: 112). In both cases, the camera's small size and mobility suggest it as a tool for capturing reality.

The digital movie camera extends this desire further, and encourages a new way of seeing, one that is open to the capturing of mistakes, errors, and randomness of the reality being filmed. Rather than tightly controlled montage – with each shot carefully planned and choreographed – the digital system allows for the uncontrolled emergence of the real into the frame, even as the manipulation and editing of those captured images is made all the more easy on desktop editing systems. It is almost as if the gains made in long-take realism are counterbalanced by the potential limits imposed on those long takes by inexpensive editing interfaces. Perhaps the urge to break up or interrupt real-time long takes is rooted in our own experience of consciousness and perception, which rhythmically 'interrupts' the flow of our own processing of reality. For while it may be true that such a thing as a ninety-minute film exists with no cuts, it is also true that no human being could ever truly experience the event, as the very act of blinking serves as a momentary cut or edit: we lose multiple frames each time we blink. There is no long take for the viewer, only fragments of a long take uninterrupted by the act of blinking, just as sleeping interrupts or pauses our conscious absorption and processing of real-time reality. 'Pure perception', Henri Bergson wrote, 'in fact, however rapid we suppose it to be, occupies a certain depth of duration, so that our successive perceptions are never real moments of things … but are moments of our consciousness' (1988: 69). Extremely long takes made possible by HD remind us that, as humans, we can never approximate or replicate the camera eye, which does not blink, but rather captures a steady stream of information. Paradoxically, long takes are techniques we can never truly experience as long takes.

Image/Text
[*Gun Crazy*, intertitles, subtitles]

In one sense, digital cinema offers a return to textuality, and a reminder of how unstable the boundaries are between image and text. As W. J. T. Mitchell has noted, the 'image-text relation in film and theatre is not merely a technical question, but a site of conflict, a nexus where political, institutional, and social antagonisms play themselves out in the materiality of representation' (1994: 91). On the most basic level, films have become more textual, broken into 'chapters' and embedded in the text of menus and optional subtitles, which provide a textual dimension just visible beneath the surface. Such image/text interplay reinforces the logic of the global marketplace, as all movies are available in languages not their own. It's not that films are subtitled with greater frequency, but rather that the prominence of text on the screen today hearkens back to early cinema, when texts and images competed on the screen, reinforcing each other's meaning. In a film like D. W. Griffith's *His Trust*, for example, the intertitle serves to prepare the viewer for the next scene, and to convey the general narrative logic of the film:

An intertitle from *His Trust*:
the alternation between text and image
in silent cinema

The alternation between text and image was common during the silent era, and provided a narrative framework for understanding film that was largely lost with the coming of sound. The re-emergence during the digital era of a certain textuality of the screen – in the form of subtitles, menus, chapter titles, and so on – returns film to its roots, even as film in its digital form moves ever further away from its analogue sources. One crucial difference is that the text on the screen today is often multilingual, casting even pre-digital films in a global context. Below: three versions of *Gun Crazy*:

The return of cinematic textuality in the digital era: subtitle selections from the DVD version of *Gun Crazy*

Today, the proliferation of subtitles suggests a foreign-language instruction class, and a further erosion of the aura of films which, after all, become commodities in a global system, marketed to different audiences. What subtitles reveal is a fact that everyone knows, but that is easy nonetheless to forget: there are no 'foreign languages', simply languages. The multiple-language options on DVDs – a feature that was not available in previous mediums, such as VHS – is a subtle reminder that the 'default' language is just one choice among many. Just as the numerous bonus and supplementary features have contextualised and demystified films, the subtitles options suggest that language itself is arbitrary.

Incompleteness

One of the consequences of the digital turn is that forms of entertainment and art – such as movies, albums and even novels – are perpetually incomplete. The model here is something like Wikipedia, where individual entries are updated at every moment. Of course, new knowledge and content is always being created, expanded, revised and updated, but traditionally these changes only registered in a visible way periodically, such as with the publication of a book or essay (the end result of writing and research) or the release of a film (the end result of months or years of production). Today, however, the ongoing production of content is visible; it can be tracked on blogs and various websites so that the 'release' of new content is really only a technicality. Films in the digital era are open source, not because viewers can alter them, but because they exist as multiple versions (in 'director's cut', and so forth) and across numerous platforms. How can a film – or any text – ever be considered 'complete' when it is forever being re-released in different versions?

Theodor Adorno – that bitterest and most brutally honest of theorists – once wrote that the 'automatic self-reproduction of the status quo in its established forms is itself an expression of domination' (1991b: 185). Technology in the digital era has made self-reproduction possible in almost every strata of society: no longer do audiences need to wait for movie studios or television networks to provide content. The 'do-it-yourself' movement – once the special attribute of punk rock but now spread to creative amateurism in almost every field – suggests, finally, that incompleteness is not a flaw, but rather a permanent state, a condition for the creation of movie content. 'Automatic self-reproduction' means, practically, that a user can – in a matter of seconds – cut the 'embed' code for a YouTube video and paste it into his or her weblog: the video appears, now, in a new context, jolted out of its previous environment. This no longer appears to be an 'expression of domination' because the user has seemingly chosen to reproduce this video. And yet, it is not the ideological content that dominates, but instead the very forms of interfaces themselves, which encourage an incomplete understanding of texts because texts are perpetually removed from their contexts ('cut') and placed into new contexts ('paste'). Domination occurs not because we only incompletely understand the hundreds of texts and images we see every day, but because the very interfaces we use to manipulate and consume remind us that nothing is permanent, that everything is partial and incomplete.

Interfaces
[genres, Lionel Trilling]

In the digital era, the interface threatens to supplant content as the primary narrative. The process of navigation and selection – DVD chapter menus, iPod screens, links on the web – suggests narrative framing and assembly. The experience of going to a theatre and sitting in the dark without participating in the selection and arrangement of narrative blocks is becoming a radical, avant-garde experience. Everyone wants to have a hand in the fashioning of stories. This is because the stories themselves have lost their charm, have been demystified. To compensate for this, it is the mechanism of arranging, ordering, selecting stories that supersedes the stories themselves. In film, the old genres are worn out. Horror, comedy, drama, sci-fi – they exist today as interactive games. Digital logic and the dominance of interfaces give easy display to our individual 'tastes'. Whether genuine choice or the illusion of choice, the interface permits selectivity and interactivity. In 1962, Lionel Trilling wrote that 'sometimes we may wonder if it is wholly an accident that so strong an impulse to base our sense of life … chiefly upon the confrontations of taste should have developed in an age dominated by advertising, the wonderful and terrible art which teaches us that we define ourselves and realise ourselves and realise our true being by choosing the right style' (1965b: 152). In this regard, the new interfaces – in promoting selectivity to the highest level – rescue cinema from oblivion by processing it through new controls that at least provide the illusion of choice. Soon, movies will be like songs on the iPod list, arranged so that the playlists consist not only of entire movies (such as a *film noir* or a horror film set list) but bits and pieces of films that can be rearranged into new ones.

Two short stories illuminate changed perceptions about interfaces in the digital era. In 1950 (when less than 10 per cent of American homes had television sets) Ray Bradbury's story 'The Veldt' served as a cautionary tale, as the screens in the children's room came alive, the lions devouring the parents who dared to try to 'turn off' the house out of fear that their children were becoming too dependent on its virtual technologies. 'But won't the shock be too much for the children, shutting the room up abruptly, for good?' the father asks a psychologist who has come to evaluate the situation. 'I don't want them going any deeper into this, that's all', he replies (1950: 16). In the end, the parents are consumed by the very technologies they purchased to secure a better life. Over fifty years later, Michael Faber's story 'The Eyes of the Soul' is concerned with characters whose home in England has a large front window that overlooks a violent, ugly street. One day a company called Outlook Innovations stops by, and installs – on a free, trial basis – a new 'window' that turns out to be a video display screen that changes the view to 'a scene of startling beauty. The house had seemingly relocated itself right in the middle of a spacious country garden' (2005: 43). The following exchange between the home owner Jeanette and the saleswoman ensues:

> 'It's a video, right?' she said shakily. To keep her awe at bay, she closed her eyes and tried to see the view through her window objectively. She imagined it as a sort of endless re-run of the same film of a country garden…
>
> 'No, it's not a video,' murmured the saleswoman.
>
> 'Well, some sort of film anyway,' said Jeanette, opening her eyes again. The geese were out of sight now, but the golden light was deepening. 'How long does it go for?'
>
> The saleswoman chuckled indulgently, as though a small child had just asked her when the sun would fall back to the ground.
>
> 'It goes *forever*,' she said. 'It's not any kind of film. It's a real place, and this is what it's like there, right now, at this very moment.' (2005: 44; emphasis in original)

The story ends with Jeanette renting the screen, whose real-time images don't so much suggest a virtual reality, but a corresponding reality, made possible by digital technologies. The story does not vibrate with the same sorts of anxieties about technology that Bradbury's did. Yes, Jeanette uses the screen to mask her social reality, but why not, when that social reality is so dispiriting? And besides, her screen does not seduce her with false, virtual images, but with real ones, just as we are surrounded by screens – at home, in offices, at airports, in shopping malls – displaying real-time realities. The old cultural fears that interfaces were potentially dangerous portals that allowed excess fantasy into our lives have been ameliorated by the dominance of reality-based content, which transforms the screen interface into a supposedly neutral window as opposed to one that seduces with imaginary content.

And yet there are no cuts in theoretical real time: in the story, Jeanette is subject to an uninterrupted stream of reality, competing with her own. So, she must impose her own cuts, which spectators have done since the beginnings of cinema. Indeed, the ability of spectators to 'edit' films was there from the beginning: viewers can select what portions or quadrants of the screen to watch. Orson Welles once commented that he preferred long, unedited takes because these were inherently democratic, allowing the viewer to *choose* what to watch on the screen. Spectators have never been the passive viewers enslaved by spectacle that they were imagined to be by the neo-Marxist theorists. Films – like reality – have their own gaps, fissures, breakdownss and ambiguities that allow for a far wider spectrum of freedom of interpretation and meaning. Cinema in the digital era puts into practice a *style* of viewing that has always been present: selectivity. I say style because not all viewers choose to interact with films in the ways that technology makes available. If, during the classical era, viewers could visually make edits on the movie-house screens in front of them, then during the digital era these edits are made at the level of interface, as viewers literally make edits by skipping forwards or backwards through a movie, or by selecting which 'alternate' ending to watch. And of course copying – legally or otherwise – a movie is also a form of interaction that is, on one level, a stylistic choice.

I refer here not to the style of this or that film, but rather to the style surrounding the viewing of a film. For today, a film's style – like its content – is secondary to the style attached to the interface. Whether it be a video iPod, a flat screen television or a laptop computer, the design and style of these objects transports the film's meaning into whatever environment happens to surround the viewing experience. Greil Marcus has written that 'Certain images in [David Lynch's] *Lost Highway* take the story that produces the images so far outside of the social that the story ceases to seem real' (2006: 114). With digital interfaces, there is a different, more physical form of detachment: movie images – shrunken down to inches and made portable – are detached from their theatrical classical-era surroundings, and displayed on screens that are themselves privately owned markers of style. Taste therefore extends beyond one's choice of which movie to view to include which 'device' to use for viewing. One of the results of bringing movies to consumers rather than bringing consumers to movies, is that they become unattached from the contexts that gave films shared meanings that transcended their specific 'content' or 'style'. In the digital era, the context of a film's playing is wherever the film is playing: on an airplane, in a car, on a bus, in the subway, at a coffee shop, in a bedroom, in a basement, and so forth. Thus, the film itself becomes edited into whatever circumstances happen to surround its showing. So, we have at least three layers of editing:

- editing within the film itself (cuts, shot/reverse-shot, dissolves, and so forth).
- editing by the viewer through the interface (fast-forward or reverse, skipping, freezing a frame, selecting alternate endings or audio commentary).
- editing by the viewer through the mobility of the screen and its placement in or movement through various environments or contexts (for instance, watching a film on a video iPod while riding a train, then continuing to watch it in a taxi, then in a coffeeshop and then finishing it in a hotel room).

While none of these iterations gives the user ability to add or subtract from the existing content of the film, it substitutes for that the ability to alter the immediate circumstances of the film's reception, and thus does provide a powerful edit function, one that – at the extreme – sutures the film object itself into the mundane realities of everyday life. For a generation of people raised with screens embedded in screens and multiple levels of windows open and displaying content simultaneously, the experience of watching a film on a single, large screen might very well be a rare experience.

iPod Experiment

[culture industry, Gorillaz, *Superman Returns*]

There is, in fact, a form of creeping CGI-surrealism that is invisible. An erased wrinkle. A deleted imperfection. A corrected mistake. A chaotic moment brought to order. The binary code of the digital commanding reality. A special effect that is so subtle that you don't notice it, or you have forgotten how to notice. The most astounding and surreal CGI moment that you will see on the screen is not the gravity-defying stunts of Halle Berry in *Catwoman* (a movie so terrifically Insane that no one dare call it the Mad, Bad-Ass Art that it is), but rather the so-called realism of a face that you think is real, but that is not. The full and unremitting power of the Culture Industry beckons you, seduces you not through Illusion that announces itself as Illusion, but through Illusion that corresponds so closely with reality and in fact improves upon it and therefore it is reality itself that becomes surreal.

The iPod (or any personalised listening device) makes possible the disruption, a way to see movies in a radically new light. Freed from dialogue (does a movie like *X-Men* need dialogue?) we are free to appreciate the radical beauty of these films and their surreal images. My own experiment along these lines occurred in August 2006. On vacation with my family at Lakeside, Ohio – a Chatauqua on Lake Erie – I borrowed my son's iPod and, in the beautiful and creaky old theatre from the 1920s, watched *Superman Returns* with the iPod set on shuffle, and volume very, very loud. I could hear no dialogue from the movie, simply a random rotation of songs by Gorillaz, The Fastbacks, Sleater-Kinney, They Might Be Giants, Rocket from the Tombs, Lavender Diamond, Guided by Voices, Flogging Molly, Grandaddy, Mercury Rev, Johnny Cash and others.

The result was almost heartbreaking in a way that is hard to explain. Perhaps it is because all cynicism and irony slips away when you are watching a sequence on the screen that synchronises in a profound way with the music you are listening to – music that you know is entirely random but that seems deliberately and carefully chosen to go with the sequence. REM's 'The One I Love' as Clark Kent and Lois Lane flirt with their eyes, or They Might Be Giants' 'Experimental Film' that happens to shuffle on just at the most surreal, reality-defying sequence of the film. But more than that, the CGI sequences – freed from their parasitical relationship to the relentless expectation of *coherence, economy and feeling* in the film – stand out as the surrealist art pieces that they are. This is made possible by digital technologies that allow for the easy duplicating, transference and portability of digital media.

Ironic Mode

In Spike Lee's film *Bamboozled*, white media owner Dunwitty challenges the 'blackness' of African-American television show writer Delacroix:

> I understand black culture. I grew up around black people all my life. If the truth be told I probably know 'niggers' better than you, Monsieur Delacroix. Please don't be offended by my use of the quote-unquote N word. I got a black wife and three bi-racial children, so I feel I have a right to use that word. I don't give a damn what Spike says, Tarantino is right.

These lines are delivered with such sincerity that their ironic framing is almost shattered.

David Foster Wallace, in his 1993 essay 'E Unibus Pluram: Television and US Fiction', offers one of the more challenging and insightful readings of the commodification of irony in postwar US culture, especially as it is expressed in literary fiction (notably metafiction) and television. For Wallace, the first-wave of postwar irony – being shown the difference between the way things appear to be and the way things are – worked to expose the 'absurd contradictions' (1997: 35) and hypocricies of American culture. Television – with its ubiquity, repetition of images and ability to 'repeat' shows over and over again – is for Wallace the ultimate ironic medium, because it has helped to transform us into *knowledgeable* viewers, that is, viewers who can see through the very narratives that constitute television. Wallace points to a host of adverts on television in the 1980s that openly mocked the fact that they were adverts, including the Joe Isuzu ads for Isuzu, which featured a creepy car salesman: 'The ads succeeded as parodies of how oily and Satanic car commercials are. They invited viewers to congratulate themselves for getting the joke, and to congratulate Isuzu Inc. for being "fearless" and "irreverent" enough to acknowledge that car ads are ridiculous and that the Audience is dumb enough to believe them' (1997: 61).

This is the same sensibility that characterises many of the graphic novels which became popular in the wake of a 1992 Pulitzer Prize for Art Spiegelman's *Maus*, including Chris Ware's *Jimmy Corrigan* (2000) and Daniel Clowes' *Ghost World* (1997) and *David Boring* (2000), drawn in a 'bluish-green tint that suggests a TV on the blink – exactly right for these lives in which much of the colour has been drained by a crippling irony and hyper self-awareness' (McGrath 2004: 33). Robert Ray has written that the very medium of television itself helped to create an ironic audience, and that 'the period's defining self-consciousness arose from a new awareness of the inescapable interrelationship of media, audience, and historical events' (1985: 268). We could say that post-1960 media – no matter what its content – was potentially ironic in the sense that it was made and consumed by people for whom the governing mythologies and narratives were relentlessly exposed and undermined by the very technologies of media. David Jay Bolter and Richard Grusin have noted that television 'acknowledges its mediation more explicitly and readily than film does' (2000: 186). Or, to get back to he who sits at the font of all this theorising, Marshall McLuhan, '[People] don't see movies on TV; they see TV' (1995: 294).

Digital technologies have further demystified the stories offered by film and television, as home playback systems make it possible to manipulate the previously fixed temporal order of film. Writing in 1993, before the advent of DVDs, critic Anne Friedberg noted that VCRs 'allow for time-shifting and playback of rental tapes' (1993: 136) and that the VCR 'becomes a privatised museum of past moments, of different genres, different times all reduced to uniform, interchangeable, equally accessible units. The videocassette transforms the size and accessibility of film experience, markets it as a booksized, readily available commodity' (1993: 139). This is pushed even further by DVDs, which accelerate the user's ability to manipulate a film's narrative and, with multiple options and commentaries, radically destabilise the aura of a primary, fixed film. As Graeme Harper has suggested, 'DVDs promote and develop the idea of film as a "game". No longer do audiences simply enter a text expecting to follow its narrative from Point A through to Point Z' (2001: 24). The implications of these recent home-based technologies of viewing had and continue to have enormous impact on the emergence of an ever-increasing ironic audience. What distinguishes and links many digital-era films is their ability to both evoke a sincere emotional response while at the same time creating the possibilities for the audience to see through the very mechanisms that elicit this response.

The films of Lars von Trier – especially *Breaking the Waves*, *The Idiots* and *Dancer in the Dark* – while distinct from camp, offer a profound awareness of film traditions and dramas. In one important sense, they share what Sontag refers to as 'the sensibility of failed seriousness, of the theatricalisation of experience. Camp refuses both the harmonies of traditional seriousness, and the risks of fully identifying with extreme states of feeling' (1966b: 287). Even more significantly, Sontag identifies in camp a tendency that is shared by many post-punk films, especially those by von Trier and others working in the Dogme 95 tradition: 'The traditional means for going beyond straight seriousness – irony, satire – seem feeble today, inadequate to the oversaturated medium in which contemporary sensibility is schooled. Camp introduces a new standard: artifice as an ideal, theatricality' (1966b: 288).

The Idiots is about a group of people who pretend, in public, to be mentally disabled. This activity – called 'spassing' – essentially tricks unwary strangers into emotional feeling for the spassers. One in particular, Karen, shows great concern over Stoffer, who has been brought to an expensive restaurant by his cohorts, where he proceeds to create a disruptive scene. In a gesture of sympathy, she walks with him out of the restaurant, only to be laughed at and ridiculed by the spassers once they reveal to her their con. Out of curiosity, loneliness and the sense of identity and community that this group offers, she stays with them, an accomplice who eventually succumbs to spassing by the end. No plot summary can do this film justice, but what I hope this minimal outline suggests is that the film's plot – which seems outrageous – in fact explores the very mechanics of audience identification that we all experience each time we watch a movie. For what is a fictional film other than a group of people pretending to be someone else (spassing) in such a way that tricks us into entering into the film's world and suspending our disbelief long enough to be moved by the emotional cues offered to us?

Tim Walters has suggested that there might be a direct connection between spassing – with its formal rules and defiant reshaping of the social world – and the very rules of the Vow of Chastity. He notes that the 'charismatic and, arguably, brilliant Stoffer should then be considered as a more-or-less direct representation of von Trier himself, someone who experiences great frustration as he tries to passionately coax his fellow malcontents to reconsider the way they function in opposition to a system they find abhorrent' (2004: 48). One scene in particular is unusually open to readings that are reminiscent of actors debriefing after a performance or, to extend Walters' argument, a director chiding his performers on the day's work. After their visit to the Rockwool factory, the group returns to the country house and, in a scene reminiscent of a college-bull session, sit on the floor in a room lit by candles and discuss the day. At one point, Stoffer says: 'Jeppe copped out right in the middle and it pisses me off.' Other characters either agree with Stoffer or else defend Jeppe regarding the quality and believability of his spassing at the factory, with lines like 'I thought Jeppe was good', and 'Where the hell was Jeppe good?' On one level, we are invited to read this as a part of the fictional world of the movie that we have entered into. On another level, the scene reminds us that the characters are not only talking about their 'performance' in the Rockwool factory for the factory manager, but also talking about the quality of their performance as actors who are playing the role of spassers in a film. In this regard, Stoffer's criticism of Jeppe's performance comes not from Stoffer the fictional character who is leader of the spassers, but from Stoffer as a sort of theatre director who is evaluating the work of his actors that day. And on yet another level, the scene recalls the very 'rules' of the Dogme 95 movement itself and its penchant for the rituals of self-criticism, critique and confessions.

This self-awareness extends to the explicitly documentary dimensions of the film itself, where von Trier – off-camera – asks the characters after-the-fact questions about the motivations for and consequences of spassing. In several exchanges reminiscent of discussions regarding who originally came up with the Dogme 95 concept and Vow of Chastity, the interviewer asks one of the spassers whose idea this all was, to which she replies, 'Axel says it was his idea. I think it was Stoffer's.' Jeppe himself says, 'It was my idea, but it was Stoffer who wanted to do something about it.' The plot of *The Idiots* involves people who pretend to be something they are not for audiences in order to elicit emotional responses, a process which makes it very difficult to know how to read the intensely emotional, even melodramatic, scenes in the film. For if the film continually reminds us of the very process by which we ourselves are being manipulated, what are we to make of the painfully intense close-ups of Karen, the woman drawn into the world of spassing? This really becomes a problem of audience identification: to which characters – if any – are we expected to extend our sympathy? Are we to view the spassers – who clearly are framed in such a way as to indicate a righteous piercing of hypocritical bourgeois attitudes towards the mentally disabled – as characters with whom we are supposed to identify on some level? Are they speaking and enacting a 'truth' that, however harsh, is sincerely expressed? It would be difficult to accept this, given that the spassers are shown to be indulgent, selfish, cruel and given to excess.

If there is any romantic appeal in *The Idiots* – if there is any uncorrupted sincerity – it comes closest to being embodied in the character of Karen, who we learn by the end of the film has recently lost her child and who has left her family, presumably out of grief or shock. She, more than anyone else in the film, questions the spassers – and Stoffer in particular – about the moral and ethical dimensions of their game. Stoffer's indignant defences of spassing as a way to expose the hypocrisy of bourgeois prejudices regarding the mentally handicapped (and perhaps, by extension, any marginalised group) are repeatedly undercut by Karen's quiet questioning. In many ways, she serves as a surrogate for the audience, one of us who wants to ask, 'why?' One of the more poignant moments comes when the group is in the woods and Karen directly confronts Stoffer: 'But there are people who are really ill. It's sad for the people who are not able like us. How can … how can you justify acting the idiot?' His response – 'You can't' – can be read as a profound, philosophic come-back that suggests it is as silly to ask about acting the idiot as it would be to ask why Dadaist art doesn't make sense. Or, it can be read as the response of a bored, sadistic, spoiled man-boy for whom suffering is a game; the sort of person whose generational blankness is described by Tyler Durden in *Fight Club*.

Looking at Yourself Looking: Avatar As Spectator

Although the changes in the technology of film, as it transforms from analogue systems to digital ones, have been profound, just as profound are the changes surrounding the concept of the viewer or spectator. Traditionally, the spectator – as constituted by Laura Mulvey (1975) and others – has been a real, flesh-and-blood person, either sitting in the dark of a theatre, or otherwise in front of a screen. Of course, it is more complicated than this. For one thing, viewers, like readers, bring multiple versions of themselves to any text. As Wolfgang Iser (1974) and other reader-response theorists have suggested, there are many potential readers constituted by a text, including the implied reader, that is, the reader implied by the text. This is someone who navigates the texts 'properly' because she understands the authorial codes and gestures that lead her to appreciate the full meaning of the text. There are other potential reader roles as well, such as the resistant reader, someone who reads against the grain and who works against the 'ideal' position that the text imagines for them. Of course, categories like these are never fixed and permanent; a single reader might alternate between such stances, at moments edging towards the implied reader, at other moments becoming the resistant reader.

But no matter how many gradations of potential readers – whether inhabiting the same reader or spread across multiple readers – the assumption was always that these were 'real' people. And for all the theory and writing about film spectators from the 1960s on, there was also the assumption that 'spectator' meant a human being sitting in front of a screen. The emergence of avatars – imagined in the fictional world of Neal Stephenson's 1992 novel *Snow Crash* – into the everyday world of the Internet, has potentially profound implications for traditional frameworks for describing and understanding the spectator. In 2007, the Sundance Channel established an area in *Second Life*, where visitors 'can watch full-length feature films in a three-dimensional screening room' (Itzkoff 2007: 28). In other words, a player's avatar can enter a theatre, and watch a 'real' movie, while the user sitting at the computer watches her avatar watching the movie. On one level, there is a special sort of horror involved in the process, a process whereby a self is split in two and watches a film from two identities and perspectives simultaneously.

What does it mean to watch yourself (your avatar) watching a movie? How do you experience a video when you see your second self watching the same screen you are watching? Of the many implications of this shift, there are two I would like to consider briefly:

1. *Although the emergence of avatar-spectators is not a radical break from traditional modes of watching movies, it is another example of how interfaces themselves have become narrative-like.*

Classical narrative film has always been in the business of creating alternate worlds that draw readers in so that, ideally, they lose themselves in the stories. As we have seen, in any interaction with narrative – whether filmic, printed or audio – there are multiple and sometimes simultaneous modes of viewing or reading that are at work. It is doubtful that audiences have ever been the naïve, mystified, passive viewers that so many film theorists posited in the 1970s. The emergence of the avatar – a visual representation of the user's self – is, on one level, a form of 'theory' made visible. The spectator is no longer a passive, distracted vessel for ideological indoctrination; viewers can actually witness representations of themselves absorbing movies. Does this 'second level' in 'second life' foster a more critical, sceptical, active viewer, someone who sees through the narrative and aesthetic codes of the media experience?

Some theorists, such as Fredric Jameson, have commented on the schizophrenic dimensions of the postmodern condition: schizophrenia offers 'a suggestive aesthetic model' (1991: 26) to describe the fragmented, dehistoricised features of the postmodern era. For Jameson, the perpetual present, signified in part by ubiquitous screens, offers a model of perception that, when Jameson's book was published in the 1990s, was radically new. Describing the work of Nam June Paik, whose 'stacked or scattered' television screens don't offer any coherent codes for viewing, Jameson suggests that some viewers adopt an 'older aesthetic' by focusing on a single screen, attempting to find order and meaning. 'The postmodernist viewer, however, is called upon to do the impossible, namely, to see all the screens at once, in their radical and random difference' (1991: 31). What was avant-garde art in the 1980s and 1990s is at least partially mainstreamed today, as users have adopted their own habits and codes for navigating multiple screens.

But the shift to watching movies in the presence of one's own avatar equals more than simply a new paradigm of spectatorship, it involves an entirely expanded narrative framework surrounding the viewing experience, a framework that is itself embedded in a narrative. That is to say, the navigation of the interfaces that culminate in one's avatar entering a 'theatre' in the virtual world in order to watch a 'real' movie, is, at its heart, a form of storytelling. Lev Manovich has wisely cautioned against utopian claims that new media is a revolutionary form of interactivity: 'All classical, and even moreso modern, art is "interactive" in a number of ways. Ellipses in literary narration, missing details of objects in visual art, and other representational "shortcuts" require the user to fill in missing information' (2001: 56). While the interactivity involved in positioning an avatar in a virtual movie theatre might only seem heightened and more pronounced than previous modes of viewership, the narrative components of the interface experience are pronounced markers of this new mode of media consumption. While it could be said that all human interactions involve some narrative components, what is different in the digital era is the foregrounding of this narrative experience. For instance, when your avatar watches a film (itself a narrative) in an online space (such as a virtual movie theatre or screening room) that experience itself is embedded in a narrative.

2. *The presence of the avatar gives lie to the 'realism' of any movie.*
In his 1948 essay 'An Aesthetic of Reality: Neorealism', André Bazin wrote that the 'objective nature of the modern novel, by reducing the strictly grammatical aspect of its stylistics to a minimum, has laid bare the secret essence of style' (2005b: 31). In like fashion, by reducing the film experience to its basest form – the interaction between the screen and the spectator – the avatar serves as a reminder of the movie's artifice. I know that postmodern cinema is often characterised as self-reflexive, but the presence of the avatar only amplifies this. This is something that writers like Chuck Palahniuk have recognised for some time, in novels like *Fight Club* (1996), *Choke* (2001) and *Lullaby* (2002), where the implied reader is never implied for too long before being made explicit. In Palahniuk's *Rant*, a character says that 'In my classroom, I tried to impress upon the students that reality is a consensus' (2007: 53). Of course we, as readers, recognise that these are precisely the instructions for reading a novel or watching a narrative film. Today's audiences learn early on that movies are 'movies' and that novels are 'novels' and that art is 'art'. And the more a writer – like Dave Eggers – pleads to have his or her work read as 'sincere', the more we suspect it is, on the contrary, ironic. The visible manifestation of this is the avatar, which serves as an obvious reminder that there is no such thing as a film apart from its viewer. But there is something else at play too, I think, and that is the reminder – perhaps a sad one, after all – that movies are nothing more than illusions.

In *A Scanner Darkly*, Arctor watches surveillance tapes of himself, and we in turn watch him watching himself. The 'scramble suit' protects him, but from what? Himself? *A Scanner Darkly* might very well be the first film of the digital era to suggest – not directly but through its visual logic – that watching ourselves is no longer enough. Instead, we need to watch ourselves watching ourselves. 'What does a scanner see?' asks Arctor at one point near the end of the film. 'Into the head? Down into the heart? Does it see into me? Into us? Clearly or darkly? I hope it sees clearly because I can't any longer see into myself. I see only murk. I hope for everyone's sake the scanners do better.' The sadness here is not the depiction of a surveillance society, but rather the fact that Arctor hopes that something else – something that might not even be human – can see into him and understand him better than he could ever understand himself. In a sense, the scramble suit that Arctor and other police agents wear to protect their identities is the ultimate avatar, as unstable and changing as the times themselves. In *A Scanner Darkly*, the split in Arctor's personality is, on one level, a consequence of the drug he is taking. But on another level, his split into multiple selves is in keeping with the process of creating and living a double life through an avatar, which serves as a projection of the self onto a second self. This hyper-awareness of self, this deep narcissism, is characteristic of the film viewing experience in the digital era, when the role of the spectator assumes an ever more visible role in the arrangement of a film's structure. In *A Scanner Darkly*, Arctor's manipulation of the surveillance tapes of himself, as he fast-forwards and freeze-frames the action, is akin to our own manipulation of the DVD of *A Scanner Darkly*.

In Jorge Luis Borges' story 'The Circular Ruins', the protagonist realises that he – like the son that he has created – is likewise a simulacrum: 'He walked toward the sheets of flame. They did not bite his flesh, they caressed him and flooded him without heat or combustion. With relief, with humiliation, with terror, he understood that he also was an illusion, that someone else was dreaming him' (1962: 63). The avatar-spectator takes these very old questions about the differences between truth and illusion to a new level: instead of a relationship between the spectator and the screen, we now have one between the spectator, the screen and the spectator's avatar, who watches the screen on an intermediary screen on behalf of the spectator. The avatar becomes a character, too, an illusion, but one projected from the flesh-and-blood spectator, and endowed with a certain degree of agency. In his influential 1975 essay 'The Apparatus', theorist Jean-Louis Baudry sought to expose the insidious effects of mystification that movies had upon film audiences: 'First of all, that taking into account the darkness of the movie theatre, the relative passivity of the situation, the forced immobility of the cine-subject, and the effects which result from the projection of images, moving images, the cinematographic apparatus brings about a state of artificial regression' (1999: 773). But what if the spectator is doubled now, in some contexts, so that her avatar also watches, and exists within, but separate from, the screen that contains the movie? Does the avatar serve as a sort of filter, straining the film's ideology so that by the time it reaches the 'primary' spectator, its power is diminished? Does the presence of our own double watching the same movie we are watching automatically double the interpretive possibilities?

Media As Its Own Theory
[cinematology, Michel Gondry, *Scream*, United States Department of Defense, video archiving]

Postmodernism was an essentially democratic movement because its metanarratives – its self-consciousness, its parody, its pastiche, its irony – always worked to make visible the codes that underlie cultural productions. Perhaps this is disputed by many of the well-meaning professorial theorists, whose dying influence still depends upon the supposed ability to demystify popular culture.

The gradual enmeshment in administrated networks of professors and theorists is especially noteworthy in the American college and university system, where vocational models of higher education have largely supplanted the older (perhaps mythical) models of the university as a utopian site of dissent and critique. If theory has been banished from today's administrated, technocratic university (which in its student-as-customer incarnation tends to regard the hard edges of theory as impractical and alienating) it has found a new home in the very forms of popular culture it once strove to demystify, rendering divisions such as avant-garde and mainstream, or theoretical and naïve, practically meaningless. In short, the theorist-professor is disappearing because media today theorises its own ideology in fairly explicit ways, both in terms of form and content. And nowhere is this more evident than in the contradictory uses to which DV filmmaking is being put. Today, the process of theoretical deconstruction – at one time restricted to the halls of *academe* – has now become our culture's new lyricism. This has been recognised not only by academics, but by the popular press itself. In his discussion of movies like *Shrek* and musicals like *Wicked*, James Poniewozik wrote that 'parodying fairy tales has become the default mode of telling them' and that 'the strange side effect of today's meta-stories is that kids get exposed to the parodies before, or instead of, the originals' (2007: 84).

In *Subculture: The Meaning of Style*, Dick Hebdige wrote of punk's ordered anarchy: 'The punk subculture … signified chaos at every level, but this was only possible because the style itself was so thoroughly ordered' (1979: 113). Today, it is in the very ordering, or administration, of newly deployed reality, signalled by shaky cameras and images that in their imperfection reveal their status as images, that we witness the final codification of deconstruction. If we look at one DV production company – the United States military – we see a rawer, more experimental aesthetic of DV filmmaking emerging, one that borrows in terms of its theory and its production tactics many of the signature characteristics of the Dogme 95 movement. How, well-meaning theorists might ask, has it come to pass that the most startling cinema of the year 2003 was the film of the captured Saddam Hussein in what looked like the prologue to a snuff movie, recorded on a Sony PD 150, the camera of choice for the US military in Iraq? Sergeant Wesley Wooden, a combat cameraman, has said that 'Basically what we're trained for is that the camera is our first weapon … We're lucky enough to carry pistols. It gives you some more protection. You can shoot and shoot at the same time' (in Heffernan 2003: 2). That it is the US military producing some of the most startling *cinéma vérité*, very much in the spirit of the Dogme 95 movement, reminds us of Paul Virilio, who has written famously that the gestures of surveillance, of vision, of speed have for a long time linked cinema and the military: 'One could go on forever listing the technological weapons, the panoply of light-war, the aesthetic of the electronic battlefield' (1989: 88).

And what, if not an avant-garde film studio, is the Joint Combat Camera Program, which is part of the Department of Defense's Defense Visual Information (DVI) Directorate. For it is the tactics of guerilla filmmaking, the New Wave, the fast-and-go immediacy of post-punk film that is described in the section on the 'Video Flyaway Kit': 'All items are fitted into one case which is easily handled by one person. It provides a single videographer with the capability to acquire video imagery, edit and compress the imagery using the laptop, and transmit the video clip via INMARSAT. In addition the INMARSAT can also be used to transmit still imagery. This is an ideal system for use by a two man documentation team.' The pre-eminence of the military as a movie production company using guerilla filmmaking tactics is understandable given the gradual incorporation of theory and irony into the major channels of cultural distribution in the 1980s and 1990s. The self-aware, ironic comments by Sergeant Wooden, who recognises that the language of warfare and the language of perception are bound together, is made possible because theory – once the province of cultural theorists and the professorial elite – has been extensively mainstreamed into popular culture over the past twenty years. And the incorporation of theory into popular culture is archived in not only the contents but the format or medium of the DVD, where films are permanently demystified, stripped of their aura in ways described by Walter Benjamin in his 1935 essay 'The Work of Art in the Age of Mechanical Reproduction'. Indeed, the self-deconstructing dimension of the films is there for all to see because they are permanently archived, easily available, and garner publicity in multiple cultural arenas ranging from amazon.com to blogs. Some of the titles in the Director's Label, DVDs by Spike Jonze, Michel Gondry and Michael Cunningham, are excellent examples, and illustrate the extent to which popular culture has absorbed the logic of theory in ways that illustrate the obsolescence of the professional theorist/critic and the emergence of a powerful new cultural form that exists at the far edges of what used to be called film or video.

Michel Gondry's 1994 video 'Lucas with the Lid Off' (available on the Director's Label collection) is an interesting example of a pop video whose self-theorising elements are radically foregrounded. Shot in one continuous take, the video is a series of over twenty shots, each one anticipated by a numbered frame that awaits the camera's arrival. In effect, we see how each tableau (more often than not featuring the singer Lucas) has in fact been pre-staged for us. In addition to the framing of our screens, we are made aware of the visual parameters of the camera itself, as it is positioned for each shot in a literal frame that anticipates the camera's arrival. The story the video tells is essentially the story of its production, although without resorting to the usual methods of revealing the camera. One is tempted to call this video – and indeed most of Michel Gondry's videos – avant-garde, although in film studies this term is usually reserved for artists whose work is considered to be largely outside the mainstream. And yet many of Gondry's films and videos are as experimental as the work of Maya Deren, Michael Snow, Hollis Frampton and others canonised in the avant-garde pantheon.

By the 1990s, irony – previously associated with the avant-garde, most notably in the Pop Art movement of the 1960s – had become incorporated into mainstream practices, a process expertly documented by David Foster Wallace in his 1993 essay 'E Unibus Pluram: Television and US Fiction', which explores the nexus between ironic modes in postmodern fiction and popular culture of the 1980s, such as Isuzu car commercials and *Late Night with David Letterman*. Letterman's relentless breaking of the codes of technical invisibility (the 360-degree rotating camera, cameras attached to a monkey's head in the 'Monkey Cam' episodes, and so on) were as experimental as any serious avant-garde films being made at the time, and drew upon Monty Python's albums (especially *Monty Python's Previous Record*, from 1972) and their *Flying Circus* television series. Later, television shows like *Talk Soup* (which premiered in 1971) further mainstreamed irony as a prime-time formula, and by the mid-1990s, with the relentless self-awareness and self-commentary of *Scream*, we witness a simultaneous outcropping of theory in disparate places, including highly commercial films, music videos, academic books and essays, and avant-garde, experimental films and websites. As Carlo McCormick has noted in relation to the emergence of the 'pop surrealism' art movement in the 1990s: 'Born outside the naïve age of generational discovery into a more complex dynamic of immediate and utter immersion, we are media-damaged beyond recognition and have taken rampant appropriation to a frenzied level of mashed-up multitasking' (2004: 11).

Indeed, in *Scream*'s famous moment where the film *Halloween* is paused so that one of the beer-toting teens can explain to his friends (*a la* a film professor) the underlying codes of slasher films, he offers an explication of the 'rules' of slasher filmmaking that echoes not only deconstructive film theory but also the rules in the Dogme 95 Vow of Chastity. If *Scream* signalled the mainstreaming of film theory in ways that helped to resuscitate a moribund genre (the slasher film), and if the Dogme 95 movement shared this same logic of self-theorising in the guise of provocation and aesthetics, then we could say that Carol Clover's book *Men, Women and Chainsaws* (1992), which similarly deconstructed cinematic rules in academic discourse, represented the last moment that a certain kind of film theory was possible. This deconstructionist approach to film – one that had enjoyed the status of authority for decades in American universities – was stripped away the moment commercial films began validating, and thus rendering obsolete, rarefied academic film theory. As we shall see, the demise of film theory as a potent unmasking force was cemented with the popularisation of media whose very form theorised itself.

Cinema in the digital age – which no longer simply uses self-reference as a narrative device but which in fact depends upon an audience which expects it – has a sort of built-in mode of deconstruction, which is also evident in other art forms from the era. Here, for instance, is a passage from the novel *Innocence* by Jane Mendelsohn:

> In class, the teacher said something about the unreliable narrator. The unreliable narrator was a device. A device for what? For creating ironic distance, she said. Oh, said Tobey. So you mean, like, it's okay to lie.
>
> No, it's not lying. It's a literary technique.
>
> Cool. I had sex with every girl in this school.
>
> That's a lie, another kid said.
>
> No, it's not, Tobey said. I'm just an unreliable narrator. (2000: 38)

Even films that are not self-referential on the level of content are on the interface level, where the film's aura is not enhanced, but reduced, by the bonus and supplementary features that reveal the secrets of its making.

What does it mean today to say that many forms of new media are embedded with the very structures of critique and theory that are supposedly the province of the theorist? Certainly, the tendency to look to artifacts themselves, rather than professional academics, for theory is nothing new. In 1969, in her essay 'Trash, Art, and the Movies', Pauline Kael sided with the potentially subversive qualities of film as opposed to the official academic culture which taught students how to read such films: 'It's appalling to read solemn academic studies of Hitchcock or von Sternberg by people who seem to have lost sight of the primary reason for seeing films like "Notorious" or "Morocco" – which is that they were not intended solemnly, that they were playful and inventive and faintly (often deliberately) absurd' (1970: 113). And auteurs of the past, such as Sergei Eisenstein and Jean-Luc Godard also theorised about film in terms of ideology and aesthetics in ways that would be familiar to us now as academic. So the notion that groups other than professional theorists are capable of offering critiques and theories that explore the deeper ideological dimensions of film is nothing new.

However, as Robert Ray has suggested, the institutionalisation of film studies as an academic discipline in the 1960s contributed not only to a productive and alert inter-disciplinary model but also to a kind of stagnation as various theoretical approaches – the Frankfurt School, semiotics, cultural studies – became codified, regularised, re-producible and defanged. Whereas many of the previous theorists – Eisenstein, Go-dard, Deren, Kael, Jonas Mekas, André Bazin – were either filmmakers themselves or else wrote independently of academic institutions, by the 1960s and 1970s in the US, film theory became almost exclusively associated with academia. Indeed, as early as 1960, in the US, the popular press was reporting on the rise of film scholarship. In 'The Day of the Cinematologist', in the *Christian Science Monitor*, we read that in 'universities the study of film production has become an accredited course. The motion picture, as a popular or even fine art, has become an increasingly likely subject for intellectuals to theorise upon. The result is a new kind of academician whom Parker Tyler calls the cinematologist' (Anon. 1960: 6). Theory became a practice, inevitably fragmenting into schools, slowly removing itself from the objects of its critique, and largely assuming that films – especially Hollywood films – were essentially naïve and untheorised at a conscious level. Film theory, it was assumed, was a tool by which to crack open the hard kernel of ideology masquerading as film.

Of course this was not the case, but because of the impermanence and unarchived nature of film, who could dispute such a claim? Until the advent of the VCR as a house-hold commodity in the 1980s, it was difficult for average film viewers to capture a film long enough to study it. Rather than widely accessible film archives, we had widely accessible archives of theory given the weight of permanence in books and journals. Today, however, theory is confronted with the object of its critique, as more and more films, previously available only in museums or on film festival circuits, make their way to affordable DVD home viewing formats, thus challenging decades of theory that depended for its authority on the obscurity and impermanence of the films it was critiquing. This is to say nothing of the proliferation of video on the web: how does the avant-garde maintain its status when it is situated no longer in obscure galleries or special art-house showings but instead is available for anyone to see, for free, at any time, on virtually any computer screen?

The proliferation of theory not only in terms of narrative content (*The Matrix*, *Scream*) but also in terms of self-revealing formats (such as DVDs with their atten-dant behind-the-scenes, deconstructive content) suggests that DV has the potential to archive the breakdown of the real even as it captures it. A film like *28 Days Later* is significant because its attempt to capture realistically a hypothetical future only high-lights the artifice of the medium. Ironically, the realism of the Dogme and Dogme-like films – notably *The Celebration* and *The Blair Witch Project*, and the Saddam Hussein tape – rests precisely in their momentary anti-realism. Although many of the films deploy shaky, hand-held cameras and self-conscious lighting as shorthand for real-ism, this only serves to reinforce the fact of the camera behind the image. We begin to recognise the visual codes of 'realism' as just that: codes that ultimately erode the very mystique of realism itself. The closer DV takes us to the Real, the more we recognise it as illusion. Keith Griffiths notes that 'what gave cinema part of its value – a confident, assured and unchallenged recording of reality, and one that was extremely difficult to modify and manipulate – has now been fundamentally changed by the new digital technology' (2001: 2).

Alas, are we to be tempted into nostalgia for the digital so soon after its appearance? Do we already yearn for the 'good old days' of early DV and the noisy proclamations of the Dogme 95 movement, or are those aesthetics yet to be found in the productions of the US military? Does the cycle of incorporation and commodification come so quickly on the heels of the avant-garde today that we are left with the stultifying aura of 'history' surrounding such movements as Dogme 95? In perhaps the ultimate cruelty, our ironic sense of theory and our hunger for deconstruction robs us even of the sedate pleasures of nostalgia, which, someone will no doubt remind us, is just another myth.

Mobile Viewing
[hand-held screens, Anne Friedberg, Siegfried Kracauer, Ramones]

But it is not just that watching a film today involves *tmesis*: film itself is moving, because its screens are mobile. On laptops, video iPods and cell phones, the shaky screens are of our shaky world. Anne Friedberg and others have explored how 'the gradual shift into postmodernity is marked … by the increased centrality of the mobilised and virtual gaze as a fundamental feature of everyday life' (1993: 4). And as Lynne Kirby has noted, as 'a perceptual paradigm, the railroad [in the nineteenth century] established a new, specifically modern mode of perception that the cinema absorbed naturally. In other words, the kind of perception that came to characterise the passenger on the train became that of the spectator in the cinema' (1997: 7). Hand-held screens have liberated not only the spectator from the theatre, but the screen as well. But liberated them from what? For decades film theory attempted to expose the 'imprisonment' of the passive spectator – with ideology sweeping over her – in the dark confines of the theatre. But now that film's aura has been thoroughly debunked, we are faced with nostalgia for the old movie houses, the prisons where our dreams were given shape and sound. Part of the problem is that having rooted out ideology and deconstructed the politics of the gaze, we are no longer sure how to react to them when we detect them.

The mobility of the screen erodes the boundary between the place of dreams and everyday life. Like books, movies have become, in the digital era, increasingly hand-held, transportable objects. In this sense, they have freed themselves from their references to live theatre, which also relied upon immobile audiences. It is perhaps to be expected that as digital images strive for an ever more pristine representation of reality, screens should likewise become detached from the fixed walls of movie houses, which served, after all, to remind audiences of the theatricality behind the movie, to assure them that they were in a place of representation, separate from the everyday world. Screens, during the classical era, were constructed places that suggested a sort of fixed portal into some other world. But screens today have leaked into the everyday world, colonising it. The secret history of the shrinking of the screen is intertwined with the shrinking of music in the form of punk in the mid-1970s. In the *New Musical Express*, Roy Carr wrote that the Ramones were 'the first group to have condensed an entire 14-track LP onto the head of a pin without any loss of definition' (1976: 21). Since then, movies have been subjected to the same thing: they have become smaller and smaller, even as they have grown in high definition.

In 1960, Siegfried Kracauer wrote that 'cinema can be defined as a medium particularly equipped to promote the redemption of physical reality' (1997: 300). The downsizing of screens – from CinemaScope to television sets to video iPods – cannot be underestimated, for between the large, fixed screen and the small, mobile one there lies a fundamental difference in the conception of physical reality. On the big screen, one reality is overlayed with another; we lose ourselves in this second, cinematic reality. On the small screen, the cinematic reality is just a piece, a fragment, of the dominant one in the same way that movies themselves are now fragmented, rendered as 'chapters' or 'scene selections' on DVD menus or clips on places like YouTube. Small, mobile screens are not a medium for watching two-hour movies uninterrupted, and in fact interruption is now an important structural component of the narrative logic of many digital-era films.

Moving Space In The Frame, And A Note On Film Theory
[continuity editing, Salman Rushdie, *The Shining*]

'It's easy to move things around in the frame, to change various visual aspects of the film, which just wasn't possible before' (in Magid 2002: 2). Although this was George Lucas referring to the making of *Star Wars Episode II: Attack of the Clones*, it might just as easily refer to us, as spectators, in the near future, when screens are not something we simply manipulate through remote controls and buttons, but rather through actual interaction with the screen itself. Lynne Kirby has noted an important difference between the relationship of audiences to screens during the silent and the classical film eras:

> Once it 'won out', classical cinema developed a system of techniques that it would perfect over the next decade (1908–17). 'Continuity editing' developed as a method of connecting shots to subordinate everything to the progress of the narrative – i.e., to what *happens*. Similarly, everything within the frame in classical film was composed to orient the spectator's attention to the most narratively significant action or object, whereas early film often filled the frame with a variety of competing characters, actions, and objects that tested the spectator's ability to discern the most significant action. (1997: 104; emphasis in original)

If continuity editing still dominates the editing logic of film today, as spectators we are developing a method of functional editing more akin to jump cuts than continuity. For what does it matter if a film is edited along the classical lines of subservience to narrative when our own interaction with that film increasingly draws upon the logic of sampling and mixing? We are at the dawn of an era when it is not only possible to mix and rearrange the existing content of a film, but when it is also possible to mix together existing video into something new, as with video mash-ups. Robert Ryang's 'Shining' – a remixed trailer for Stanley Kubrick's *The Shining* set to Peter Gabriel's 'Solsbury Hill' – suggests a heartfelt, sentimental family drama. It offers a glimpse into a possible version of the film, one buried beneath its surface. The humour comes from the disjunction we feel watching the clip: we have seen Jack Torrance before, and he is a monster. But here he is a loving father, who is redeemed by his family from his own demons. More than simply an ironic reworking of the film, the mash-up reveals the *possibles* of the film, the paths not taken. The mash-up works not because it is so far removed from *The Shining* that we know, but rather because it corresponds so closely to a possible version of the film lurking within the film.

Spectators' instinctual, almost sensual, understanding of film means that they are mostly attuned to these nuances and secret passageways that run through films. If there is one central reason that film theory has withered, it is because it failed to acknowledge viewers' deeply complex understanding of film itself. Spectators tend to deconstruct films in their minds; in fact, this deconstruction is fundamental to our relationship with film, the best of which offer many layers of sometimes contradictory meaning. Paradoxically, digital culture – in which we are prompted continually to rearrange data, information and images – has made it abundantly clear. The act of *interpreting* a film, which used to involve simply thinking and writing about it, now involves the physical manipulation of the film through its interface. This process itself is an act of deconstruction; a film's meaning is taken apart not only by our thinking critically about it, but by our physical interaction with it through its interface. Formalist explications, for instance, of cause and effect in film, are perhaps irrelevant in an age when spectators are no longer prisoners of time in a film.

In *Imagined Communities* (1983), Benedict Anderson addressed the struggle of the big capital T Theories (for example, Marxism) to make sense, on a personal level, of the profound tragedies (for example, the death of a child) on our lives. So too film theory, in its historical turn against aesthetics and 'appreciation', and in its quest to decode ideology, has by-and-large neglected to account for the fact that film retains its appeal to audiences not because they are completely seduced by it, but rather because they are not. In Salman Rushdie's *The Satanic Verses*, an Indian film star named Gibreel Farishta falls through the air after the plane he is on explodes. He is reported as dead. His image on movie posters and signs begins to decay, to fade, to implode, to disappear: 'Even on the silver screen itself, high above his worshippers in the dark, that supposedly immortal physiognomy began to putrefy, blister and bleach; projectors jammed unaccountably every time he passed through the gate; his films ground to a halt, and the lamp-heat of the malfunctioning projectors burned his celluloid memory away' (1989: 16). Paradoxically, the end of analogue and celluloid portends not the death of the image, but its replication everywhere, all the time.

Natural Time

[chronometricals, Dressed to Kill, Herman Melville, The Science of Sleep]

Digital movie cameras are not even called digital movie cameras now: they are called cell phones. Cinematography is simply one of many functions – and certainly not the most important – an almost throwaway feature. Soon movies will become so little they will disappear. The dethroning of the way movies are shot means the dethroning of movies themselves, the best of which only serve to remind us that the bad old days of ideology at least produced objects worthy of deconstruction. Michel Gondry's *The Science of Sleep* is not an empty movie because it has nothing to say but because what it has to say is empty, and perfectly reasonable. The time-shift machine that Stephan invents is not an act of fantasy, but a confirmation of the skip-ahead and pause functions of our time. The movie struggles to find some coherent point of reference not because it is a shallow postmodern trick, but because the audience itself is unstable, whirling. That the movie cannot commit to a point of view is, of course, read by the critics as its great achievement.

In *Adaptation*, during the scene when Kaufman meets the movie producer to pitch his idea for the adaptation of *The Orchid Thief*, he tells her: 'I don't want to cram in sex or guns or car chases. You know? Or characters learning profound life lessons. Or growing, or coming to like each other, or overcoming obstacles to succeed in the end.' Of course, moments like these – when the film we are watching reminds us we are watching a film – are nothing new. From the beginnings of cinema, when in Edwin S. Porter's *The Great Train Robbery* one of the bandits aims his pistol at us, on the other side of the screen, and fires, to the classical era, when Norma Desmond (Gloria Swanson), in *Sunset Blvd.*, looks directly into the camera when talking about her 'audience', to Jean-Luc Godard and beyond, movies have, occasionally, been about themselves. The difference is that what was once a gesture that called attention to itself is today the dominant narrative. The reason there are so many supplementary features on DVDs is because in peeling away the narrative layers of the 'feature' film, what is revealed is a more compelling story than the one told by the film itself.

But in a larger, metaphorical sense, the rejection of traditional editing (cuts, shot/reverse-shots, and so forth) offers a basic return to natural time, uncut except for the blink of your eyes and your sleep. There is no shot-reverse/shot in our everyday experience; we are creatures of the long take, trapped in our own gazes.

But we must go back further. For at the heart of modernity lies a break with natural time, and a radical scepticism and sadness. A key text here is Herman Melville's novel *Pierre; or, the Ambiguities*, published in 1852, the year after *Moby-Dick*; a disastrous novel, which a contemporary reviewer called 'One long brain-muddling, soul-bewildering ambiguity' (Spengemann 1996: xx). Written during an era of advances in synchronous time, the most bizarre section of the novel occurs roughly mid-way through, when Pierre finds clutched in his hand (how it got there he doesn't know) a worn pamphlet, with its concluding pages missing. This is a lecture entitled 'Chronometricals and Horologicals' by one Plotinus Plinlimmon, a rumination on human time, heavenly time and God which basically calls into question the nature of truth itself. On one level, the pamphlet trades in a sort of obvious relativism, one made more pronounced by the standardisation of time and technologies designed to measure time ever-more accurately, such as the chronometer:

> Now in an artificial world like ours, the soul of man is further removed from God and the Heavenly Truth, than the chronometer carried to China, is from Greenwich. And, as that chronometer, if at all accurate, will pronounce it to be 12 o'clock high noon, when the China local watches say, perhaps, it is 12 o'clock midnight. (1996: 211)

The discussion deepens into a more unsettling discussion of time and relativity:

> But though the chronometer carried from Greenwich to China, should truly exhibit in China what the time may be at Greenwich at any moment; yet, though thereby it must necessarily contradict China time, it does by no means thence follow, that with respect to China, the China watches are at all out of the way. Precisely the reverse. For the fact of that variance is a presumption that, with respect to China, the Chinese watches must be all right; and consequently the China watches are right as to China, so the Greenwich chronometers must be wrong as to China. (1996: 212)

In the theatre, watching a film like *Russian Ark*, we the audience experience time in the same manner as the characters on the screen did. Our ninety minutes is their ninety minutes, and vice versa. It is fellowship, in the dark. This is 'personal cinema' in a new sense, as our affinity with the actors on the screen offers, paradoxically, a new form of humanism, even as new technologies like RFID (Radio Frequency Identification) tagging threaten to reduce us to statistics about what we purchase and where we move. In movies, traditionally, such mobile long takes were considered, paradoxically, 'breaks' from realism, from the natural order of storytelling, even as they captured a certain reality in a very special way. They called attention to themselves. The museum sequence in Brian De Palma's *Dressed to Kill*, as the camera glides along with Angie Dickinson, sometimes observing her, sometimes adopting her gaze, is often singled out from the movie as an example of style (or, more typically, as an example of style over substance). Once upon a time, these real-time segments were self-conscious, in part because they were technically difficult: making them involved heavier cameras, great lengths of film, and expense. As DV and HD arrived, some of these obstacles disappeared. Inevitably, the traditional long take was regarded as art precisely because it was so difficult. With the democratisation of technology, the cheapness, the risk-free conditions of experimentalism (if the long take doesn't work, just try it over again, since no film was wasted), made techniques like mobile long takes more possible than ever, less rare, and perhaps less of an aesthetic choice than a practical function of making movies with small digital cameras.

Which brings us to the question of art, of aesthetics, terms that for so many years in film theory and criticism have suffered, revealed by Marxist and post-Marxist theory to be the mystifying agents of ideology. As digital media has made the previously invisible mechanisms of cinematic storytelling visible – and in fact has turned these into art – film theory finds itself out-theorised by movies themselves. A film like Steven Soderbergh's *Bubble*, produced in 1080i HD format and released in January 2006 simultaneously in theatres, on DVD and on high-definition cable television, is both a film and an event about the making-of and the distribution-of the film. It is the fact of storytelling – rather than the story itself – which fascinates today, and which is the dominant marker of the digital era. Here is Soderbergh discussing filmmaking in the digital age:

> When the changeover from film to digital happens in theatres in five or ten years, you're going to see name filmmakers self-distributing. Another thing that really excites me: I'd like to do multiple versions of the same film. I often do very radical cuts of my own films just to experiment, shake things up, and see if anything comes of it. I think it would be really interesting to have a movie out in release and then, just a few weeks later say, 'Here's version 2.0, recut, rescored.' The other version is still out there – people can see either or both. (In Jardin 2006)

This is why larger social critiques of the dehumanising dimensions of digital cinema (such as that of Jean-Pierre Geuens (2002)) do not really ring true. Sean Cubitt's suggestion that 'the digital corresponds so closely to the emergent loss of an ideological structure because it no longer pretends to represent the world' and that 'digital media do not refer. They communicate' (2004: 250) aptly captures the feeling of human loss in the midst of digital special effects and evermore spectacular scenarios.

Other pioneers in digital independent filmmaking, such as Alejandro Adams and Lance Weiler, discuss the shift to digital not just in terms of the aesthetics of the movies themselves (in Weiler's case *The Last Broadcast* and *Head Trauma*) but also in terms of 'do-It-yourself' distribution. As Brian Holcomb notes, the 'studios have the contracts with the owners of all the major theatre chains and the financial muscle to be able to spend a cool 10-15 million dollars in advertising to make sure their product has a high profile and is available to be seen in all of the major markets … Until now, if an independent filmmaker did not sell their film to a major studio/distributor, they would find out soon enough that they reached the end of the road' (2007: 1–2). A newly emerging alternative, however, suggests something very much different: 'Now that a filmmaker can bypass the need to make costly film prints, he or she can burn their finished film to DVD, screen it theatrically through digital projection, or make it available for download' (2007: 2). And yet the allure and mystery of watching films together in the dark with strangers is perhaps a pleasure that will not be eradicated by new technologies. Alejandro Adams – whose film *Around the Bay* is among the finest and most moving of the new wave of independent digital films – has written about the pleasures of watching his film on the big screen, where all the triumphs and flaws of a film are magnified.

Walter Benjamin's early speculations about the effects of mass reproduction were wildly ambiguous: while reproduction threatened to jar a work of art out of its original contexts, stripping it of its aura, it also facilitated a sort of demystification that allowed for healthy scepticism. The easy reproduction and mass distribution of self-made work today would seem to suggest that new or previously marginalised ideas and aesthetic forms could merge into the mainstream with more ease, if not least because much less capital is needed to reach audiences. This is not the reproduction of ideologically dominant ideas, but rather of ideas that were formally confined to small communities who lacked the means to 'broadcast' and reproduce them in the media. And yet how to talk about this, how to theorise it, remains highly contested. I have a colleague who insists that the 'conservative' elements of culture are always co-opting new and potentially dangerous and subversive ideas, slightly modifying them and recirculating them back into mass culture. And we could extend this argument even further: the very technologies of digital reproduction encourage a parasitical dependence on technology. As Marshall McLuhan and others have noted, content and the medium used to deliver content (such as a television, a computer, a mobile phone) are part of the same narrative. So one could say the content of digital reproduction is always, at some basic level, the idea of digital reproduction itself.

Nonlinear
[random access]

Nonlinear is the name of a book by Michael Rubin, first published in 1991, and subtitled *A Guide to Electronic Film and Video Editing*. Rubin was not the first to use the word 'nonlinear' to describe a process of editing in the video and digital age, but his book was among the first to popularise the term, and to describe not only a technical process, but a way of thinking. 'As you know', Rubin wrote, 'traditional videotape editing is, by definition, *linear*. It means that you make the first edit, commit to it, then make the second edit, and so on, starting at the beginning of your project and ending it at the end … "Nonlinear" is the key word describing the new computerised editing systems that are designed for cutting in a film-like style' (1991: 6; emphasis in original). Written on the cusp of the digital and Internet revolution, *Nonlinear* captures the chaos of the times, as Rubin shifts – in this first edition of the book – between highly technical descriptions of editing processes, and larger, more global discussions of the consequences of the shift from analogue to digital. The question that haunts the book, and that is never directly asked, is this: does this relatively new, emergent form of editing have the potential to radically change the very narrative logic and structure of films themselves? When the source material is digitised for editing, and becomes part of a digital database available for almost instantaneous recall, how does this impact on the entire notion of linearity? Of course, linearity was always a construct, and imposed the idea of order upon a fractured but coherent filmmaking process as most films themselves are shot out of chronological sequence, and later edited together.

Symbolically, nonlinear editing corresponds to traditional film editing that took place on uprights and flatbeds: in both cases, images are managed and rearranged in order to tell a story. But the random access and virtually instant recall of the database fundamentally alters the way we perceive of the relationship between the shots in a film. Lacking a physical presence or embodiment, the fragments to be edited together appear *only* on the screen. As Rubin has noted, traditional film editing involved dailies, which were 'broken down into small rolls, each containing one take. Racks of these little rolls are brought to the editor' (1991: 24), a process illustrated famously in Dziga Vertov's *Man with a Movie Camera*. While the idea behind linear and nonlinear editing is similar – the arrangement of fragments into an order that expresses the story – the lack of physical film and the immediate availability of images in nonlinear systems suggests a technology that makes more possible than ever the nonlinear potential of time. Whether movies like *Memento*, *Eternal Sunshine of the Spotless Mind*, *Run Lola Run* and *Inland Empire* are byproducts of the general logic of nonlinear editing systems or not, it could be said that far from being avant-garde, they will come to be known as some of the films that began to naturalise the concept of nonlinearity and repetition. In *Run Lola Run*, the several different versions of the same event tell the story not only of Lola and her boyfriend Manni, but of the process of nonlinear editing itself, whereby shots and sequences are pieced together in potentially endless configurations, each one telling a slightly (or drastically) different story. Again, it is not that the ability to rearrange and resequence time in movies is new with nonlinear editing, but rather that the ease and speed whereby the database can be accessed and summoned means that more experimental, even radical representations of time in cinema are possible.

Pausing
[Roland Barthes, Man Ray, *The Ring*]

Paradoxically, the new technologies take us back to the oldest forms of criticism, a criticism that, at its heart, is a form of exegesis. The New Critics, with their close readings and worship of the text, were not buried by the postmodernists, after all. They are alive, like zombies, always coming back. Perhaps they never went away to begin with. While digital technologies provide the ability to create endless layers of context and multiple frames around a text (in the form of DVD bonus features, alternate endings, remixes, parodies, pastiches, and so forth), they also make it possible to freeze, capture and disseminate cinematic images. Of course, film theory and analysis based upon a film's stills or even publicity shots is nothing new. What is crucially different, however, is the ease by which a film's images can be captured today, and the availability of inexpensive (often free) technology that makes freezing and capturing a film's image possible. And so despite the relentless speed of information and images today (x number of new videos are posted on YouTube every day) it is possible to use this technology to slow down – to freeze, even – the images around us. As Roland Barthes noted in his writings on the 'third meaning' (see 1977a), the contemplation of film stills allows for an alternative form of knowledge, one that exists on the periphery of critical acceptability. For instance, as noted in the introduction, the pause button on DVD players makes it possible to notice correspondences such as these, from Gore Verbinski's *The Ring* and Man Ray's *Le Retour à la raison* and *L'Étoile de mer*.

In 1935, Walter Benjamin wrote: 'With the close-up, space expands; with slow motion, movement is extended. The enlargement of a snapshot does not merely render more precise what in any case was visible, though unclear: it reveals entirely new structural formations of the subject' (1968: 250). The correspondences between the avant-garde film within the commercial, genre film *The Ring* and the short avant-garde films of Man Ray can only be traced fitfully and incoherently. The digital era – and that vast archive of previously obscure images, texts and films that it makes easily

Blurred faces in *L'Étoile de mer* and *The Ring*

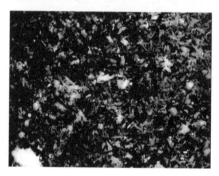

Bodies in *The Ring* suggest the idea of bodies in *Le Retour à la raison*

available (both Man Ray films cited above are freely accessible on the web) – is still young enough that the methods of film criticism have not yet hardened into path-dependent orthodoxies.

Seventy years after the destruction of time through montage, the total freezing and capture of the image renders montage as just another series of frozen moments. In late postmodernity, the fragment has been put to use as a building block – the myth of total cinema, of the long take, of real time, replaces the fragment as the pre-ferred form. 'Photographic reproduction,' Benjamin suggested, 'with the aid of certain processes, such as enlargement or slow motion, can capture images which escape natural vision' (1968: 222).

But what the digital makes possible is the absolute disruption of moving images, the very basis of cinema itself. Today film is captured in freeze-frames on laptop com-puters, and reduced to images on cell phones. In fact, before too long distinctions be-tween movies and other forms of moving images (for instance, television shows) will be meaningless: when you are watching (glancing at?) something on your cell phone, does it matter if it was originally a 'movie' or not? Today, movies still open on movie theatre screens, and then again on television, computer and cell phone screens. Like everything else, they are made to adjust to on-demand lifestyles. The loss of the 'aura' that Walter Benjamin wrote about in the early twentieth century is now complete. In fact, the dispelling of the aura is itself a dominant narrative mode, not only in terms of plot (see *Stranger Than Fiction* or *Adaptation*) but in terms of interface, as well (DVD menus, on-demand movies on cable, and so forth). There are no secrets left for movies to confess, so they confess to having no secrets: this is what the supplements and bonus features on DVDs amount to. Such elaborate confessions make the demystifying job of theorists and academics irrelevant: the confession has already been tendered before the interrogator arrives. The serious, frowning Marxists of the 1960s and 1970s gave way to those who practiced the safer art of university-sanctioned cultural studies. But today even they are faced with students whose blank faces in film classes represent not boredom, but rather the secrets to the mysteries the dutiful professors believe they are unveiling. The tendency to 'see through' movies was there from the beginning of modern cinema. Home and amateur movies developed as correctives to studio-financed films, rendering a sort of in-home film school long before there were academic film schools. Popular magazines and books from as early as the 1920s 'deconstructed' the techniques and languages of filmmaking. And in newspapers such as the *New York Times*, there were frequent articles devoted to abstract, non-commercial cinema. Representative is a 1952 piece, 'The Case for Abstract Art Films', that surveyed the various types of abstract films and other art forms of the era, particularly their experimental approaches to light. 'For such artists', the article suggested, 'just as forms are not conceived as static entities and just as space is not immutable and measurable by a network of perspective, so light itself has no constant intensity or fixed source' (Louchheim 1952: X9).

The task today is not to see through movies, but rather to find ways to resist the total colonisation of space and time by new media. In a 1973 column for the rock magazine *Creem*, Richard Robinson wrote 'what will happen when there is so much media available that everyone will have access to total communications remains to be seen' (1973: 82). Today, viewers have unprecedented access not only to movies, but to their still frames as well, as the 'pause' button allows for the complete disruption of the time-flow that has traditionally constituted movies. The ability for everyday spectators to freeze films at will suggests that the primary stories that movies tell are no longer within the films themselves. Rather, the dominant stories are now the stories that surround the films, stories that can be stopped and started or even skipped over. Pausing and freezing images makes possible the destruction of the very myths upon which cinema was built, and makes theorists out of an entire generation. But even as the 'pause' function releases spectators from the tyranny of the moving image, it also elevates these images to a position of unprecedented dominance. In 1970, Jack Gould wrote in the *New York Times* about a breakthrough in technology – Electronic Video Recording (EVT) – that had been developed by CBS. This precursor to VHS allowed for the stopping of moving images for study:

> After tinkering around with an EVR unit at home, this writer concluded that its implications and possible applications border on the staggering. For fun, a segment of 'The Prime of Miss Jean Brodie' was stopped and made into a still picture. In leisurely fashion, one could examine the exquisite pastel colour shadings, discuss the director's

intent and appreciation of composition, and then run the whole scene a second time. (Gould 1970: 4)

This ability to pause, to symbolically freeze time, is a reflection of how digital cinema is haunted by its analogue past, when a movie really was a film strip comprised of individual, discrete frames that could be held before a light and pondered almost as miniature photographs. And in pausing a film to ponder its images, we pause ourselves, momentarily.

Punk

[betamax, Jimmy Carter, Richard Meltzer,
UK economy in the 1970s]

The incompatibility between Einstein's theory of general relativity and subsequent quantum theory (about which Einstein was notoriously sceptical) comes down to, according to many physicists, differences in scale. According to Michio Kaku, 'general relativity is a theory of the very large: black holes, big bangs, quasars, and the expanding universe … The quantum theory is precisely the opposite – it describes the world of the very tiny: atoms, protons and neutrons, and quarks' (2005: 186). The widescreen, deep focus compositions of the classical analogue era were likewise products of big studios. The miniaturisation of technology, and the shrinking of the screen and the emergence of micro-budget and no-budget cinema are another form of quantum cinema, one characterised by the digital code (discrete numbers), pixels and the shrinking of film down to the size where literally hundreds of hours of it can be stored on a laptop computer. For now, the incompatibility of analogue and digital is masked because most theatrically distributed digital films are projected in analogue, as 35mm film.

The segmenting of screens into smaller and smaller sizes – into little YouTubes – portends the end of one dream, and the beginning of another. The Big Screen was always a doppelgänger anyway, a vision of our imperial selves, projecting onto the world. In the US, the 1970s put an end to the sort of dream that fuelled the big screens. The incoherence of the Vietnam War (who won?), the Watergate scandal and subsequent resignation of Richard Nixon, the OPEC oil crisis, the disintegration and near bankruptcy of great cities like New York; while these events alone did not curtail expansionism, they made possible a smaller thinking that demanded smaller screens. During this period, the UK was also in a period of deep recession, with unemployment reaching 6.4 per cent in June 1976. As one commentator has noted, the 'world's financial markets were losing confidence in Sterling as the British economy stumbled. The Treasury could not balance the books' (Casciani 2006). In his infamous 'Crisis of

Confidence' speech given in July 1979, Jimmy Carter actually said: 'The symptoms of this crisis of the American spirit are all around us. For the first time in the history of our country a majority of our people believe that the next five years will be worse than the past five years.' He also said this: 'As you know, there is a growing disrespect for government and for churches and for schools, the news media, and other institutions. This is not a message of happiness or reassurance, but it is the truth and it is a warning.' These are not things that can be said without consequence. Carter's words were either the recognition and confirmation of what was already known, or else they were a statement of a new vision, a new dream out of the nightmare of the 1970s, in the same way that the gritty minimalism of punk was a new dream. In this vision, reduction becomes a virtue, rather than a sign of weakness. Austerity becomes a virtue, a badge of honour. 'Serving its radical function, the Ramones' debut drives a sharp wedge between the stale ends of a contemporary music scene bloated with greying superstars and overripe for takeover', a reviewer said of the Ramones' first album when it was released in 1976 (Sculatti 1976: 66).

But what if takeover means, along the way, disappearing? The birth of mainstream video (which would give way to the pristine wish of digital) happened during this era of dirt, disintegration and near economic collapse. Around this same time, Sony introduced Betamax (in 1975), selling approximately 55,000 units to American dealers in 1976 (see Wasser 2001: 72). In his autobiography, Sony's Akio Morita wrote that 'In the fifties and sixties, popular programmes in the United States and later in Japan caused people to change their schedules. People would hate to miss their favourite shows. I noticed how the TV networks had total control over people's lives and I felt that people should have the option of seeing a programme when they chose' (quoted in ibid.).

In his book *Gulcher: Post-Rock Cultural Pluralism in America (1649–1980)*, avant-garde rock critic Richard Meltzer included a final chapter that began, 'Now it's your turn to write a chapter and it's the last one so you get the last laff' (1972: 143). The chapter is a list of 159 words, each one followed by a number: 'The words of this finale have already been written for you and they're listed in alphabetical order, all you gotta do is just put em back in sequence and the numeral *following* the word indicates what the desired sequence is' (ibid.; emphasis in original). Published in 1972, the book is a riot of absurdity camouflaged as theory or, more likely, theory camouflaged as absurdity. The disorientated, incoherent punk scene of the 1970s was in some ways a rough draft for the digital revolution of the 1990s, which in its early formulations (such as the Dogme 95 movement) offered a disorder so alluring that it could not possibly last. As Howard Hampton has noted, 'punk was, briefly, a smarter free-for-all: anyone could join, and nobody had the slightest clue where it was going' (2007: 182). The controlled chaos of the early Dogme films – simplicity conditioned upon strictly simple rules that, paradoxically, fostered bursts of anarchy – was a blood relative of punk's desire for authentic, amateur creation freed from the structures of studio overkill.

Realism

[Accenture, Dogme 95, RFID technology, Paul Virilio]

Digital cinema is haunted by a double logic: the striving for ever greater realism via a technology and interface that continually calls attention to the artifice of the medium. This is why the avant-garde is no longer avant-garde: DV has incorporated the logic of self-reflexivity into texts themselves. When the technology itself reveals its processes – such as DVDs showing how films are made – then is it still a radical gesture when films deconstruct themselves? The very interface itself – navigating a menu – means that we have to be a more ironic audience when it comes to viewing the film.

Filmmaker and writer Alejandro Adams has written against what he terms the 'cult of naturalism' in the digital era, whereby films are purposely made to appear 'naturalistic' which, ironically, means that they end up looking a lot like reality TV:

New Naturalism glorifies removal, subtraction. The director tells the actor to do less, as close to nothing as possible. The director assumes the viewer wants less, as close to nothing as possible. It is a matter of amateurising, roughening: deadpan acting, clumsy camerawork. Naturalism is, compulsorily, about being natural, and in nature dynamic actors and tripods don't occur as they do in Hollywood movies. New Naturalism rejects tripods and trained actors because tripods and trained actors are inextricably bound to the Hollywood conspiracy. (2007: 3)

And yet real time, natural time, is the revenge of the real upon all our interfaces. Jean Baudrillard has written that it is 'a good thing we ourselves do not live in real time! What would we be in "real" time? We would be identified at each moment exactly with ourselves. A torment equivalent to that of eternal daylight – a kind of epilepsy of presence, epilepsy of identity. Autism, madness. No more absence from oneself, no more distance from others' (1996: 53). The yearning for real time in digital culture is a desire to recover natural time, so fragmented by modernism. Paul Virilio has written about the destruction of time, of the body, in modernism. Streaming audio. Streaming video. The continuity promised by the real-time flowing of information. Digital technologies, such as RFID (Radio Frequency Identification), theoretically make possible a one-to-one correspondence with perceived reality in ways that make films like *Minority Report* seem quaint. RFID tags are designed, as Katherine Albrecht and Liz McIntyre note, to use 'electromagnetic energy in the form of radio waves to communicate information at a distance' (2006: 13). Already, they are used by thousands of companies to track inventory; of course, they can be used to track human beings, too. Glover Ferguson, Chief Scientist for Accenture, has said that 'I want to talk about RFID as one element in what I believe to be a much larger movement toward putting reality itself online' (in Anon. 2005b: 1). One of Accenture's goals is to create a world in which 'for every physical entity or event, there is a virtual, cooperating double' (Anon. 2005a: 1). This is not Baudrillard talking, nor is it some conspiratorial science fiction movie script. 'The Accenture Object Information Exchange shows how the concept of the virtual double will work, making an object's information available to an array of potential users' (Anon. 2003: 1). Cinema's increasing ability to capture reality in real time – with HD storage devices that free cinema from the 'cuts' that characterised the classical era – is part of this same movement to make a double of reality.

And yet, how to account for the return of the human in digital cinema, especially the films of the Dogme 95 movement, or David Lynch's *Inland Empire*? *The Celebration* is a film of human bodies, of human faces. It is reality itself that is the special effect in Dogme. Lars von Trier's reputation as a cold director, as almost anti-human in his treatment of his actors, is paradoxical in light of the fact that he makes the most humanistic works of the early digital era. *The Idiots*, *Breaking the Waves* and *The Kingdom* are crammed full of human faces; long, lingering shots affirm over and over the contours of the face, the body. Even *Dogville* – in all its Brechtian staginess – cannot hide its excessive humanism. In fact, the fictive world laid bare, stripped of mimesis, only serves to drive us deeper into the humanism of the characters who are all the more real to us against the fake props, the chalk outlines of their world thrusting the characters beyond fake, into the real. That von Trier chooses to practically torture his characters, moving them compulsively deeper and deeper into Dante's rings, does nothing to take away from the harsh sentimentality of his films. 'Humans aren't really that good', von Trier has said and yet in their brutality his films demonstrate that – if not good – they are at least interesting. 'When you use a hand-held camera, the search for the object becomes part of the story' (in Smith 2003b: 151).

In Margaret Atwood's novel *Oryx and Crake*, two characters -- Jimmy and Crake – play a game of chess with each other on two computers:

> 'Why don't we use a real set?' Jimmy asked one day when they were doing some chess. 'The old kind. With plastic men.' It did seem weird to have the two of them in the same room, back to back, playing on computers.
>
> 'Why?' asked Crake. 'Anyway, this *is* a real set.'

'No it's not.'

'Okay, granted, but neither is plastic men.'

'What?'

'The real set is in your head.' (2004: 77; emphasis in original)

This is our conundrum, too: we like to be able to say that this film or film genre is 'realistic' and that one is not, but in the end, when it's all on the screen, who is to say what is real and what is not? I will leave it to the poets and philosophers to parse this, but let me venture: 'realism' in art (films, novels, music, paintings, sculptures, and so forth) is a condition of the world illuminated, briefly, through a process that breaks in some way with a previous process. The process of digital filmmaking – the rendering of images through a binary code – is a fairly drastic break from the analogue method, where the ephemery of 'reality' was captured on the very real fact of the film itself: one could literally see that captured reality on a filmstrip held up to the light, frame by frame, 24 frames per second. *The real set is in your head*. Of course. We judge a film's realism against that which we know to be real. But once the symbolic, physical link between the realism *in our head* and the realism on the screen has been severed, what are the consequences? On some level, the process by which analogue systems – such as the motion picture camera – captured and represented reality was knowable. But what is knowable about digital systems, and their binary codes? My argument – and really the argument at the heart of this book – is that the return to humanism (i.e., the small and intimate stories of the Dogme 95 movement, the extreme close-ups of faces in *Inland Empire*) in digital cinema is a compensation for the inscrutability of digital systems themselves. The technology is awesome, and even frightening (its seemingly eternal databases), and one cultural response to that is to make stories with that technology that are intensely realistic in their portrayal of human beings and their relationships. The numerous digital effects in a film like *Eternal Sunshine of the Spotless Mind* (for example, the covers and spines of the books gradually turning white in one of the bookstore scenes) is used in the service of a story which is almost old-fashionedly romantic and heartbreaking: there is nothing about this film other than its characters, who are human beings so hurt and scarred by love that they pay to have its memories erased from their minds. And thus, a curious footnote to these early films of the digital era: as the technology used to create and project them becomes evermore abstract, their stories remain relentlessly concrete and human.

Real Time

[Ann Arbor, Koji Suzuki, Lars von Trier]

According to Paul Virilio, the digital era is marked with the closing-of-the-gap between real time and represented time:

> With paradoxical logic, what gets decisively *resolved* is the reality of the object's *real-time* presence. In the previous age of dialectical logic, it was only delayed-time presence, the presence of the past, that lastingly impressed plate and film. The paradoxical image thus acquires a status something like that of surprise, or more precisely, of an 'accidental transfer'. (1994: 64; emphasis in original)

As Daniel Frampton has noted, 'the film experience is not strictly analogous to real-world audio-visual experience' (2006: 151). It is not that distinctions between the 'real world' and the 'filmic' world are passé, but rather that they are increasingly irrelevant. Gene Youngblood has written that 'today cinema represents reality; tomorrow it will *be* reality' (2003: 161; emphasis in original).

But it already was. 'Hundreds Now "Shoot" Movies of Their Own', proclaimed a headline from the *Washington Post* in 1926, where readers learned that 'hundreds of persons are "shooting" their own motion pictures, many as a pastime but others for utilitarian reasons' (Anon. 1926: R14). A 1927 editorial in the *Christian Science Monitor* noted that – in something that sounds like a pre-video sharing system, 'other signs of the times in the direction of amateur effort are the film exchanges where professional films of all manner of subjects can be bought for individual home libraries. News reels, natural history series, scenic features, golf lessons, travel films, comedies, and even new releases of well-known photoplays are now to be had from the various exchanges' (Anon. 1927: 15). And, writing from London, Godfrey Lias noted in 1933 an early form not of garage rock, but what might be called 'garage cinema': 'Some of the richer [amateur cinema] clubs have real studios. Most of them haven't. Garages, however, make efficient substitutes' (1933: 5).

This presents a paradox, for if part of our understanding is that reality is that which happens, and art is that which represents, then what to make of a movie that is *happening* in front of us? Even the most fantastical subject matter (a movie about trees turning into flesh-eating lizards that defy gravity) is real in the sense that we are watching something happening; when we are watching, we are in the presence of the reality of the film unfolding. This is of course not a new question, and it is not unique to film. But cinema, perhaps because of its approximation of real-time storytelling made evermore possible by extensive long takes that aren't dependent on film stock, pushes us ever closer to a recognition that, as Youngblood suggests, cinema is reality itself. In Bret Easton Ellis's novel *Lunar Park*, the narrator opens an e-mail attachment that contains a video of his father's last night on earth: 'The camera then crossed the hallway and stopped again. It had a vague and maddening patience' (2005: 179). The camera – with no hint of who is holding it or who is doing the filming – floats throughout the father's house, finally showing him turn towards the camera before the image turns to darkness and he presumably dies. In an odd moment, the narrator suggests that there was, in fact, no camera, and that he was 'seeing something through the eyes of a person' (2005: 180). This prospect – that a person and a camera could possibly be the same thing – is given new credence in the digital era, when the real-time, long storage capabilities of HD make possible a continuous recording of reality that lasts for days, weeks or perhaps even months. If one of the unique historical markers of humanness was that we perceived the world and recorded it into our memories, then the digital archive – which is approaching the point where it, too, can hold an uncut, real-time recording that spans years – threatens, even if only in an initial, small way, to intrude on what was a human and animal capability.

On the most basic level, video does not need to be 'processed'; it can be shot and uploaded for the world to see in a matter of seconds. The distinctions between 'live' and 'taped' events are fast evaporating. At some point, events and representations of those events have become one and the same thing. This is not true of other mediums – such as books – for which the process of production still results in a lag between the creation of the object and its dissemination. There is a perfectionism, still, in other mediums that cinema has jettisoned. The shaky cameras of Lars von Trier from the Dogme 95 era are rooted in this punk desire to eschew so-called professionalism. 'The reason why I laid down the Dogme rules or put a camera on my shoulder', von Trier has said, 'was to get away from all this perfectionism and concentrate on something else' (in Smith 2003: 149). To 'concentrate on something else'. But on what? At the end of the day, what Dogme revealed was that its strategies were no more radical than reality TV, which was already rummaging through 'something else' – but for what? That question – and the circle that it made – turned out to be Dogme's greatest contribution. For the technique itself – shaky camera, improvisation – was already there in the likes of John Cassavetes and others.

The searching, hand-held, shaky camera in the digital era – in films and television shows ranging from *Homicide: Life on the Streets* to *The Blair Witch Project* to *The Celebration* to *Tape* – was considered almost hysterical in the new millennium, before

9/11. It is not so much a case of the application of historical methods to cinema, as it is the application of cinema to history. To the good liberal humanists of the West, cinema is a symptom of history, an archive that 'tells us' something about the time. But what if cinema is not the symptom, but the cause? Of course this is unprovable, unteachable. It makes no sense; film is not a cause, it is an effect.

Avant-garde cinema – and cinema itself – is special because it is an event; it is something that happens somewhere, and that *somewhere* attaches itself to the meaning of the film. I remember *Requiem for a Dream* so well, in part, because my wife and I crammed into the ridiculously small, red seats at the State Theatre in downtown Ann Arbor with the serious University students and the older woman a few rows down who withdrew from her purse an entire hamburger wrapped in tin foil. I remember running to our car afterwards in the rain. I remember the man who said, to no one in particular, as we left the theatre and stepped into the street, 'This is okay – I need to wash that movie off me.' That the postmodern event is 'nowhere' is a commonplace of critical theory, and nowhere is this clearer than in the detachment from place of contemporary cinema.

But it is more than this, at last. For cinema began as the nickelodeon, with individuals peering at the tiny moving images alone. And home movies, which entered mass culture in full force by the 1920s, have always restricted the event of movie watching to small groups of people. But today, it is the sheer routine expansion not only of the archive, but of the original filmic object itself, which shows just how dubious our old notions of permanence were. In a culture where permanence is associated with being out-of-date, or unfashionable, how can you speak of a tradition? After all, the revelation that cinematic tradition is really just the skillful and publicised manipulation of technique – i.e, montage, long takes, split screens, melodrama, close-ups – means that tradition itself is just a technique.

But a technique for what? If anything, the massive public archiving that digital media makes possible (for instance, I can call up scores of clips from Hitchcock films and watch them for free on the Internet) reveals that, historically, technique corresponds – sometimes obviously, sometimes obliquely and mysteriously – to moments in time. The Cold War and the long take. The 1960s and the iris dissolve. The 1970s and the split screen. The 1990s and speed ramping. These are all, we know, cinematic techniques and cultural techniques, simultaneously. Does our own era's fragmented screen reflect a global dissolution of a different sort? 'The video mutated. Through copying, it evolved until a new strain emerged. It's still lurking out there somewhere. And it's taken a completely different form' (Suzuki 2006a: 172). In Koji Suzuki's novel *Spiral* it is the invisible reproduction – not of sleeper cells but of images – that threatens humanity. In 2005, I lent a friend a copy of Richard Linklater's *Tape* on DVD, because he had heard that Ethan Hawke's performance was outstanding. When he returned it to me a few weeks later, I discovered an extra DVD in the case, a burned copy of the movie, an illegal reproduction. Like the characters in the film, I wondered if I was in the midst of some sort of stealth betrayal: my digital copy of *Tape* had been taped and given to me, as a gesture of thanks or as a reminder that, as the front of the DVD box says, 'some things can't be erased'.

As much as the digital image masks the conditions of its own production in its clean, error-less perfection, it is also true that a fundamental feature of the digital era is a powerful return to history. Indeed, the desire (even fetish) for filmic preservation, restoration and remastering takes us back, inexorably, to a film's origins. For to 'restore' a film is to acknowledge that it has a past that makes restoration necessary. This past is a gap that must be bridged from the present. When theorists such as Fredric Jameson refer to the 'dehistoricising' features of the postmodern condition, they do so at the expense of the vast archives of retrievable information that make the past ever more available in the present. And yet Jameson's larger point that the proliferation of post-modern space can lead to a sort of schizophrenic exhaustion in the subject (too many choices!) is crucial. Thus the paradox of the digital era: even as the historical imaginary is more available than ever, it is brought 'online' at such an alarming rate that it tends to become unreal.

The Real You

[Siegfried Kracauer, Malcolm Le Grice, *Tape*, Andy Warhol]

In the chapter 'The New Realism' in *From Caligari to Hitler*, Siegfried Kracauer criticised the new realism in German film during the 1920s:

> New Objectivity marks a state of paralysis. Cynicism, resignation, disillusionment: these tendencies point to a mentality disinclined to commit itself in any direction. The main feature of the new realism is its reluctance to ask questions, to take sides. Reality is portrayed not so as to make facts yield their implications, but to drown all implications in an ocean of facts. (2004: 165–6)

And yet Kracauer was responding to a moment in time that was not yet able to replicate reality at a level that threatened to create a virtual double of reality itself. Today, one can dispense with technique and simply film what the camera sees, and post it onto the web. More than ever before, what defines reality in digital cinema is the medium itself, which remains as the last threshold between the real and the representation of the real. A film like *Tape* – shot on digital video – suggests that it is only the degradation of the image which confers upon the hotel room in which it was shot the status of art. Paradoxically, the slightly out-of-focus, messy image rendered through the digital video camera creates the illusion of reality more fully than a sharply focused, high-definition, image. At one point in *Tape*, after Vin gets his old high-school friend Jon to confess to a date-rape of a shared high-school acquaintance, Vin reveals that he has taped the conversation. 'If you're such a different guy than you were ten years ago,' Vin tells Jon, 'then you shouldn't mind apologising for something that the real you in effect didn't even do.' In digital cinema, the status of the 'real you' is precarious: it is reproducible in terms of image and sound, and yet we resist this replication by forcing it and compressing it into narrative. Digital systems – which can create a perfectly reproducible one-to-one representation of 'reality' – suggest a copy whose seamlessness is only broken by the limits of duration. Although films like George Lucas's *Attack of the Clones* were shot digitally, it wasn't until films like Alexander Sokurov's *Russian Ark*, Steven Soderbergh's *Bubble* and David Fincher's *Zodiac* – shot on a Thomson Viper FilmStream camera – that tape was eliminated altogether from the digital process. According to Peter Mavromates, one of the producers of *Zodiac*, 'this is a literal tapeless process, because we record to hard drives, shuttle back and forth to the edit room, where we load the data, back it up and convert it to editable media' (in Goldman 2006: 1). In that same article, Fincher laments that we 'live in a world where we still have to exhibit on film, at least for now' (ibid.). Yet from another perspective, the traditional analogue, film-based process at least symbolised the relationship between images and their sources in the real world. In Chuck Palahniuk's novel *Lullaby*, one of the characters looks out over the Nevada desert and says that 'None of this is native, but it's all we have left … Almost nothing in nature is natural anymore' (2002: 110).

Until the day that someone makes a movie that unfolds on the screen in continuous, uninterrupted months and years – not hours – we can remain secure in our immunity from total cinematic reproduction. Andy Warhol – with his *Screen Tests* and *Chelsea Girls* (the latter directed with Paul Morrissey) – expanded film into the realm of real time in radical ways that digital cinema is only recently beginning to experiment with again. In *Experimental Cinema in the Digital Age*, Malcolm Le Grice has noted that 'Mass media, particularly television, have progressively created a cultural schism between the representation and the physical object. Instantaneous transmission of images and sounds across space has created a cultural habit of reading the electronic representation as if it were present. Our discourse with the real has become a discourse with the represented image' (2001: 311). The prevalence of mobile, portable screens (laptop computers, cell phones, and so forth) since the 1990s transforms the 'present'-ness that Le Grice describes into an everyday phenomenon that further blurs the distinctions between 'the real' and representation. It is as if representation itself has become so ubiquitous, so prevalent, that it threatens to displace what could be called some form of primary reality. Of course, scepticism and anxiety about 'virtual reality' is nothing new; the rise of the novel as an emerging popular genre in the eighteenth century, for instance, was met with resistance in Europe and America by those who worried that its realism would lure readers away from the 'real world' of work and productivity. But there was a difference: print-based virtual reality depended upon its users' literacy for its functionality, whereas there are multiple literacies at play in the digital era. Playing a video game, watching a movie, using the Internet – these each involve their own often overlapping codes and grammars.

Remainders

In *What Is Cinema*, André Bazin recounts the story of watching a film with friends; technical difficulties meant that the film stopped and started several times: 'Every interruption evoked an "ah" of disappointment and every fresh start a sigh of hope for a solution' (2005a: 59). But beginning with the advent of video-based home viewing systems in the 1970s, interruption gradually emerged as part of the logic not only of films, but of film viewing itself. Iconic films of the digital era – such as *Run Lola Run* or *The Blair Witch Project* – with their rapid, multiple cuts and sudden shifts of perspective, acknowledged what spectators already know: that stories are composed of pieces, and that it is really in the stitched-together transitions between pieces where the heart of the story often lies.

In *28 Days Later*, which was shot on a Canon XL-1S digital video camcorder, interruption is crucial to the opening minutes of the film itself. In the 'making-of' feature that accompanies the film on DVD, director Danny Boyle notes that he decided to shoot on digital video for a variety of reasons, one being that 'this is the way we record our lives. We're surrounded in the city by cameras. They're everywhere. And they're all these DV cameras; all types of them and they're recording our every motion all the time.' The film opens with a series of violent news images of revolutions, protests and anarchy from around the globe, cut together at an alarming and disorientating pace. It is only after a few minutes that we, as spectators, realise we have been watching footage directly off a television screen, as the camera slowly pulls back to reveal that we are in the primate research centre, and have been watching these screens. As the camera pulls back further, we see a chimp strapped to a table. Then the camera tracks across the room to another television monitor, this one showing a grainy, closed-circuit image of masked people in an outside hallway, who turn out to be the animal rights activists who will shortly enter the room, free the chimps infected with rage and set in motion the epidemic. The multiple framings that the film opens with –

The shift from narrative time to 'real' time in *28 Days Later*

as perspective shifts from the real time of the film to the time in the television frames – suggests a disintegrating and disordered world, a world verging on catastrophe. It makes sense that the film's second sequence – which occurs '28 Days Later' – begins with Jim waking up in a hospital room and proceeds for approximately 13 minutes with no substantial dialogue. As he wakes up in the hospital room naked – as if just born – Jim will emerge into a world where all the old, familiar objects take on new meaning. A bank of phones with their receivers dangling, soda machines with their fronts smashed in, cars left abandoned in the middle of streets – none of these objects in themselves is strange; they are only strange in the context of no human beings. Outside of their use value, they mean nothing: there is no social value attached to them, which makes them haunted.

The first question Jim is asked after taking refuge with two other survivors is 'Who are you?' It is both a simple and a complicated question, for Jim does indeed remember his name and even the circumstances that landed him in the hospital just prior to the outbreak. However, on another level, Jim does not know who he is, because all the familiar relationships to people, to work, to the larger social order, have vanished. He has been reborn into a world violently purged of signification, which is only made possible when there are human beings to interpret signs. In the post-apocalyptic world of *28 Days Later*, objects don't mean what they used to because their context has been stripped away. Cormac McCarthy's novel *The Road* – which tells the story of a father and son as they journey across a devastated and largely deserted United States – is similarly haunted by objects that are fast losing their meaning: 'He [the father] went through the house room by room. He found nothing. A spoon in a bedside drawer. He put that in his pocket … He went back out and crossed to the garage. He sorted through tools. Rakes. A shovel. Jars of bolts and nails on a shelf. A boxcutter' (2006: 101). In both works, the world is littered with objects – with *things* – that have become unattached from the systems that produced them and gave them meaning. In *28 Days Later*, the digital look and feel of the film makes it both more real and less; the authentic, degraded images appear more naturalistic while at the same time drawing attention to the fact that they were shot with digital cameras. It is significant that the only portion of the film shot on 35mm was the ending, as the three survivors signal a jet for rescue. The immediate brutality of the post-epidemic world, which was shot in digital, has given way to the warmer, traditional aesthetic of analogue film. In this regard, the film's ending is both hopeful and forward looking, and nostalgic.

The significance of *28 Days Later* is not that it was shot expertly with digital cameras, but rather that it portends a new aesthetic of the remainder, of things left over, of objects that no longer have fixed meanings. In order for this aesthetic to have the power and lure of illusion, it must dispense with the classical era materials and technologies that enabled the cinematic representation of a coherent world. Perhaps it is not coincidental that the dominating ideologies of the twentieth century – such as fascism and communism – co-existed with the emergence of analogue cinema. The splintering and disintegration of those ideologies, especially following the collapse of the Soviet Union – has likewise coincided with the rise of digital technologies, whose material presence is disembodied and more difficult to locate. Because digital filmmaking allows for the storage of images as information in hard drives, it is possible to overshoot, to shoot in excess, to collect far more visual data than will ever be included in the 'final cut' (if such a concept even exists anymore) of a film. According to Anthony Dod Mantle, 'For *julien* [*donkey-boy*] Harmony [Korine] wanted to shoot eighty hours of material. That would have meant a devastating budget if it were to be shot on film' (in Macaulay 1999: 2).

The 'remainders' in a film like *28 Days Later* – the abandoned cars, the rubbish strewn about, the grocery stores stocked with rotting food, even the dead bodies – are reinforced by digital technology itself, which allows for filmic excess and remainder. The forces that threaten to destabilise and overthrow Western civilisation are no longer enormous nation states and armies, but nature itself, in the form of viral epidemics, or small, highly disciplined groups of insurgents or terrorists. What they leave in their wake are the remainders of civilisation, and the new cinematic apparatus that imagines such destruction is itself predicated on the production of excess or 'bonus' footage and information. In fact, in a film like *28 Days Later*, the remainders exist not only on the level of content (the detritus of abandoned cities) but on the DVD features itself, whose multiple levels of information – including the director's audio commentary, the three alternate endings and the deleted scenes with optional commentary – offer remainders from the film. Or perhaps the film itself is the remainder, a by-product of the bonus features?

This confusion between primary and secondary is similar to postmodern novels by the likes of David Foster Wallace (*Infinite Jest* (1996)) and Mark Danielewski (*House of Leaves* (2000)), where the primary, main narrative is so overridden with footnotes, asides and nested narratives that the primary text itself is destabilised in a sort of textual chaos. But unlike those examples, which were received as deliberate experiments modillions, or even trefoil, Tudor, stilted horseshoe, ogee, lancet, or equilateral arches, most probably resembling basket handle though without any sign of a key-stone, pier, spandrel, voussoir, springer, or impost.

Picture that. In your dreams.

"The content of photographs will NEVER be changed or manipulated in any way."

Mark Danielewski's novel *House of Leaves*: textual chaos

or forays into the avant-garde, the elevation of secondary, 'bonus' materials on DVD is fully part of commercial, mainstream culture. There is nothing 'experimental', per se, about a movie that takes a back seat to all the supplementary material on DVD. It is as if, cynical about and bored by the endless variations of genre, we have become attached to a new category – the remainder – to compensate. In William Gibson's novel *Spook Country*, one character says that 'when you look at blogs, where you're most likely to find the real info is in the links. It's contextual, and not only who the blog's linked to, but who's linked to the blog' (2007: 65). The vast linkages today between different types of media and different interfaces (for example, a movie like *Apocalypse Now* available in theatres (re-released and restored), on television, on VHS, on DVD and on the Internet which is itself available on computers, on mobile phones, and so forth) is a form of distraction raised to the level of narrative. The very architecture of social networking sites like Facebook works against the notion of a primary text, because the primary text is the user, who selects options out of a myriad of choices, in the same way – but on a much larger scale – that movies are becoming mere selections from vast databases of moving images.

The question is: what are the aesthetics of the remainder? Are there any common or shared characteristics of the extra or leftover features that have grown to challenge the primary text? We could look to the bootleg, in music, as one of many historical precedents for the remainder in digital cinema: 'extra' tracks that somehow shed new light, new ways of understanding, on the primary song. Yet part of the mystique and aura of bootlegs was that they were marginally elicit: they were not official. They were unsanctioned, available in the shadowy margins. And their relationship to the author – the auteur – (for example, Bob Dylan) was ambiguous. But the most important thing was that they were extras, recorded versions of songs that were not cleaned up or perfected or overly produced. In the digital era, the remainder becomes so complete that, in some cases, it operates upon its own aesthetic principles. Here are two examples:

1. *McSweeney's Issue No. 11* DVD

Issue No. 11 (published in 2003) of the literary/arts journal *McSweeney's Quarterly Concern* (published by author Dave Eggers) features a DVD that is made up entirely of bonus features, including 'Deleted Scenes', 'Extra-Deleted Scenes', 'Behind the Scenes of the Deleted Scenes and Extra-Deleted Scenes', and 'Outtakes from the Deleted Scenes, Extra-Deleted Scenes, and from Behind the Scenes of the Deleted Scenes and Extra-Deleted Scenes'. One feature is 'The Editing of the Making of McSweeney's Issue No.11 DVD (with Audio Commentary by John Hodgman and Sarah Vowell)', which is nothing more than footage of the DVD editor at work editing on his computer. At one point, Vowell comments on the process in a way that is both funny and theoretical:

> Back in the old days when it was tape and razor blades and splicing … don't you think that would make for a slightly more action-packed making of the DVD? But the very idea that it is a digital enterprise in and of itself precludes that. Have you ever noticed how in the digital age every act of computing involves some sort of metaphor for the old analogue equivalent, like 'scrolling down' or 'cut-and-paste'?

Her suggestion that there is nothing of interest to watch in the 'making of the digital editing of' a film hints at a larger truth: that the entire process and production of making a digital film becomes the remainder whose basic information is disembodied, hidden in machines that are accessed by keypad and mouse clicks. But even more significantly, what Vowell's commentary – and the entire Issue No.11 DVD – shows is that media critique and even theory has migrated away from the academy and back into popular culture, where it once resided in the works of writers like Marshall McLuhan, Pauline Kael or Andrew Sarris, who were known not only to film scholars, but to more general readers, as well. Indeed, the Issue No. 11 DVD is, beneath its humour, a deconstruction of the very notion (and absurdity?) of the remainder in digital cinema, a remainder which invites the most thoroughgoing deconstruction of its host, the primary text.

2. Audio Commentary released separately from film

With *Clerks II*, director Kevin Smith attempted to release a commentary track that people could listen to in the theatre while watching the film, although worries about distracting others watching the film without the audio track prevented him from doing so. More recently, the screenwriter/director John August released audio commentary for the film *The Nines* for free in two different formats: m4a and mp3. His website details guidelines for listening to the audio commentary while in the theatre: 'Be respectful: If you're listening to the commentary, sit away from other people, so they're not hearing it.' In one sense, this suggests how information flows today in discrete streams or channels, that, taken as a whole, constitute the entire movie-watching experience. 'Deconstruction' no longer happens solely at the hands of media theorists and academics, but within the very structures of media itself which, forged into evermore digital streams, reveal movies to be collaborative composites rather than unified wholes. The ideological power of movies – their ability to 'lose' the audience in their myths – is shattered when those myths are *already* deconstructed through the very apparatus of watching the movies. An audio commentary track available to take into the theatre on an iPod or other device suggests a stance outside the internal world of the movie itself.

In the specific instance of *The Nines*, the movie becomes a game, a puzzle to solve via a remainder (the added audio track that comments on the process of making the movie) that conspires against the illusion that has been so central to narrative filmmaking. Even a director like David Lynch, who in the past has been reluctant to discuss the meaning of his movies, has spoken more openly about this and about the filmmaking process on the bonus features on the *Inland Empire* DVD. In instances like these, the remainder (the unused footage, the deleted scenes, the audio commentary, the making-of documentaries) threatens the very aura of film, or video, itself. I know there is the risk of nostalgia in this line of argument, but there is something lost when the remainder – which acts as an agent of deconstruction – lays claim on the viewer as the primary text. In *Reading Comics*, Douglas Wolk writes that '"Change over time" is roughly the same thing as narrative – one thing happens, then another thing happens' (2007: 130). Although the prospect of time-shifting introduced by videotape recorders in the 1970s threatened the linearity of the film viewing experience, the basic unit of film remained stable. That is, despite its medium (the theatre screen, the television set) a film's narrative coherence was immune – or at least shielded – from the demystification that extra knowledge can bring.

In fact, it is audiences themselves who now watch movies in theatres with the anticipation that future versions and releases of the movie for home or personal viewing will include data and information that will alter their understanding of the film. In other words, the revolution in cinema is no longer that technology has elevated the remainder to a much more prominent status, but that our *expectations* as viewers and consumers prepare us to understand that films exist in multiple versions, and that our experience of a film at a theatre is only an experience with one version of that film. The remainder is, in some ways, the logical outcome of modernism, which relentlessly divided reality into shards and fragments. But more than that, I think, the remainder is the necessary by-product of two technological and cultural forces: speed and the archive. For the rapid pace of information flow creates ever more content, which in turn is archived in ever larger databases and archives. In terms of film and video, far from being erased, the past is brought into greater visibility and focus. We are practically drowning in the present; we are practically drowning in the past. Television series just one or two years old are released on DVD with enough bonus materials to fill an entire disc. Because it is not possible to archive – and make available for fast retrieval – vast amounts of information, vast amounts of information are now archived. It is now possible to conceive that, in a place like the US, what used to be called the bonus or extra materials surrounding a film (i.e., its remainders) are the primary artifacts of cinema itself.

Sampling
[continuity, mistakist cinema, real time]

If classical cinema sampled its reality only after it was very carefully constructed, then digital cinema returns to the site of reality for its samples. Is this to say that digital cinema is somehow more real or authentic than classical? Not at all. What we are talking about here is gestures, tendencies, approaches. The elimination of the sound stage does not liberate cinema so much as return it to the sound stage of nature, the natural world. This accounts for the schizophrenic nature of digital cinema in these, its early stages. On the one hand, the term *digital* suggests the elaborate, expensive, micro-managed, soulless, perfectionist aesthetic of George Lucas's last three *Star Wars* films. On the other hand, it conjures the homemade, imperfect, intimate, mistakist cinema of *The Blair Witch Project*, *The Celebration* and *Tape*, films where digital does not imply cold, anti-human technology, but rather intimacy, spontaneity and imperfection. This is achieved not necessarily through the close-up, but rather through the camera's intimate proximity to its characters. The miniature DV camera shrinks space, collapsing distance (emotional and physical) and bringing us face to face with a mediated reality no more false than pre-digital realities of analogue, painting or simply words.

Digital culture is not only the culture of bits and fragments, but of continuity. A return to the long day, the long night. A desire so strong that we are creating an entire machinery to duplicate real time – a real time machine. We want a double-life for ourselves: our real life and our real life mirrored in real time. Like the detective who slowly realises she is investigating herself, we realise that we are finding ourselves behind every new digital technology, no matter how cold. Is this return to pre-classical real time a response to modernity's fracturing of time and space? For it is real-time reality today that is the new avant-garde, stunning us with its unpredictability. Real time shows us that reality does not need to be deconstructed in painting or film; allowed enough time, it deconstructs itself. Modernism – epitomised in cinema by films like *Man with the Movie Camera* – totally destroyed time; the ultimate hubris. God's world fragmented and rearranged. Paul Virilio writes about this in *Art and Fear*, noting that 'In the end, "modern art" was able to glean what communications tools now accomplish on a daily basis; the *mise en abyme* of the body, of the figure' (1994: 35). He goes on to argue that 'Today, with excess heaped on excess, desensitisation to the shock of images and the meaninglessness of words has shattered the world stage' (1994: 36). Compare this to Walter Benjamin's claim in 1935 that film's

> illusionary nature is that of the second degree, the result of editing. That is to say, in the studio the mechanical equipment has penetrated so deeply into reality that its pure aspect, freed from the foreign substance of equipment, is the result of a special procedure, namely, shooting from a particular camera angle and linking the shot with other similar ones. The equipment-free aspect of reality here has become the height of artifice; the sight of immediate reality has become the [unattainable] blue flower in the land of technology. (1968: 222)

Digital cinema counteracts this with two tendencies: (i) the long take, which allows for a greater degree of reality and its mistakes to unfold; and (ii) self-consciousness not only in terms of technique (such as shaky cameras, boom-mics and other equipment allowed in the frame) but also in the interface itself. Viewers fully see movies now as Hollywood products: the 'making of' bonus features strip away illusion.

In this regard, media in the digital age 'samples' reality with such continuous sweep that reality is returned to us as something that is indistinguishable from reality itself. Digital storage devices make it possible to archive enormous sets of data. If narrative is, at its heart, the selection, arrangement and strategic release of information for dramatic purposes, then the ability to record and store ever vaster amounts of data perhaps suggests the emergence of new forms of storytelling that places into the hands of the audience the task of shaping information into stories. As in the 'Choose Your Own Adventure' books that allow readers to select various narrative threads that lead to various outcomes, the process of shaping stories in the digital era becomes fundamental to the stories themselves. The challenge for film theory is to create narratives as surprising and enlightening as films themselves. Marcel O'Gorman has used the term 'remainder' to describe a hopeful turn in academic discourse, a turn that embraces a certain playfulness that can result in the fiercest form of critique: 'the remainder is the "other" of academic or scholarly language. It is deemed as nonsense or rubbish, classified as "cute" or juvenile' (2006: 4). In digital media, it is the remainder which has been elevated to the status of primary, as with bonus or supplementary features on DVDs. Digital media theory is only beginning to answer this with its own languages of the remainder.

Secondary Becomes Primary
[auteur, DVD]

What if we think of the supplementary features on DVDs not just as simply bonus material, but as new forms of digital cinema? Perhaps the new auteurs are not the film directors, but the DVD producers, such as Laurent Bouzereau, who is Steven Spielberg's DVD producer, or Michael Gillis who said in a *New York Times* article on the emerging power of DVD production companies that 'We're really a virtual studio' (in Moerk 2005: 2). The experience of watching and rewatching films today is inextricably related to the multiple interfaces that stand between viewers and the films themselves. When Van Ling, who has worked closely with James Cameron and George Lucas on the production of the elaborate, multilayered DVD versions of their films, speaks (in an essay accompanying the 'Extreme DVD' version of *Terminator 2: Judgment Day*) about catering not only to movie buffs but 'film students' as well, he is acknowledging what has long been known among users but not properly acknowledged among film theorists: that the specialised knowledge upon which 'film studies' rested has been dispersed among spectators for some time now. Speaking about the *Star Wars* DVDs, Van Ling noted that he 'was contracted by Lucasfilm to create the DVD menus, design the navigation, and supervise the overall production of the DVD itself' (2005: 2). His work, and the work of other DVD producers, is much more than simply tacking on distracting options to the main feature. As Graeme Harper and others have suggested, the 'supplementariness' of DVDs and their bonus features is a sign of what Harper refers to as the 'cinema of complexity', that makes 'the centre of the DVD not the film itself but what has, until now, been considered auxiliary material in the practice of film viewing' (2005: 98).

In fact, we could go further: it is not that 'bonus' materials on DVDs are considered auxiliary, but that cinema itself is becoming auxiliary to a larger, global digital literacy of which cinema is only one small part. In 'Is a Cinema Studies Degree Becoming the New M.B.A.?', Elizabeth Van Ness noted that at the University of Southern California, 'fully half of the university's 16,500 undergraduate students take at least one cinema/ television class' (2005: 1). These students are the inheritors of what the children in the 1970s were only beginning to discover with small home computers and early experiments with computer/video interface. The cover of the journal *BYTE*, from 1976, shows two brothers at play on a computer hooked up to a television screen – an early, homemade example of video interface. In the accompanying article – 'It's More Fun Than Crayons' – Richard Rosner notes that while 'I have been putting microcomputers using microprocessors together for almost two years, it wasn't until I hooked up the TV to my present system that my family took interest. Now, when I walk in the door after work, the kids corner me asking me which one can use the computer first' (1976: 26–7). The television screen as the interface for new computer technology not only reverses Marshall McLuhan's notion that the content of new media is old media, but it is also a reminder that media content is never just about 'content', but is also about the 'coolness' or 'style' of its delivery devices, something that Apple Computer has learned very well. Perhaps it's not surprising that as movies have become things that we can personally own (like books have been for a long time) and watch at leisure in our homes, the ways of manipulating them have expanded to the extent that – perhaps – the manipulation of their content has become nearly as important as the content itself. Even a film on DVD such as *Inland Empire*, which has no chapter titles but which does offer the ability to skip ahead, is a radically different film once we have watched the material on disc two, which includes 211 minutes of unused footage, as well as behind-the-scenes material and ample footage of David Lynch speaking about the making of the film. Even if Lynch – or any director – refused to discuss the meanings or possible interpretations of the film, it is inevitable that we understand it in new ways once we have 'mixed' it in our heads differently based on the related features that shed new light on the process of the film's creation.

Self-deconstructing Narratives

[Dave Eggers, playlists and menus, *Only Revolutions*]

And yet what about the ways that digital cinema, such as those early films of the Dogme 95 movement, has resurrected a sort of intimate humanism in cinema, and at least the illusion of natural time? For all of the talk of Lars von Trier, Harmony Korine and other directors associated with the principles of the Dogme 95 movement as ironic or even anti-humanist directors, their films – eschewing special effects – dwell almost exclusively on the human form, on human interactions, on human stories. *The Blair Witch Project*, despite the attention paid to its formal and technical characteristics – is fundamentally an intimately-told story about three people. The fact that their lives are mediated through camera lenses serves to highlight, rather than diminish, their humanity. And exchanges like this one suggest not so much an ironic debunking of 'reality' but a sort of sad awareness of living in such a thoroughly mediated age:

Josh:	I see why you like this video camera so much.
Heather:	You do?
Josh:	It's not quite reality.
Mike:	Reality says we've gotta move.
Josh:	No but it's totally like filtered reality man. It's like you can pretend everything is not quite the way it is.

This self-awareness – more specifically the awareness that media itself is a filter that threatens to hijack and displace the so-called real – is such an important part of media itself in the 1980s and 1990s. James M. Moran has written that MTV's *The Real World* – which debuted in 1992 – 'suggests that at least for those generations bred on television and video cameras, reality is difficult to extricate from its mediation' (2002: 145). The self-deconstructing features of so much new media – such as the basic interfaces to DVD – were already part of the content of mainstream books and movies. In fact, it is in those very books that were often dismissed as overly ironic that some of the most pointed critique unfolded. In Dave Eggers' book *A Heartbreaking Work of Staggering Genius* (2000), the narrator auditions for *The Real World*. A woman interviews him – and videotapes it – to see if he is what they are looking for for the show. At one point, he deconstructs the identity politics of the series, listing the requisite ingredients:

> So, let's work this out. First, you'll get a black person, maybe two – they'll be hip-hop singers or rappers or whatever – and then you'll get a couple of really great-looking people, who will be nice to look at but completely ignorant and prone to terrible faux pas of taste and ignorance, their presence serving two purposes: they a) look wonderful on screen, and b) also serve as foils to the black person or people, who will be much sharper and savvier, but also easily offended, and will delight in raking the dumb people over the coals week after week. So that's three or four people. You'll probably throw in a gay guy or a lesbian, to see how often *they* can get offended, or maybe an Asian or a Latino, or both. Or wait. A Native American. You should get a Native American! That would be so great. (2001: 204; emphasis in original)

Like the sequence in the film *Scream* – where one of the characters pauses the film *Halloween* that is playing on VHS at a party and deconstructs the 'rules' of the horror/slasher genre – these lines are really a form of theory. Do you need a professor to tell you that a show like *The Real World* is a carefully constructed – but seemingly natural – melange of various racial, ethnic and sexual identity types, or that the show both reflects and shapes popular attitudes about identity, or that for some viewers, the 'gay' person or the 'ethnic' person functions as a sort of informant into the lifestyle of 'the other'?

The prevalence of interfaces in digital media – DVD menus, iTune playlists, even web browsers – are the extension of self-deconstructing stories that gained mainstream currency in the 1980s and 1990s. By the 1970s, public discourse was already shifting from the content of media to the medium of media. Hugh Beville, who had been NBC's vice president in charge of planning, noted that 'Since its earliest beginnings, the electronic media have held their audience in a form of temporal tyranny. ... Now viewers are able to tape any show from any station's schedule and replay it at their convenience' (1977–78: 84). In a preface to the 1979 Video Programs Index catalogue, Ken Winslow wrote about the 'movement now underway to turn the 40-year-old home TV receiver into an interactive, integrated function "infotainment" terminal' (1979: iv). Today, with iPods serving as pure fetish objects, it is clearer than ever that content is really only an excuse to explore the medium. For it is so-called content that serves the medium. A show like *24* is fractured into small, floating screens because it is to be watched on small, floating screens. The stately long takes of classical cinema were performed for the expansive screens which attempted to fill your entire field of vision.

Is it any surprise that the navigation of interfaces has threatened to supplant content as the primary narrative, when, in our age of relentless reproduction, content itself has lost its charm? The popularity of books like Mark Danielewski's experimental novel *Only Revolutions* (2006a) – which at one time would have been consigned to the avant-garde fringe – suggests a renewed interest in what we might call the *display* of stories. *Only Revolutions* (published not by some obscure art press, but by Random House) involves shrinking fonts, mathematically precise symmetries, copious marginal notes, upside down text and blank verse, and is very much a display of the physicality of the book as an object in the digital age. Such objects of display are not weak gimmicks to cover up narrative emptiness, but rather testaments to how the storytelling process itself – in both cinema and in books – has become, practically, a genre.

'The thing that I saw very early on was how the book itself could describe this relationship', Danielewski told students at Columbia University, 'whereby you have Hailey's side here and Sam's side here and they're as far apart as you can imagine. And then slowly through the book they get closer and closer until at the very middle, they actually touch. And it's at that place that they actually see each other accurately' (2006b). The book performs its story, foregrounding the structure itself as an element of storytelling: the characters in the book actually 'meet' when their texts meet. The demands upon the reader – periodically turning the book upside down to shift between Hailey's and Sam's stories, deciding whether or not to read the historical notes in the margins, and so forth – are similar to the forms of viewer interactivity required by DVDs. And even the publisher's note, included on the inside dust jacket ('The publisher suggests alternating between Sam & Hailey, reading eight pages at a time') has echoes of the DVD menu function. On another level, books like *Only Revolutions* and *House of Leaves* (2000) are nostalgic for the physicality of the print age (which is always predicted to end but has yet to) in the same way that Quentin Tarantino's and Robert Rodriguez's *Death Proof* and *Planet Terror* yearn for the materiality of pre-digital movies in all their glorious mistakes.

Today, so many films are 'shaky' not solely because the cameras are compact and lightweight and easy to carry in one hand, but, more significantly, because the vision that lies behind them is shaky and uncertain. Writing about *cinéma vérité* from the 1960s, Gilles Deleuze remarked that in 'the cinema of poetry, the distinction between what the character saw subjectively and what the camera saw objectively vanished, not in favour of one or the other, but because the camera assumed a subjective presence, acquired an internal vision, which entered into a relation of simulation ("mimesis") with the character's way of seeing' (1989: 148). There is a generation of directors for whom the unsteady camera is not just an aesthetic choice, but a philosophical one. Of course it is not a choice at all, but a certain stance, a particular way of seeing the world. Filmmaker and writer David Mackenzie has proclaimed 'no more storyboard logic – let's throw it to the wind and see what happens. One of the great hopes for the creative future is amateurism' (in James 2001: 24). This desire for spontaneity, for rawness, for amateurism goes back to punk, and before that to *cinéma vérité*, and before that to the Beats, and before that to Dadaism, and back and back. Indeed, for every expansion of professionalism into the art of filmmaking, there have been movements to return (or to keep) filmmaking amateur. Writing in the *New York Times* in 1936, John Markland noted the rise of amateur filmmaking, suggesting that even 'bridge players annoy their partners with irrelevant remarks about panorama shots and haze filters and business men disrupt conferences to argue the relative merits of F.2.7 lens and F.1.9 in cinematography. The vernacular of moviemaking is no longer confined to Hollywood' (1936: C3). What is new is not the desire to shake up the world of movies, but rather the ability to shake it up so cheaply.

The tendency among cultural critics remains to unmask, to demystify, as Charlie Gere does in his provocative book *Digital Culture*: 'Digital technology's ubiquity and its increasing invisibility have the effect of making it appear almost natural … This naturalisation is problematic, in that it has distinct political repercussions' (2002: 198). But what if, rather than hiding in ideological invisibility, the objects of digital culture announce themselves as created objects at every turn? What if these objects openly theorise themselves, because they are made and consumed by those for whom theory has become a style that calls attention to itself? This seems to me to be the most revolutionary aspect of digital cinema in all its attendant forms: that it recognised – long before academics and theorists – that audiences had already absorbed the tools of deconstruction, that they already knew that movies were 'just stories'. In 1973, Raymond Williams described the process by which the dominant culture maintains its hegemonic hold within a society, noting a 'selective tradition … the way in which from a whole possible area of past and present, certain meanings and practices are chosen for emphasis, certain other meanings and practices are neglected and excluded' (2001: 169). With the rise of digital media in the global marketplace, one has to wonder if the sway of tradition is quite so powerful. As one small example, the increasing availability of 'foreign' films on DVD in the United States suggests the opportunity for people – even those living far from certain cities which, in the past, might have been the only places where such films could be seen – to experience previously excluded forms of cinematic art. The cinematic avant-garde, as well, is now a part of everyday life, as places like YouTube archive not only the traditional avant-garde (such as Stan Brakhage, Maya Deren) but emerging avant-garde filmmakers, too. As Aaron Hillis has suggested, experimental video artists are turning to content-delivery systems like YouTube to 'catch the attention of the hypnotised masses who are growing more and more accustomed to getting their "art" between checking e-mail and the RSS feed' (2007: 1). Deconstruction is no longer an academic theory, or a method of reading texts or viewing films. Rather, deconstruction has become part of the fabric of everyday life, woven into the technologies that surround us.

Shaky Camera
[Jonas Mekas]

In 1962 – over thirty years before the Dogme 95 movement – Jonas Mekas wrote, in a section of his article 'Notes on the New American Cinema' under the heading 'A Note on the "Shaky Camera"', that 'I'm sick and tired of the guardians of Cinema Art who accuse the new film-maker of shaky camera work and bad technique. ... Only this kind of cinema contains the proper vocabulary and syntax to express the true and the beautiful' (2000: 105). And in 1998, Lars von Trier, in describing *The Idiots*, said that the 'film was made in five weeks and I've shot about 90 per cent of it myself, with a small hand-held camcorder for amateurs. This gives a great difference in that if the camera is curious, it's really you yourself who are curious' (in Iversen 2003: 127).

With the rise of the fluid, global marketplace during the years in between those two quotes, the shaky camera has transformed from a technique to a way of seeing the world. And the digital code itself, weightless information transmitted through firewires, cables and wireless nodes, is as free-floating as the camera. An issue of *Film Culture* (which Mekas was still editing) from 1975 advertised a book on moviemaking that featured the type of 16mm hand-held camera used by the avant-garde, but that soon would be replaced in the home market by video cameras.

In some ways, it makes sense that with the collapse of totalising systems of thought (fascism, communism) and the end of the Cold War, our 'vision machines' would become smaller, less fixed, the sorts of machines that record fragments rather than grand narratives. Even though the advertisement stresses the do-it-yourself ethos that marked the punk era, it still promises to instruct readers how to create 'professional looking' films. In the not too distant future, however, the very idea of 'professionalism' would be dispensed with, as films like *The Blair Witch Project* took advantage of small cameras to create movies that prided themselves on the complete appearance of complete amateurism.

Roll your own.

MOVIE MAKING is the place to begin, a primer in filmmaking—in both Super 8 and 16mm formats—for the intelligent adult. In simple step-by-step process the authors take you through the art of film (writing a treatment, a storyboard, a script, the problems of continuity, directing, editing) and the craft of film (the principles of photography, sound recording, lighting, lab procedures, animation, etc.). With this book and a modest amount of equipment you will soon produce professional looking, artistically satisfying films.

MOVIE MAKING

A Guide to Film Production
SUMNER GLIMCHER
and
WARREN JOHNSON
Illustrated $9.95

COLUMBIA
UNIVERSITY
PRESS
New York, New York 10025

An advertisement from the journal *Film Culture*: amateurism that still promises 'professional' looking films

Shoot! [Si Gira]

Shoot! is a novel by Luigi Pirandello, serialised in the Italian journal Nuova antologia in 1915 and translated and published in English in 1927. Narrated by a cameraman, Gubbio, who 'shoots' films for Kosmograph Studio, and unfolding across the course of several of his notebooks, the work is a form of fierce film theory disguised as a novel, or else a novel disguised as film theory. Tom Gunning notes that 'Pirandello's comments on film in Shoot! played an important role in Walter Benjamin's "The Work of Art in the Age of Its Technological Reproducibility"' and that 'Benjamin drew specifically on Gubbio's discussion of the camera's alienating effects on film actors' (2005: ix). Shoot! describes filmmaking as a process that – literally – drains the life from the actors, the human beings who perform before its cameras: 'Here they [the actors] feel as though they were in exile. In exile not only from the stage but also, in a sense, from themselves. Because their action, their *live* action of their *live* bodies, there, on the screen of the cinematograph, no longer exists: it is *their image* alone, caught in a moment, in a gesture, an expression, that flickers and disappears' (2005: 68; emphasis in original).

In the digital era, all is reversed: people go before the camera precisely to reproduce '*their image* alone' with full knowledge and no sadness that this image will disappear as soon as the projector turns off. This is because the projector does not ever turn off today. It is available for perpetual call-up on multiple screens. Gubbio describes the camera as 'a huge spider watching for its prey' (ibid.). With the viral-like spread of motion picture cameras into cell phones and city streets in the form of surveillance devices, one could say that the spiders are everywhere, and that we are all, on some level, actors or performers. Our deeply ingrained sense that we are on camera – or potentially on camera – much of the time in our public lives must have ramifications for the way we behave, the way we carry ourselves, even the way we think. One could go so far as to say: we have shaped ourselves to the desires of the cameras that we have made. Like the character in Elia Kazan's A Face in the Crowd, the camera has secured a gradual change in us that, perhaps, only strict and harsh theory can awaken us to.

The bitter end of *Shoot!* is also strangely predictive of the reality-based media of the digital era, as a movie scene that Gubbio films between a tiger and a man ends not with the tiger's death, as intended, but with the destruction of the man: 'I heard there in the cage the deep growl of the beast and the horrible gasp of the man as he lay helpless in its fangs, in its claws, which were tearing his throat and chest; I heard, I heard, I kept on hearing above that growl, above that gasp, the continuous ticking of the machine [the camera], the handle of which my hand, alone, of its own accord still kept on turning' (2005: 212). The continual gaze of the camera, which in the early twenty-first century required the presence of a human operator, is today possible without any human presence. At the end of *Shoot!*, reality and fiction collapse into one, as the narrative movie scene being filmed becomes terrifyingly real; the man's death is no special effect, but a fact recorded by the camera. Cast in this light, the novel's earlier theories about how the camera creates the illusion of '*live* action' and '*live* bodies' take on a new meaning, serving as ironic forecasts of the novel's plot.

Simultaneous Cinema

[database, Einstein, Eisenstein, *Memento*, multiple screens, quantum entanglement]

In 1930, a strange and funny confusion briefly brought together – figuratively, not literally – two giants of the twentieth century. According to Sergei Eisenstein's biographer Oksana Bulgakowa, in 'early January 1930 Eisenstein spent a short time in Holland. He was welcomed by dozens of reporters at the Rotterdam airfield – they had mistaken him for Einstein' (2001: 104). Although Eisenstein was not Einstein, Einstein was on his mind. Just five months earlier, Eisenstein published a radical essay on sound in film – 'The Filmic Fourth Dimension' – that specifically referenced Einstein:

> The fourth dimension?! Einstein? Or mysticism? Or a joke? It's time to stop being frightened of this new knowledge of a fourth dimension. Einstein himself assures us:
>> The non-mathematician is seized by a mysterious shuddering when he hears of 'four-dimensional' things, by a feeling not unlike that awakened by thoughts of the occult. And yet there is no more common-place statement than that the world in which we live is a four-dimensional space-time continuum.
> Possessing such an excellent instrument of perception as the cinema – even on its primitive level – for the sensation of movement, we should soon learn a concrete orientation in this four-dimensional space-time continuum, and feel as much at home in it as in our own house-slippers! (Eisenstein 1977a: 69–70)

Eisenstein's playfulness here, his easy-sounding familiarity with Einstein's theories of the space-time continuum, suggests a cinema that is as much about exploration as it is about spectacle. This is the cinema of science, of discovery, of a sort of avant-garde investigation into reality. Eisenstein's vision of cinema as 'an excellent instrument of perception' reminds us how, early on, the function of cinema was debatable, and not taken for granted. Cinema could penetrate ever deeper into reality by destroying familiar ways of seeing, by challenging the very frameworks of the real. In *The Emergence of Cinematic Time*, Mary Ann Doane notes how 'this dilemma of discontinuity and continuity becomes the epistemological conundrum that structures the debates about the representability of time at the turn of the century' (2002: 9).

As Scott MacDonald has suggested, surrealist filmmakers – including René Clair and Luis Buñuel – 'continually confront one of the central assumptions of conventional cinema: the idea that the individual personality and social and political relations among individuals are basically rational and understandable' (1993: 3). And earlier, in the 1880s, Eadweard Muybridge, whose 'deepest concerns seem to have been scientific' (MacDonald 1993: 10) used film to study and to document motion, taking roughly 200,000 images during this period (see Musser 1990: 50). Cinema as a tool to penetrate into the workings of physical reality constituted one of the supreme gestures of cinema in its early years. Indeed, Muybridge was something of a hero to the New American directors of the 1950s and 1960s. As Thom Andersen noted in a 1966 issue of the journal *Film Culture*, 'Muybridge considered himself a scientist, not an artist' (1966: 23). As reality splintered ever more deeply under modernism's gaze, movie cameras served as machines for deconstructing the visible, not with an eye towards destroying it – as would be a tendency during the postmodern period – but rather with an eye towards understanding it. In 1927, Albert Einstein wrote to Hedi Born that if 'one wants to get away from this vagueness one must take up mathematics. And even then one reaches one's aim only by becoming completely insubstantial under the dissecting knife of clarity. Living matter and clarity are opposites – they run away from one another' (in Born 2005: 92). Cinema's emergence during modernism is traced continually upon its surfaces, which are concerned with the play of light, the staging of action and the rhythm of editing, all of which attempt to impose clarity upon the mad chaos of reality. The rise of the American studio system – with its continuity, its invisible editing, its order – was the culmination of this thinking, organised around pictures and sound. In an advertisement from a 1928 issue of *Amateur Movie Makers*, the Cinematic Accessories Company advertised a 'dissolving device' that would allow the procurement of 'the beautiful, smooth, even-timed fade-outs, fade-ins, dissolves and other camera tricks of the professional'. But the destruction of natural time was more than a trick; it was an effort to impose a new order on reality. In this regard, movies were – as they are today – experimental no matter how conventional their plots, because they involved, as this advert suggests, the manipulation of real time through fade-ins, fade-outs, dissolves and other techniques.

The notion that films could be instruments of discovery is something that has informed and haunted them from the beginning. In his 1960 book *Theory of Film*, Siegfried Kracauer wrote:

'I ask that a film *discover* something for me', declares Luis Buñuel, who is himself a fiery pathfinder of the screen. And what are films likely to discover? The evidence available suggests that they assume three kinds of revealing functions. They tend to reveal things normally unseen; phenomena overwhelming consciousness; and certain

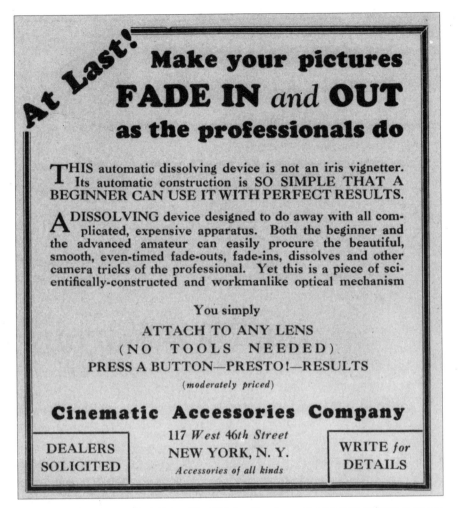

At Last!

Make your pictures FADE IN *and* OUT as the professionals do

THIS automatic dissolving device is not an iris vignetter. Its automatic construction is SO SIMPLE THAT A BEGINNER CAN USE IT WITH PERFECT RESULTS.

A DISSOLVING device designed to do away with all complicated, expensive apparatus. Both the beginner and the advanced amateur can easily procure the beautiful, smooth, even-timed fade-outs, fade-ins, dissolves and other camera tricks of the professional. Yet this is a piece of scientifically-constructed and workmanlike optical mechanism

You simply

ATTACH TO ANY LENS
(NO TOOLS NEEDED)
PRESS A BUTTON—PRESTO!—RESULTS

(moderately priced)

Cinematic Accessories Company

| DEALERS SOLICITED | 117 *West 46th Street* NEW YORK, N. Y. *Accessories of all kinds* | WRITE *for* DETAILS |

From the magazine *Amateur Movie Makers*, May 1928: breaking down and rearranging reality to create narrative

aspects of the outer world which may be called 'special modes of reality'. (1997: 46; emphasis in original)

Eisenstein's argument was that editing itself was an unintended form of investigation that revealed the underlying ideologies of Western culture. 'The structure that is reflected in the concept of Griffith's montage is the structure of bourgeois society,' he wrote in 1944 (1977b: 234). As Stephen Kern has argued, the turn of the nineteenth century hinged in many ways on a shattering and reshaping of ideas about perspective, not only in the fields of science and physics, but art and film as well. The cubists, writes Kern, 'abandoned the homogeneous space of linear perspective and painted objects in a multiplicity of spaces ... One explanation for multiple perspective was that it enabled the cubists to transcend the temporal limitations of traditional art' (1983: 143). This shattering of time – at the same time that Einstein's theories were overturning Newtonian conceptions of a stable, absolute space and time – was a cinematic possibility that was never really seized upon. In this regard – formally – the television series *24* was not that much different from the film *Timecode*. Both rely on multiple frames to convey events unfolding simultaneously but in different locations. But whereas *Timecode* unfolds in four distinct long takes – with no edits, no cuts – *24* uses multiple screens sporadically, right before and immediately following commercial breaks and during moments of intensity. Such films – as well as other media ranging from cable news shows to the multiple real-time windows of a web page – signal not so much a postmodern break with older versions of representation, but an elaborate extension of simultaneous multiple perspectivism that characterised, as Kern has argued, physics and art in the early twentieth century. There are hints of it everywhere, including in 'The Futurist Cinema', a 1916 essay that called for 'cinematic simultaneity and interpenetration of different times and places. We shall project two or three different visual episodes at the same time, one next to the other' (Marinetti *et al.* 1916). Rejecting the emerging logic of narrative cinema – crosscutting or parallel editing – the futurist idea of showing simultaneous time simultaneously on the screen was, ironically, a call for a form of representation that was no more radical than crosscutting, but that came to be perceived as avant-garde or 'arty'. Peter Weibel imagines a future where 'every member of a cinema audience would be able to watch a different movie' with the help of a quantum computer that allows each viewer to watch a separate film 'resulting from the same stock of probabilistic values' (2003: 600).

For why, we might ask, is showing two or more events that are occurring at the same time in parallel editing fashion (cutting back and forth between them) considered 'realistic', while showing simultaneous events on the screen at the same time considered 'experimental' or at least self-conscious? One could argue that today – with the prevalence of ever more divided screens, such as cable news, the Internet itself, and so forth – split and multiple screens are losing their caché as art statements. The self-conscious split screens of Brian De Palma are everywhere today. Coming to mainstream fruition in the late 1960s in such films as *The Thomas Crown Affair* and *The Boston Strangler*, the split screen suggested dissolution – as the 1960s was collapsing in on its own dreams – but also an effort to break free from a single point of view. In *The Boston Strangler*, especially, director Richard Fleischer did not so much make a movie with multiple screens, but made a multiple-screen movie with occasional single screens. In one striking sequence, a smaller screen of an elderly woman who has just unwittingly buzzed the strangler into her apartment complex is embedded in a larger screen revealing a point-of-view shot as the strangler makes his way up the apartment building stairs. In another, the sombre television announcer warning women not to let strangers into their homes is revealed on multiple screens, so that the announcer appears twice, speaking the same words, in different contexts. On the left, the serious television announcer; on the right, the women watching the serious television announcer. These overlapping present moments soon evolve into a multitude of shifting screens, as many as four or five simultaneously that provide a kaleidoscopic real-time version of the unfolding investigation. The return in recent years of split and multiple screens – which were neglected in mainstream cinema in the 1980s and 1990s, with the exception of some films by Brian De Palma and others – coincided with the emergence of the Internet and the multiple-window interface of early MacIntosh computers that allowed for the amateur manipulation and mixing of text and image, prefiguring the video and music mixing now prevalent in even the most functional of media devices, such as mobile phones.

The multiple screens that seeped into mainstream cinema in the 1960s encouraged a form of space-shifting on the audience's part, as viewers could, in a very rough way, 'edit' the films themselves, selecting which screen quadrants to view at any given moment. As Norman Jewison (2005) has said of his film *The Thomas Crown Affair*, 'we realised that the eye is the only selective organ in the body and therefore you could take in more than one image at the same time as long as there wasn't a lot of sound'. In *The Thomas Crown Affair*, multiple screens are used not only to show events unfolding simultaneously in different locations, but also to reveal future events, as near the end of the film, when Thomas Crown (Steve McQueen) and Vicki Anderson (Faye Dunaway) are on the beach (in the upper left screen quadrant) talking, while the rest of the screen begins to fill with images from the robbery that is to take place in the future. In some ways, these multiple screens imagined, symbolically, Sony's 'time-shifting' revolution. A Betamax advertisement from 1980 shows the silhouette of a man sitting in a chair, holding a remote control up: 'Experience the freedom of total control' the caption reads. At the bottom of the picture is a list of Sony Corporation trademarks, including BetaScan and Time Commander. BetaScan, introduced in 1979, allowed viewers to watch video in fast-forward mode, while Time Commander, introduced in 1980, made possible frame-by-frame advance, variable speed slow motion, and relatively clear and stable freeze-frames. Another Sony advertisement, also from 1980, promised (in an eerie premonition of the film *Eternal Sunshine of the Spotless Mind*) to free 'you from the restraints of time, memory and circumstance'.

The unprecedented manipulation of images and sound promised in the Sony advert so thoroughly demystifies video – and movies watched on video – that the theoretical work of cultural studies/film scholars suddenly seems quaint, if not redundant. Stripped of its aura, its magic, reduced to slow motion, freeze-frames and timers, film is already demystified as just another everyday object broken down to fit into the busy schedules of viewers. Of course, we might retort, are viewers being offered choice and freedom, or just the illusion of choice and freedom? 'In television', Silvio Gaggi has written, 'it is the proliferation of irrelevant choices that produces a specious freedom that obscures increasingly powerful constraints on imaginable possibilities' (1997: 121). And yet, if part of film's sway over us was dependent on the invisibility of its structure, doesn't the ability to select and rearrange bits and pieces of that structure suggest a deepening knowledge on the viewer's part that acts as a form of theory?

In essence, cinema's ability to represent multiple versions of reality simultaneously is a form of theoretical physics, disguised as narrative. In physics, the 'many world'

The time-shift revolution: moving images demystified not by theorists, but by consumers

theory has gained ascendancy lately, as what was once mere theory is now demonstrable. Niels Bohr's notion that observation determines the final state of an electron – and by extension reality itself – is nicely summarised by physicist Michio Kaku:

Before an observation is made, an object exists in all possible states simultaneously. To determine which state the object is in, we have to make an observation, which 'collapses' the wave function, and the object goes into a definite state. The act of observation destroys the wave function, and the object now assumes a definite reality. (2005: 153)

While such an astounding notion remained in the realm of pure theory for decades, experiments in the 1970s, and then again in the early 1980s, confirmed that in fact the measurement of photons determined their spins. According to Brian Greene:

There is now overwhelming evidence for this so-called quantum entanglement. If two photons are entangled, the successful measurement of either photon's spin about one axis 'forces' the other, distant photon to have the same spin about the same axis; the act of measuring one photon 'compels' the other, possibly distant photon to snap out of the haze of probability and take on a definite spin value – a value that precisely matches the spin of its distant companion. And that boggles the mind. (2004: 115)

Because digital cinema operates on what Lev Manovich has called database logic, it allows for the arrangement of that database in ways that change not only the screen, but the very ways in which time is represented. As Gene Youngblood has noted, traditional cinema's use of crosscutting or parallel montage to indicate simultaneous events gives way in digital cinema to what he calls parallel event-streams: 'Digital code offers formal solutions to the "tense" limitations of mechanical cinema. Past, present and future can be spoken in the same frame at once' (2003: 158). In a film such as *Memento*, this happens both on the level of content and of medium. The film is about the condition of being lost, a condition simulated on the special edition version of the DVD release, where there is no menu of options in the traditional sense, but rather a dizzying array of choices with only the most minimal of instructions or prompts. In the film's opening scene – which is actually the final scene chronologically – Teddy attempts to 'remind' Leonard who he is:

Leonard:	I'm Leonard Shelby, I'm from San Francisco and I'm –
Teddy:	That's who you *were*, you don't know who you *are*.
Leonard:	Shut your mouth!
Teddy:	Let me take you down in the basement and show you what you've become.

The dark secret at the heart of *Memento* might not be that Leonard has forgotten who he 'really' is, but rather that he is several selves at once, that he is both the upstanding 'Leonard Shelby, from San Francisco' *and* a serial killer. Leonard is a database character, enacting properties assigned to him by some code that within the world of the movie remains forever hidden and inscrutable. But another level – on the material level of the DVD as object – the veil is lifted and Leonard is the product of the user's interven-

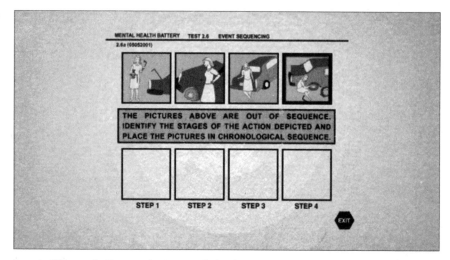

From the DVD menu for *Memento*: the viewer is asked to shape time by selecting the 'correct' sequence in order to view the film in chronological order

tion. If users can navigate the special edition DVD correctly, they can watch his story unfold chronologically. For instance, on disc two, if users answer a series of questions correctly, they are presented with the screen that asks them to put the images in chronological order.

Perform this task correctly, and the movie begins to unfold in a linear fashion. The feature is a playful acknowledgement of the viewer's identification with Leonard Shelby, whose short-term memory likewise exists in temporary segments that are not in chronological order.

Experimental filmmaker Malcolm Le Grice has written that a 'major characteristic of digital systems is the fundamentally nonlinear way information [data] is stored and retrieved' (2001: 315). In *Memento*, the 'loop' that Leonard is stuck in that drives him continually to hunt down and kill his wife's attacker over and over again is echoed in dialogue from different points in time that sounds the same, but is slightly different. For instance, while the dialogue quoted above between Leonard and Teddy comes from the beginning of the movie (but near the end of the plot), this exchange between them comes from near the end of the movie (but near the beginning of the plot):

Teddy: You haven't got a clue, have you? You don't even know who you are.
Leonard: Yes, I do. I don't have amnesia. I remember everything about myself
            up until the incident. I'm Leonard Shelby, I'm from San Fran…
Teddy: That's who you were, Lenny. You don't know who you are, who
            you've become since the incident. You're wandering around, play-
            ing detective … and you don't even know how long ago it was.

In the section of his book with the heading 'The Persistent Illusion of Past, Present, and Future', physicist Brian Greene reminds readers that 'reality encompasses all the events in 'spacetime' (2004: 139). That is, all events – past, present and future – exist at a specific point in spacetime. Time seems to flow to us because of the way we perceive it: 'moments of time come to life when they are illuminated by the power of consciousness' (ibid.). It is revealing that Greene's example to help illustrate this is still frames in a film, which exist whether they are illuminated or not. Just because we do not happen to see certain frames illuminated on the screen, does not mean they do not exist, any more than the fact that we cannot perceive the past does not mean it does not exist. Filmmakers such as Christopher Nolan have noted that linearity as the dominant narrative mode has more to do with the medium itself than with the way we experience reality:

> To me it really is a question of finding the most suitable order for releasing information to the audience and not feeling any responsibility to do it chronologically, just like we don't in life. I think it's TV that's really held back the development of cinematic narrative, because with TV you have to be able to switch it on ten minutes before the ending to understand the entire show – that's the nature of the medium. And films have been tailored towards that. I think DVD and video and just the birth of VHS really changes that. (In Kaufman 2001)

And elsewhere, Nolan has said that 'once VHS came along, you could control the timeline – while you watched it' (in Anthony 2001: 59).

Films such as these, created by people raised on the time-shifting capabilities of VCRs and, later, other digital technologies, attempt to give some sort of formal structure to the notion that readers or viewers create meaning via interaction with texts and movies. This is something that Charlie Kaufman – who has written the screenplays for such films as *Being John Malkovich*, *Human Nature*, *Confessions of a Dangerous Mind*, *Eternal Sunshine of the Spotless Mind* and *Synecdoche, New York* – has directly addressed:

> There's something about movies that's very safe because they usually play out in a certain way, and also because they're *done*. They're *dead*. It's not like theatre where anything can happen, where somebody can screw up their lines, or there can be some kind of new interaction or chemistry between people. It's just this dead thing that you're watching, and I don't like that about it. So, if you force people to interact with the movie in a new way, then you're forcing them to see different things and their minds to interact. (2002: 129; emphasis in original)

In this regard, YouTube is not simply a collection of videos, but rather a vast experimental film, with literally hundreds of thousands of scenes, with new ones being added every minute. Unlike previous avant-garde cinema, YouTube is not shown to a select audience, only to be confined to obscurity or legend by its unavailability, nor is it dependent on archivists and scholars to maintain its status as art. Pre-digital experimental films – like Andy Warhol's *Empire* – achieved the status of art because of their event status, their scarcity, which conferred on them the aura of legend. Stripped of context and aura, something like *Empire* today would come and go on a video sharing site like YouTube or Blinkx without fanfare. The erosion and collapse of distinctions between avant-garde and mainstream mean that cinematic experiments, such as simultaneous cinema, are returning to their roots in science and physics, disciplines for which investigation is a primary goal. There is a contradiction that lies at the heart of digital media, which is this: even as media objects become more fleeting and come and go with greater frequency (for example, an extremely popular video on YouTube will be displaced by another extremely popular video within days or hours) they are at the same time more permanently available because of the ease with which they can be copied and stored. Siegfried Zielinski has said that the 'basic digital unit is becoming a new abstract currency' that produces 'symbols and programs, which prospectively include art that is realised exclusively within the framework of media networks' (2006: 273–4). These networks are also, simultaneously, archives, though how permanent is anyone's guess. In some ways, the proliferation of user-submitted videos featuring the mundane, everyday activities of 'amateurs' hearkens back to cinema's earlier era and the promise of the 'professional amateur'. A 1937 article in the *New York Times* on 16mm film noted that 'perhaps 90 per cent [of amateur moviemakers], however skillful, confine themselves to highly personal records such as "Baby Playing with the Dog" or "Cousin Bob Changing a Tire on the Old Family Chariot When We Had a Breakdown While on Our Vacation in the Adirondacks Last Summer"' (Sterling 1937: 3). The article goes on to note that such productions 'exist in a sort of semi-vacuum' (ibid.); a problem which meets its opposite today, when there is a potential audience for everything, but nobody cares.

In fact, we have only begun to consider the question of how future generations will 'restore' today's digital artifacts. Ironically, the digital era – when films, music and so forth, have an uncertain physical dimension and presence – has inaugurated a powerful movement to restore and archive old media, such as films. Obscure movies that, prior to the advent of DVD would never have been made available to general audiences for reasonable prices, today circulate widely for purchase or rental. The disembodiment of images in the digital era (what does the physical *source* of that video stored on your computer actually look like?) is matched by the fact that the digital archive has grown so fast, and that it includes not only new 'popular' material, but also older, more obscure, experimental work. The strangeness of the digital landscape – usually ignored by academics in the humanities who, unfortunately, have forgotten how to be pleasantly surprised by anything – is that the radically subversive and the most mainstream fare co-exist within mouse clicks of each other on the Internet. This fact of everyday life has passed beyond its ability to be coolly explained away as 'postmodern flatness' or 'surfaces', and has taken on the dimensions of a new paradigm of knowledge that has yet to be mapped by most theorists. The collision of 'high' and 'low', of obscure and familiar, of self-consciously artistic and openly commercial, has effectively put into practice what was once in the realm of theory. 'Everybody complains about the insipid programming content of TV', wrote John Swenson in an article in the rock magazine *Crawdaddy* in 1974, 'but few people realise that there is an alternative form of the medium which could effectively decentralise the major networks' hold on your television experience' (1974: 32). The advent of video, followed by digital, signalled a decentralisation that few could have foreseen in 1974, a decentralisation that suggests that cultural coherence and shared meaning occurs not at the level of content, but rather at the level of interface.

Small Screens

[Václav Havel, seduction]

Pauline Kael once wrote that audiences 'want the theatre screen to do what the television screen can't do: overpower them' (1994: 283). This is still true today, and helps to explain why so many people still go to see movies in theatres despite their increasing availability for home and mobile viewing. There is a desire to be dominated by the image; we want to be overwhelmed. In attempting to understand his fellow citizens' tolerance and even desire for the totalitarian systems that oppressed them during the communist era, Václav Havel wrote that such systems were not flukes of history, or aberrations. 'Neither is it [a totalitarian system] the product of some diabolical higher will which has decided, for reasons unknown, to torment a portion of humanity in this way. It can happen and did happen only because there is obviously in modern humanity a certain tendency towards the creation, or at least the toleration, of such a system' (1986: 53). One of the problems with the cultural studies model of film and media theory was that it too often assumed a passive subject who simply needed to be awakened to the fact that they were being dominated by seductive images and stories of dubious ideological character. One explanation for the rise of postmodern cinema is that, having grown tired of the same cinematic seductions repeated over and over again, audiences turned to films that did not hide, but in fact revealed, their mechanisms of seduction. It is not that audiences wanted to break the spell of ideology, but rather that they wanted to see the code of the spell. The shrinking of movies down to little screens that are portable erases any lingering hints of mystification: there are no mysteries to movies today. In some ways, this is in keeping with the project begun by minimal art and minimalism: a simplicity so severe that it becomes almost ornate. Small, portable screens cannot help but reveal the contours of their making: unlike the theatre screen, there is no dark surrounding the hand-held video screen: portable theatre screens mean that theatres follow us everywhere. 'Few people', Kenneth Baker has written, 'foresaw the growth of the mass media in America into a nexus of institutions having almost instant simultaneous access to millions of homes, and thus potentially to every citizen's consciousness' (1988: 29). In the past, there was at least the illusion of protection from the screens: one had *to go* to the movie theatre or cinema, one had to *turn on* the television. In a word, screens were scarce, and, being scarce, retained a mystery.

According to Alain Robbe-Grillet, the artificial nature of cinema and the experience of viewing cinema was what, in fact, constituted its spell: 'it is the very conventions of the photographic medium (the two dimensions, the black-and-white images, the frame of the screen, the difference of scale between scenes) [that] help free us from our own conventions' (1965: 168). As screens have become less scarce and more portable, surrounded by the regularity of everyday life, we find ourselves no longer in need of being freed from our 'own conventions', because the screens themselves have adopted our conventions. Of course, they always did, but the trick was in making us forget this fact. It did not take theorists to 'demystify' movies; they began to do this for themselves as soon as they began the migration to television and later to videotape and later to digital interfaces. The 'male gaze' was imposing and even dangerous on the gigantic screens of the 1940s and 1950s, but more like a parody of itself on videotape in the 1970s, when it could be frozen, analysed, exposed and deconstructed with ease. 'Time-shifting' – the hallmark of home videotape systems in the 1970s – was really about the shifting of expectations: audiences still wanted illusions, only cleansed of the dangerous, exciting ideologies that coursed through them. Here is the difference: *Jaws* was an 'ideological' movie, but *Rebecca* was an ideological movie. The power and mystique of movies was never just derived from the stories they told, or even their various techniques; it was also derived from the size of the screens and the darkness of the theatre, which inspired belief. A pocket-sized *Citizen Kane* inspires awe, but of a different sort.

And yet, audiences still pay to sit in the dark and be dominated by gigantic images, an experience that offers the best remaining hope for seduction.

Target Video

Founded in 1977 by Joseph Rees, Target Video, out of San Francisco, was instrumental not only in documenting the nascent California punk scene, but in making a theory out of the medium of videotape and even looking beyond this to the speed that would characterise technologies of the digital era. 'Punk demonstrated a fascination with technology and machines', Charlie Gere has written, 'not so much as musical tools, but as symbols both of the passing industrial era and of the coming information age' (2002: 171).

Capturing both live performances and staged music videos before there was such a thing as MTV, Target Video worked quickly and cheaply with consumer equipment at the dawn of the home consumer video age, eschewing perfection for the raw immediacy of real time. Marshall McLuhan once said that when 'an inexpensive play-back for video tape is available, the film will become as portable as a book after Gutenberg' (1995: 290). A little over a decade later, Rees put this theory into practice. At the time, he said that 'video's worked out to be the ultimate medium for new wave because it's very fast; it instantly documents an event and also we can distribute this information very rapidly' (1980: 34). The speed and spontaneity of video was a mystery, a contradiction. It was a contradiction because it was a medium of instantaneous emotion, destroying the time-lag between the live event and its memory in the archive. And yet the very nature of the archive is that it preserves events so that they endure long beyond the moment of their original creation and performance. Rees started with borrowed video equipment: 'It was definitely faster and easier to use for instant feedback of the events. I had free access to a local cable channel in San Francisco where I could show the material hours later' (ibid.).

Rees glimpsed the future of music video in 1979, while attending the 'first rock 'n' roll video conference ever', in Los Angeles. Realising he had to pay $100 to attend, he snuck into one of the presentations: 'The room contains a TV monitor and about 35 slickly-dressed types standing around it watching Elton John doing the same over-produced thing, "Midnight Special"-style. Checking out the brochures lying around announcing upcoming videodisc shows, I soon realise nothing new in programming is in the offing and that the strategy of the companies involved is to feed the public the same garbage they have done for years' (ibid.). Although in its early years MTV did play some adventurous, bizarre and even avant-gardish videos (DEVO comes to mind) this was largely because the station was in need of content. By the mid-1980s, most music videos on the network had become what Rees had predicted: 'Arista and more of that bunch are spending *lots* of dollars to develop the video-album or "videogram" market. It's the same Big Business versus the Artist problem all over again: artists now recording will have to struggle with overproduced visuals, i.e. special effects colouris-ing, dry ice, star filters, etc., and the high costs of live production running from $10,000 on up' (ibid.; emphasis in original).

For Rees, punk was part of the inevitable overturning of the old order which was, for that generation, the 1960s. The 1970s, he said recently, were a time of 'boredom, rejec-tion of cultural styles, the pure desire and intensity of the young artists to make their statements and the natural cultural roll-over. As any new wave movement, it [punk] rejects the old and creates a new language' (2008). As fast·and amateurish as punk, video – as he conceived it – was the perfect medium for that language. Although his-tories of the rise of video technologies still tend to underemphasise the importance of video as a tool to document and create 'music videos' in the years preceding the emergence of MTV in 1981, when music videos became a highly formalised genre, video practices and aesthetics were an important precursor to digital video. These videos – shot on video cameras that were frequently owned by colleges and universi-ties – were not quite documentaries, and they were not quite narratives. Videos from the mid- to late-1970s of bands such as the Ramones and the Cramps occupy a sort of lost spot in the history of video and cinema, as they were not filmed by notable auteurs but frequently by amateurs whose choices about framing, editing, and so on, were motivated by the circumstances of capturing live performances.

Time, Memory
[Walter Benjamin, Maya Deren, YouTube]

The database. 'Archive fever'. In the late 1920s, Walter Benjamin wrote that 'collecting is a form of practical memory, and of all the profane manifestations of the penetration of "what has been" (of all the profane manifestations of "nearness") it is the most binding' (1999: 883). Today's archives are of a different sort, as videotape is given new life by that which supposedly replaces it. Just as movies made their way to television, videos make their way to the Internet, preserved on places like YouTube that host enormous databases of old, obscure clips. In 2007, my university invited a serious scholar to lecture about how postmodernism had flattened out and forgotten history; he said many things, including that we had lost touch with tradition. And yet, is it not true that, despite our best efforts, it is a fact of the digital era that we cannot escape the overbearing past? It is there, at every turn, on every channel, on every web page, waiting to be clicked. If anything, we are drowning in history. History in the digital era has a stranglehold upon us. The historical archive in the digital era makes itself possible by creating users who internalise the very rules that create them. The digitalisation of cinema – on DVD and other formats – has chained film to the history of film. The bonus material on DVDs (which in sheer length outstrips the 'feature' presentation) forces a historical grounding that positively makes viewing a film a 'scholarly' experience. There is no escape, in the digital era, from the relentless historicising that renders all cinema simply a product of an era. 'We were trying to tell five stories at the same time, and so we all went up to the Montreal World Festival [1967]', Norman Jewison says on the director's commentary on *The Thomas Crown Affair* DVD, and immediately we see that the radical multiple screens were a product of a specific time, a specific place. We are taught a *lesson*. There is no mystery, after listening to Jewison's commentary, to the film anymore. There is no genius, just a group of people (the director, the film editor, and so forth) who happened to go to Montreal and see the film *A Place to Stand* by Christopher Chapman. Of course, this is how art works: everything is influenced by something. But in the digital era, this fact moves from the background to the foreground. Even those accused of being the most notorious products and promulgators of postmodern shallowness and cynicism in cinema – such as Quentin Tarantino – habitually refer to older cinematic styles and traditions, to older ways of viewing, to older ways of making movies. The French New Wave. B-Movies. Drive-In Movies. Grindhouse Movies. It is not even nostalgia, because the past is everywhere, enveloping us. What Neo needed to awaken from in *The Matrix* was not a false world, but a world so overcome by its past that the real-time present was violently repressed.

Some of the most radical – and beautiful – pre-digital films that experimented with time and memory were those by Maya Deren. *Meshes of the Afternoon* and *At Land*, especially, subjugate linear 'clock' time to psychological time. Both films – but *Meshes of the Afternoon* particularly – hint at conventional Hollywood genres such as crime drama and murder mystery. In *Meshes of the Afternoon*, Deren's multiple selves repeating the same action several times suggest a database logic we might associate with a film like *Run Lola Run*, where Lola repeats her quest to secure money to save her boyfriend. In one regard, the user's ability to manipulate units of time in cinema today parallels the activity that used to be the domain of the director or editor. George Lucas has said that it's 'easy to move things around in the frame, to change various visual aspects of the film, which just wasn't possible before. It's the same kind of thing that you find in still photography if you use Photoshop' (in Magid 2002: 3). Although film viewers cannot use (yet) the DVD to alter the content within a frame, they can manipulate the general sequence of a film. And some DVDs – such as the special edition of *Memento* – offer a recut or extended or differently sequenced version of the film that help make visible the choices that, as Robert Ray and others have argued, were rendered invisible during the classic Hollywood era.

Time-Shifting

[Philip K. Dick, Michel Gondry, Brian Greene]

Is it possible to speak of a before and after today, when everything is present, and in the present? Digital interfaces – the computer screen, the iPod video screen, cell phone video, DVDs – scramble and make it possible to scramble past, present and future in unprecedented ways. José van Dijck has wondered whether or not 'digitisation is, ultimately, a cultural process that is slowly changing the way we remember ourselves' (2007: 372). Our control over the screen is really a loss of control over time. In Philip K. Dick's 1966 novel *Now Wait for Last Year*, the drug JJ-180 lashes people back and forth across time, destroying boundaries between past, present and future. At one point, the protagonist – Eric Sweetscent – comes face-to-face with his future self: '"So I've gotten fat; so what?" his self of 2056 said' (1993: 182).

It's not just that movies today – such as *Following*, *Amores Perros*, *Memento*, *21 Grams*, *Eternal Sunshine of the Spotless Mind*, *Babel* or *Inland Empire* – experiment with time more frequently and radically than in the past. Instead, the very structures and interfaces of new media promote time-shifting. Indeed today, the interface to a movie functions as a narrative as much as the movie itself. The signatory gesture of digital technologies is that they allow us to experience and shape time in ways that equate to the nonlinear nature of the stories we consume. Time-shifting happens not only in movies themselves, but in the way we experience them through interfaces that in fact reify their increasingly nonlinear logic. We are prepared for the anarchic time-cuts in Michel Gondry's *Eternal Sunshine of the Spotless Mind* – especially near the end as Joel's memories literally bleed into each other and dissolve – because we have already become so familiar with manipulating data and databases in our everyday lives, in the form of downloading, uploading, transferring, file-sharing, burning, and so on. We find the radically disturbing implications of *Eternal Sunshine of the Spotless Mind* – selective manipulation and even destruction of memory – rather sadly humorous and non-threatening not simply because the tone of the movie is frequently light, but because the easy manipulation of digital data is something that we do every day. In the same way, *The Science of Sleep* (also directed by Gondry) features a 'one-second time travel machine' built by Stéphane for Stéphanie that allows the user to jump back or forward one second. Prior to using the invention, Stéphanie says that 'randomness is very difficult to achieve'. In the digital era, the effect of randomness is achieved through careful planning and manipulation of the database, as what appears to be a more natural rendering of reality is in fact the product of technologies that are as manipulative as the classical era, analogue technologies. As Stéphanie moves herself backwards and forwards out of present time, we see that she is simply – like Gondry, the director – editing the film in ways that give the illusion of time travel. She is, in fact, cutting the film in such a way that the characters travel backwards (into the story already told) and forwards (into the story not yet told). Even further, she is doing what viewers do when they fast-forward or reverse to different points in a movie on their DVD player or computer. The manipulation of time is, fundamentally, a choice made on the level of database. In *Eternal Sunshine of the Spotless Mind*, as Joel is preparing to have his memories of Clementine erased, Dr. Mierzwiak tells him that 'we'll start with your most recent memories and go backwards'. Like organising and managing text, audio or video files, there are, as they say, choices to be made, such as: shall the files be organised and accessed in chronological, or reverse-chronological order? In *Memento*, Leonard archived and organised his memories with tattoos and Polaroid snapshots, because as he moved forward in time, he forgot the immediate past. In *Eternal Sunshine of the Spotless Mind*, the administered elimination of memory means that Joel can (supposedly) move forward in time without the burden of selective past memories. And, of course, we as viewers can skip past scenes in the movie itself, eliminating them forever from our own consciousness.

Physicist Brian Greene has noted that – from the point of view of physics – there is no discernable reason why we are locked in to linear time:

> time seems to relentlessly march forward. Whereas in space, which Einstein taught us was related to time, you can go left or right or back – you are completely free – your motion in space. Why is your motion through time not free as well … the main puzzle is that when you look at the laws of physics they seem to show no distinction between what we call forward in time and what they call back in time. Future and past are on equal footing from the point of the underlying equations. So why are they on such different footing from the point of view of everyday experience? (in Birnbaum 2004: 2)

Guillermo Arriaga, the screenwriter of *21 Grams*, has said that 'I have a short story that has been recently published that also goes back and forth all the time. I think this is the way we tell stories on a daily basis – we never go linear. For example, if I want to tell you how I met my wife, I will never begin at the very beginning … I think this is the natural way to tell stories' (in Curry 2003: 3). This is echoed by Gus Van Sant, who, in describing the collage aspect of *Elephant*, has said that 'Things don't have beginnings and ends in our lives, and if you want to make storytelling lifelike, you have to play by the rules of reality, which is that nothing is connecting, nothing is making sense' (in Said 2004: 18).

This method of telling stories – skipping back and forth in time, compressing and decompressing swathes of time – is deeply linked with technologies that foreground this process. Mark Stephen Meadows has noted that 'digital media, with things like back buttons and the ability to accelerate, decelerate, link, and close, changes how time is used in narration' (2003: 51). The question is no longer, *how do these interfaces enable users to manipulate time in movies?*, but rather, *how are these interfaces a new form of narrative?* In other words, could it be that the very process of digital media navigation – selecting which scenes or chapters to view on DVD, or which screen version to select, or which alternate ending to watch – could it be that this process itself is a basic form of storytelling, insomuch as it allows the user some degree of freedom in selecting and arranging narrative bits and chunks? If I want my ending to *28 Days Later* to be a happy one, and I 'select' the happy ending, am I not contributing to the shape of the narrative? In 1999 – in two influential articles published in the *New York Press* – Godfrey Cheshire predicted that in the digital era, movies could be continually re-edited and released in different versions to satisfy audience demands and expectations. 'There can be hundreds of versions of a given film', he wrote (1999: 5).

In 1996 – at the dawn of the digital era – writer David Foster Wallace (who was himself often singled out as a postmodern narcissist) published a Very Long Book, *Infinite Jest*, whose plot involved a media company that proposed new ways to deliver content to viewers:

> And so but *what if*, their [InterLace TelEntertainment] campaign's appeal basically ran, what if, instead of sitting still for choosing the least of 504 infantile evils, the vox- and digitus-populi could choose to make its home entertainment literally an essentially *adult*? I.e. what if – according to InterLace – what if a viewer could more or less *100% choose what's on at any given time?* Choose and rent, over PC and modem and fiber-optic line, from tens of thousands of second-run films, documentaries, the occasional sport, old beloved non-'Happy Days' programs, wholly new programs, cultural stuff, and c., all prepared by the time-tested, newly lean Big Four's mammoth vaults and production facilities and packaged and disseminated by InterLace TelEnt. in convenient fiber-optic pulses that fit directly on the new palm-sized 4.8-mb PC-diskettes InterLace was marketing as 'cartridges'? Viewable right there on your trusty PC's high-resolution monitor? … Self-selected programming, chargeable on any major card … What if, Veal's spokeswoman ruminated aloud, what if the viewer could become his/her *own* programming director; what if s/he could *define* the very entertainment-happiness it was his/her right to pursue? (1996: 416; emphasis in original)

The concept of viewer choice and selectivity, which has always haunted cinema and television, is a fundamental part of the logic of digital media, and its most visible sign of postmodern excess. If digital poetics is about anything it is about the confusion between symptom and critique: the most notorious digital-era writers, filmmakers and theorists stand at this crossroads. They are both symptoms of postmodernism's failures, and critics of it. In a 1993 interview, Wallace was asked about one of his contemporaries, Bret Easton Ellis, whose novel *American Psycho* had recently been published: 'We've all got this "literary" fiction that simply monotones that we're all becoming less and less human, that presents characters without souls or love, characters who really are exhaustively describable in terms of what brands of stuff they wear' (in McCaffery 1993: 131). Of course many readers and critics have accused Wallace himself of precisely this shallowness, and yet Wallace identifies an attention to surfaces that is a fundamental characteristic of a digital era when images are so easily transferable across multiple platforms.

Tmesis:
Skimming and Skipping
[Roland Barthes, Carol Clover, *Not Another Teen Movie*]

In *Cybertext*, Espen Aarseth refers to Roland Barthes' use of the term *tmesis*, noting that 'even the most classical narrative carries with it an invitation to discontinuous reading', or 'skipping' (1997: 47). Here is Barthes, from *The Pleasure of the Text*: 'Yet the most classical narrative (a novel by Zola or Balzac or Dickens or Tolstoy) bears within it a sort of diluted tmesis: we do not read everything with the same intensity of reading; a rhythm is established, casual, unconcerned with the *integrity* of the text; our very avidity for knowledge impels us to skim or skip certain passages' (1975: 10–11; emphasis in original). With the advent of videotape, and then DVDs, what was already implied in the relationship between the spectator and the film text was made explicit. If, during the classical era, viewers could not 'flip through' a film as they would a book, in the digital era flipping or skipping through a film often constitutes its central pleasure. In 1950, one commentator noted that 'television, like radio, is subject to that tyranny of time that … affects its ready and convenient use' (Siepmann 1950: 349). But in our exhausted, ironic stance towards narrative – a stance made possible by time-shifting – it stands to reason that time-shifting itself has become the operational logic of so many films, ranging from *Pulp Fiction* to *Eternal Sunshine of the Spotless Mind*. Because the act of deconstructing film is no longer something we 'apply' to film (if it ever was), but rather now something that is central to film's very being. The poster for *Not Another Teen Movie*, for instance, openly parodied and mocked what film theorists might call the film's *insidious reification of stereotypes or its complicity with hegemonic gestures of racial taxonomies*. The characters are featured on the poster, each one 'labelled' and decoded as 'the popular jock' or 'the desperate virgin' or 'the cruellest girl'.

In 1992, film scholar Carol Clover explored the 'final girl' character type in her book *Men, Women and Chain Saws*; in 2001 the poster for *Not Another Teen Movie* extended popularised film theory in ways that suddenly vindicated film theory and thus made it obsolete. Raised in a media environment where narratives figure their own

THE TOKEN BLACK GUY

THE POPULAR JOCK

THE PRETTY UGLY GIRL

THE COCKY BLONDE GUY

THE OBSESSED BEST FRIEND

Not Another Teen Movie: film poster as film theory

deconstruction as material for the narrative itself, film studies classes and textbooks that attempt to teach students to 'see through' movies are met with bewilderment by students, not because they don't understand what they are being asked to see but rather because they already see it. At one point in time, it was largely in the realm of 'art' that objects (paintings, experimental fiction, avant-garde cinema) referred openly and sometimes ironically to their status as 'constructed' things. 'The impulse behind Minimalism', Kenneth Baker has written, ' – the drive to clarify the terms in which art takes place in the world – motivated visual artists working independently in various countries in the 1960s' (1988: 10). And if a film does not deconstruct itself, we can't help but deconstruct it in the very act of interacting with it via the interfaces of home, personal or mobile viewing.

Undirected Films

[André Bazin, *The Blair Witch Project*, *Dancer in the Dark*, Abbas Kiarostami, *Timecode*]

Ironically, in the post-author age, the author is far from dead. In fact, there was no death of the author, except perhaps on the pages of academic journals and books. The problem with film theory was that it read Roland Barthes' proclamation with pure seriousness, with no humour or irony. Of course culture rolls on – with or without its critics – and so while the 'Death of the Author' was enshrined as Cultural Studies Truth #1, the author concept shifted, transformed and re-emerged as strong as ever. The death of the author was everywhere, a fact seemingly confirmed by the emergence of the Internet and hypertext, where distributed, networked, collaborative discourse seemed to validate the end of the hegemonic author.

But where Barthes' essay was outrageous, shocking and provocative – after all, it captured a particular countercultural moment – its enshrinement in academia (especially in the US) locked it down into a prison of administered seriousness. As Robert Ray has suggested eloquently in his 2001 book *How a Film Theory Got Lost*, film theory once it became part of the institution of academia, grew in to something stale and predictable, path dependent, a sad and tired parody of its original energy. Of course, most artists continued to produce as authors, even as they themselves theorised about the death of the author. Jim Sullivan, chief technology officer at Kodak Entertainment Imaging Services, has said that 'When you disconnect the image from a known medium like film and go into the digital world, you end up with integers in a computer that mean nothing' (in Kaufman 2003: 1):

> The hybrid film-digital workflow has also changed a familiar postproduction workflow. Even if they're acquired on film, images are now handled and manipulated by numerous digital devices that convert, compress and translate colour space, resolution and every other factor that makes up an image. In a perfect world, metadata will keep track of what happens to each image at each stage of the process. In turn, this makes

it possible to track changes, end up with a filmout or digital projection that looks the way the cinematographer meant it to look, and to archive the finished product with a permanent record of artistic intent. (Kaufman 2003: 1)

Digital cinema foregrounds a tendency that has been unfolding for some time in cinema: the distribution of the concept of the auteur across many fields. Or, to be more precise: today's cinematic auteurs are not the film directors, but interface inventors, creators and designers. The auteur theory, after all, was always the luxury of academics, as most filmgoers are attracted to the film itself, and its actors, rather than the name of the director. Famous contemporary directors – such as Quentin Tarantino, Spike Lee, Jim Jarmusch, Lars von Trier, David Lynch – prove the exception rather than the rule.

Indeed, the concept of the film director itself is a product of economic and cultural circumstances. As Tom Gunning suggests, in film, 'the director was an even more recent concept' (1991: 45). Gunning notes that recent scholarship on early cinema by Charles Musser and others reveals that the primary mode of production in the early years was that of collaboration: 'the concept of the director as a unifying force was not a factor' (1991: 46). Andrew Sarris's claim – in his essay 'Notes on the Auteur Theory in 1962' that 'the first premise of the auteur theory is the technical competence of a director as a criterion of value' and that a 'badly directed or an undirected film has no importance in a critical scale of values' (2000: 132) – was only true until the arrival of the camp sensibility ('so bad it's good!'). Auteurism confirmed what was essentially a theory of taste. As Michel Foucault and others have shown, the concept of the author, as we conceive her today, is a relatively recent phenomenon. 'There was a time', Foucault writes, 'when the texts that we today call "literary" (narratives, stories, epics, tragedies, comedies) were accepted, put into circulation, and valorised without any question about the identity of their author; their anonymity caused no difficulties' (1984: 109). Recent experiments with films where the director is either absent or diminished (*The Blair Witch Project, Ten, The Boss of it All*) are, in some strange way, echoes of film's very beginnings, when the role of the director was only emerging, and when there was so much experimentation with emerging forms of technology. Most of the videos on places like YouTube – and many of the most popular ones – are not even thought of by viewers as having been 'directed'. And yet at the same time, the very architecture of YouTube conspires to make us think in terms of the auteur, as links to other videos off to the side of the main video are organised around headings like 'Related' or 'More from this User'.

Undirected films – those films where the director is literally absent or where the concept of director control is challenged – are made possible by new technologies, such as smaller, sturdier DV and HD cameras and Global Positioning Systems. Eduardo Sánchez, co-director of *The Blair Witch Project*, has explained how the actors (who were also the camera operators) in the film were directed – minimally – from afar:

Once they got into the woods, they had a handset, a GPS handset that they used. Dan [Myrick] and I had actually spent three weeks prior to the shoot scouting out all the locations and programming all of those different locations in the woods. Basically, the directing notes – once they got into the woods – would say something like: 'Go to Point One, be there by three o'clock.' And then the character information would give them information as to what scene to play out on the way there or once they got there. We tried to give them as little information as possible. (In Anon. 1999a: 3)

In the case of *The Blair Witch Project*, the uncontrolled design of the film is matched by the uncontrolled method of directing. By removing themselves from the actual scene of the film – Daniel Myrick has said that 'We directed them [the actors] as best we could by remote control' (in Anon. 1999a: 2) – the directors ceded control to the actors, suggesting a vision of the director as someone who leaves choices about camera angles, camera movement, dialogue, and so on, in the hands of those who traditionally had very little control over these elements: the actors. This turns film theory on its head. Traditional, serious discussions about the intricacies of *mise-en-scène* or lighting, for instance, are less important when amateurs are calling the shots. A new aesthetics – which foregrounds chance, randomness, even amateurism – displaces the careful professionalism of the experts.

Of course this has been a distinctive part of cinema from its earliest years; directors from Dziga Vertov to Agnès Varda to John Cassavetes have experimented with ceding some element of control and allowing the chaos of everyday reality to seep into their films. And the pages of the journal *Film Culture* – especially during the 1950s and 1960s – were regularly devoted to manifestos that called for the same spontaneity outlined in the Dogme 95 manifesto. In his 1961 essay 'For an Uncontrolled Cinema', Richard Leacock wrote that 'ever since the invention of the "talking picture", it has been blithely assumed that films are an extension of the theatre in that you cause a story to be acted out before an audience (the camera) under controlled conditions. Control is of the essence' (2000: 77). He went on to write that many

of us have, like Renoir, become 'immensely bored by a great number of contemporary films'. If we go back to the earliest days of cinema we find a recurrent notion that has never really been realised, a desire to utilise that aspect of film that is uniquely different from theatre: to record aspects of what did actually happen in a real situation … Here, it would be possible for the significance of what is taking place to transcend the conceptions of the filmmaker, because, essentially, he is observing that ultimate mystery, the reality. (2000: 78)

In an era when cameras and surveillance in public spaces is ever more possible and frequent, the concept of 'the director' – as someone who imposes an overarching vision and meaning onto images – becomes less important than the fact of recording.

This sensibility is made explicit in the Dogme 95 'Vow of Chastity' manifesto, written by Lars von Trier and Thomas Vinterberg. Rule #10 reads: 'The director must not be credited'. Ironically, this repudiation of 'personal' filmmaking – one line from the 'Vow of Chastity' reads 'I swear as a director to refrain from personal taste' – has led to the rise of von Trier, and to a lesser extent Vinterberg, as a formidable, well-known auteur, whose films are greeted with strong emotions, ranging from puzzlement to disdain to effusive praise. But again, such manifestos and simple experiments with the absent director cannot be separated from the new digital technologies that give rise to new narrative forms. One director in particular, Abbas Kiarostami, has spoken of how digital cameras have made possible new approaches to filmmaking. His film *Ten* was shot with digital cameras attached to the inside of a moving car. With simple cutting back and forth between the occupants of the driver and passenger seats of the car, Kiarostami – who was nearly entirely absent as a director – has managed to make something of almost haunting beauty. As one commentator noted, Kiarostami 'goes one step ahead by declaring the absence of "the director" himself. There is no one looking through the camera and correcting the actors or prompting them' (Haridas 2002: 2).

In the documentary that accompanies the film on DVD – '10 on Ten' – Kiarostami addresses many of the practical and theoretical possibilities of digital filmmaking. Speaking of *Ten*, he says that 'I would like to point out that it was impossible to make a film like this without using the digital camera'. Later, he explains how small, hand-held, DV cameras changed his approach to filmmaking, especially the making of his film *ABC Africa*. I quote Kiarostami at length because what he says directly addresses the relationship of this new technology and the concept of the director, which he defends:

> I felt that a 35mm camera would limit both us [the film crew shooting *ABC Africa*] and the people there, whereas the video camera displayed truth from every angle, and not a forged truth. To me, this camera was a discovery. Like a god, it was all-encompassing, omnipresent. The camera could turn 360 degrees, and thus reported the truth. An absolute truth. Directing was spontaneously and unconsciously eliminated, by which I mean artificial and conventional directing. Though eliminating the director doesn't eliminate the auteur, of course. This camera gives both the director and viewer the possibility of discovery. In this way, the camera eliminates the artifice so implanted within the industry. It gives you the possibility of expanding the dimensions of cinema, and getting rid of the clichés, traditions, imposed forms and pretentious aesthetics … This camera frees cinema from the clutches of the tools of production, capital and censorship. (2002)

In *Ten*, the stationary camera does not allow for escape. In the first segment, 'Mother & Son', the camera is fixed on the son for nearly the entire segment, until the very end, when we see a few minutes of the mother as she parks the car. The segment – which lasts approximately 19 minutes – is recorded in one long take, punctuated by several fairly unobtrusive jump cuts that remind us – despite being drawn into the fierce emotionalism of the mother/son argument – that there is a camera, and that what we are watching has been edited, however minimally. One source of power in the sequence derives from the contrast between the fixed camera and the arguing and screaming that periodically erupts between mother and son over the subject of the mother's recent divorce. When the son expresses anger that his mother falsely accused his father of being a drug-user at the divorce trial, she responds: 'It was a good way of getting a divorce. The rotten laws in this society of ours give no rights to women! To get a divorce, a woman has to say that she is beaten or that her husband's on drugs.' This – the emotional high-point of the argument – is captured flatly and without comment by the camera. There is no wild camera movement to suggest heightened emotionalism, as in *The Celebration* or *The Blair Witch Project*. There is no swelling music. No radical editing.

The foregrounding of the camera as narrator is also strong in *Timecode*, which has become a canonical film in the newly emerging pantheon of digital cinema. Famously shot with no cuts, in real time, with four different cameras, the film is divided from beginning to end into four equal quadrants on the screen – one for each camera – each one following a character. Viewers are free to act as their own editors, at least in a limited way, by deciding what quadrants to watch, although we are encouraged to watch specific quadrants as the sound is more dominant in one quadrant over the others. (On the DVD version, however, users can control which quadrant they would like to listen to.) One of the first overlaps comes when Julian Sands arrives, in the lower two quadrants, to deliver massages to the film crew working in the next room. At this moment, we see him from two different perspectives, each one offering a slightly different version of the same reality unfolding at the same time.

In this regard, André Bazin stands as the godfather of digital cinema, as his appeal

Timecode: the viewer as editor

to realism via specific techniques – such as the long take – are more fully realised in digital cinema. Bazin's well-known defence of depth-of-field shots and long takes suggests a sort of democracy of viewing for the spectator, an openness to the accidents of reality that is echoed by many of today's digital filmmakers. Bazin writes that 'while analytical montage only calls for him [the spectator] to follow his guide, to let his attention follow along with that of the director who will choose what he should see, here he is called upon to exercise at least a minimum of personal choice' (2005a: 36).

Of course, to publicise a film as non-directed draws attention to the very concept of the director. One of the fundamental contributions of Lars von Trier lies not so much in his films themselves, but in the way that his films have changed the way we think about films. *Dancer in the Dark* – with its famous 100 cameras – serves as a reminder that cinema is really about the imposition of choice upon variables; those choices constitute narrative. If a film like *Dancer in the Dark* is radical it is because it reminds us what was possible in cinema all along. Stig Björkman, who was present during shooting on the set, noted that 'thanks to the 100 cameras shooting the equivalent of twenty full-length features not many retakes are needed' (1999: 10). If the medium was always the message, then non-directed films remind us again that what we are watching when we are watching a film is really the history of the film's making. It used to be that 'good' films made it possible for us to forget this, and to lose ourselves in plot, story and atmosphere. But in the digital era, all our technologies conspire to dispel the illusion of cinema.

In the director's commentary for *Timecode*, Mike Figgis discusses the humanising aspect of digital filmmaking, specifically in relation to the art of acting, as it allows cast and crew to look at what has been recorded quickly and to fine-tune performances. The same was true of Steven Soderbergh's film *Bubble*, shot with Sony HD cameras on location in Ohio with a cast made up entirely of non-professional actors whose only auditions for the film were interviews about their lives. The film – which was shot in approximately 18 days with an entire crew of no more than twenty – was edited as it was filmed, day-by-day. Soderbergh has said that 'we could all sit down … we would watch the movie a lot, because I would cut every night. We would just transfer the HD right into my computer and cut … On the last day of shooting, we watched the whole film' (2005). And because practically every scene was shot with available light, and because each actor was individually wired for sound, there was very little obvious technological interference for the non-professional actors to manage, providing, according to Soderbergh, more naturalistic performances. And if there is not a warmth to the performances, there is a warmth and a glow to the look and feel of the film itself. *Bubble* is also significant in that it is one of the first digital/HD features (Michael Winterbottom's *In This World* is another) that looks markedly different – and more 'film like' – than earlier digital features from the Dogme 95 movement that had a pixillated, rough, hand-held aesthetic. Ironically, *Bubble* looks so 'good' that it almost appears to have been shot on 35mm film, although Soderbergh suggests that he was not trying to replicate the look of film: 'It [HD] has its own aesthetic. It's not video. It's not film. It's something else' (2005).

Again, a paradox: the 'cold' binary logic of digital systems allows for an ever-greater expression of humanism. For many critics, digital is synonymous with a sort of anti-humanism. In his foreword to the 2004 edition of Bazin's *What is Cinema?*, Dudley Andrew writes that 'today the digital has lodged itself in the heart of postmodern image culture. Inhuman, cold in their perfect technical reproducibility, digital images not only can ignore the artist, they can ignore all reality beyond the monitor' (2005: xvi–xvii). Yet this is a limiting view that doesn't account for the unpredictability and chance involved in both the production and reception of creative works. In an interview (with Jason Silverman) on the eve of his 85th birthday, Jonas Mekas noted that once 'you change the technology – from a film camera to a video camera, or from an 8mm camera to 16mm – you change completely the content' (2006: 3).

Marshall McLuhan and others recognised some time ago that technology is its own message, and to suggest that digital images 'ignore all reality beyond the monitor' is to forget that the monitor itself – whether a screen in a theatre, a television screen, a computer screen, a cell phone or an mp3 player – creates a new reality of viewing for the spectator. Alain Robbe-Grillet once wrote that the 'style of the novel does not seek to inform, as does the chronicle, the testimony offered in evidence, or the scientific report, it *constitutes* reality' (1965: 160; emphasis in original). While it is true, as Daniel Frampton has written, that what 'is significant about film is that it shows us a whole new reality' (2006: 155), that reality can never be separated from its medium. That is, we are always *seeing* film on something, on some screen, large or small. At those transcendent moments when we feel as if we are actually entering into the world of the film, we are doing so through a specific medium that makes our experience of the film possible in the first place, regardless of whether or not the film transports us to another world. As Frampton and others have noted, film theory has too often ignored the sheer emotional pleasures of film watching (2006: 154), but isn't there good reason for ignoring these pleasures, assuming that viewers can experience them without the aid of film criticism or theory? And yet the immersion of the audience in the interface between themselves and the screen is, at last, a humanist gesture. Birk Weiberg has asked, 'what can be done to overcome linear narration and deconstruct the author's authority without forcing the user to assume the responsibility and not always pleasant duty of co-authorship'? (2002: 7).

The latest blows against the auteur theory of the director cross barriers between academic, avant-garde and commercial cinema. Lev Manovich's and Andreas Kratky's *Soft Cinema: Navigating the Database* – a small book and DVD that captures samples from their video installations – consists of films that rely on machines, rather than human beings, to shape and edit the three films. Like Dogme 95's 'Vow of Chastity' Manovich specifies four directions (rules?) that governed the making of these films, including:

> 2. Using a set of rules defined by the authors, the Soft Cinema software controls both the layout of the screen (number and position of frames) and the sequences of media elements that appear in these frames.

3. The media elements (video clips, sound, still images, text, etc.) are selected from a large database to construct a potentially unlimited number of different films. (Manovich & Kratky 2005: 2)

Directors like von Trier have experimented along similar lines, not only with the '100 cameras' technique of *Dancer in the Dark*, but also with *The Boss of It All*, made in five weeks, and without a camera operator. Instead, von Trier relied on a process that he called 'Automavision' which, he says, allowed the camera to tilt, pan or zoom, and which was 'developed with the intention of limiting human influence … For a long time, my films have been hand-held. That has to do with the fact that I am a control freak. With Automavision, the technique was that I would frame the picture first and then push a button on the computer. I was not in control – the computer was in control' (in Macnab 2006: 3).

Indeed, is it even possible to speak of a film's director today when film itself is part of an enormous, global network of business and distribution modes? Films exist as films, but also as trailers, clips, video games, flash animations, novelisations, mash-ups and DVD chapters available to be 'played' in multiple sequences. The film's director is becoming an afterthought, someone who creates 'content' that is made available in different mediums and across multiple platforms. I told someone the other day that I had watched *Timecode*. 'Which version?' she said. In this case, the digital cameras allowed for the movie to be filmed in one single take lasting a little over ninety minutes, something not possible with film-based cinema, where camera magazines typically hold no more than twenty minutes of film stock, thereby necessitating at least one cut every twenty minutes. This allowed Figgis to shoot 15 complete versions of *Timecode*. Sometimes one version was filmed per day, sometimes two. According to Figgis:

> We were able to watch the entire film that afternoon … So it was the first time in history, I would say with confidence, that the cast and crew have watched the finished product on the first day that they shot it … which means that for the first time ever, actors are aware of how they relate within the film, what their context is, and what the overall emotional tone of the film is. (2000)

Indeed, what often gets lost in scholarship on digital cinema are discussions of human performance. Bruno Lessard is right to remind us that 'in the evaluation of the "digital" revolution, performance has to be considered in its digitally remediated forms' (2005: 112). In this regard, the loss of the director is more than compensated for by the re-emergence of the actor. Small, relatively lightweight digital cameras – by stripping from the process of filming the elaborate spectacle of large, heavy, cumbersome cameras – have made possible a different style of acting, one which allows for longer stretches of performance captured by a smaller camera that does not need to 'cut' every twenty minutes.

Viewer Participation
[Chris Ware]

Today, audiences expect participation in the narrative unfolding of cinema, even if this simply means activating the film, or rearranging its order. If in 1945 viewers arrived at a theatre and waited for the projectionist to start the film, today audiences want to press 'start' themselves. Many people who read novels do not know how to write them; many who enjoy listening to music have never performed it. But many people who watch movies do know something about how to make them; they have held a DV camera; they have made short films. This very simple act of participation – enabled by digital technologies – is a form of deconstruction. 'What you do with comics', Chris Ware, a graphic novelist, has said, 'is take pieces of experience and freeze them in time' (in Raeburn 2004: 25). The ability not only to freeze, but to manipulate the data that underlies movies today is a form of what we might term progressive nostalgia. That is, as radical as it seems, our manipulation of movies today is akin to our age-old manipulation of books. After all, the book is a technology that allows users to stop, start, skip forwards and backwards, and pause. The ability to 'select' multiple options from DVD and computer interfaces is a practical form of nostalgia, disguised by 'futuristic' technology.

There is a special kind of loss at play here, and it is for good reason that critics are reluctant to talk or to write about it, fearing they may be accused of wallowing in nostalgia. This loss – the loss of mystery or aura surrounding a film – is in fact something that was so vigorously hoped for by the Marxist, cultural studies, feminist and other critics of the 1960s and 1970s. But what was the price to pay for demystification, for rendering the 'invisible' system visible and exposing ideologies? Irony, perhaps. Audiences today have indeed learned to 'see through' movies, and only the most deterministic, dogmatic theorist would claim that interactive technologies that allow viewers some degree of deconstructive control over films have merely replaced one form of mystification with another.

In some ways, the ability to manipulate the temporal order of a film remediates the traditional ability to *select* what portions of the screen to watch in classical cinema. Orson Welles once suggested that he preferred long takes and deep focus because it was inherently democratic: it allowed the viewer to exert some measure of will and choice over which faces, objects and actions to observe on the screen. As screens for watching movies and video have shrunk and become more mobile (computers, cell phones, iPods) the traditional aesthetics of *mise-en-scène* are transforming to meet the new conditions of the screen. In fact, one could say that the act of manipulating the temporal order of a film is akin to manipulating the classical screen with our eyes. In the past, we 'selected' which portion of the screen to focus on, our eyes darting continually from quadrant to quadrant. Today, we select which *units* of the film to watch (DVD chapters, scenes, clips, screen grabs), our eyes darting not so much across the screen as between chapters, fragments. Reproducible across various formats, cinema now is everywhere, in bits and pieces, available to be reappropriated and reassembled, free from the darkened theatre of the classical period. The participation of the viewer now fully extends into the realm of editing, broadly defined, as users watch films in bits and pieces, skipping over parts, lingering on others, in the same way that they might read a book. We could say that the primary gesture of the film spectator in the digital era is to impose herself onto the film, redirecting its flow and in time, perhaps, re-editing its content.

Virtual Humanism: Part 1
[André Breton, CGI, third meanings]

And there are other memorable bits and pieces, visual highlights of a movie with no particular interest in coherence, economy or feeling.
– A. O. Scott, *New York Times* review of *Pirates of the Caribbean: Dead Man's Chest* (2006)

A society, as it becomes less and less able, in the course of its development, to justify the inevitability of its particular forms, breaks up the accepted notions upon which artists and writers must depend in large part for communication with their audiences. It becomes difficult to assume anything. All the verities involved by religion, authority, tradition, style, are thrown into question, and the writer or artist is no longer able to estimate the response of his audience to the symbols and references with which he works.
– Clement Greenberg, from 'Avant-Garde and Kitsch' (1939)

The above quote by A. O. Scott – from his review of *Pirates of the Caribbean* – hints at a truth that Scott probably did not intend. He is right that a CGI-dominated movie like this is made up of 'bits and pieces' and 'visual highlights' that taken as a whole lack 'coherence'. The film is a pastiche of crazy, reality-bending set pieces and impossible images that teeter on the fantastic. In speaking about making the sea-chase movie *Master and Commander: The Far Side of the World*, special effects supervisor Nathan McGuinness has said that the 'biggest challenge was that there was never really a ship at sea' (in Feeny 2004: 2). Now, we have become so accustomed – so numb – to the radically incoherent images made possible by CGI that we have forgotten (or never learned) to see them for the avant-garde art that they are. Stop almost any run-of-the-mill CGI genre film – ranging from *Twister* to *The Day After Tomorrow* to *Spider-Man 3* – and you will see frozen before your eyes the most astounding and startlingly composed images, images that were they printed on oversized canvases, framed and hung in an art gallery would constitute surrealist art of the highest order.

Here is a paradox of our digital era: today's most radical and experimental moving images occur not on the avant-garde edges of society, but rather in the Heart of the Beast: Hollywood. It is in Hollywood movies – and in CGI blockbusters especially – where the most bizarre, transgressive and experimental images and sequences lie, a radically refashioned understanding of the real. But before we go forward, we must go back, for context is everything. Because these CGI movies actually hearken back to early cinema, when the rules for what movies should *be* were not yet established or formalised. This early (what used to be called 'primitive') cinema, is what film historian Tom Gunning has called the 'cinema of attractions' (1990: 56). It is too easy to forget that in the early days, no one knew what movies should do, or what they would be for. The notion (taken for granted today) that movies should be narratives – that they should essentially tell stories with basic coherence and clarity, with beginnings, middles and ends – was a concept that did not catch hold for many years.

The very first projected film – by the Lumière brothers in France in 1895 – *Workers Leaving the Lumière Factory*, is just that: 45 seconds of silent footage showing workers leaving the factory. No cuts. No edits. The film is more documentary than narrative. According to Gunning, it was not until about 1908 – when modern cinema as we know it had been around for over ten years – that *telling stories* became the main, the dominant, the expected thing that movies did. Up until then, movies were often more interested in 'the display of curiosities' or 'attractions' in part because the shock of simple movement on the screen – any kind of movement – was still such a novelty (see Gunning 1991: 37–42). Some titles of the Lumière films from the 1895–97 period are: *Baby's Dinner*, *Demolition of a Wall*, *Snowball Fight* and *Lion, London Zoological Garden*. Films from the US were also, largely, less interested in telling formulaic stories than in simply showing things. Here are three titles of US films from the 1890s and early 1900s: *Sky Scrapers of New York City from North River*, *President McKinley at Home* and *The Dog and his Various Merits*.

Why is it important to remember this? Because these early movies were not about telling ordered, logical stories that moved with relentless determination from point A to point B as much as they were about the thrill of sheer movement upon the screen. The medium was new. There were no established rules yet about how a movie should look, or how it should tell its story or even if it *should* tell a story. In this sense, the use of computer-generated imagery to create set pieces *with no particular interest in coherence* hearkens back to the pioneers of early cinema. These early movies were made up of *visual highlights* and more often than not displayed little interest in the *economy* of storytelling. Movies were about the absurd beauty of moving things. Which is to say: they were about themselves. Of course movies – in Hollywood especially with the rise of the studio system – soon adopted what has been called an assembly-line mode of production where aesthetic risk was minimised and each facet of creation was tightly controlled. And yet forms of radical incoherence persisted, finding expression in avant-garde and surrealist movements, which juxtaposed shocking and unexpected images with the banality of everyday realism, especially in films from the

1920s and 1930s by the likes of René Clair, Hans Richter, Man Ray, Luis Buñuel and Maya Deren, whose short films *Meshes of the Afternoon* and *At Land* are as menacingly alluring as anything today by David Lynch. Please do not let the age of these films deceive you: they are almost unimaginably beautiful, stunning and surprising, and if we want to peel beneath the surface to see the wild transgression of CGI in movies today, we need to look to its sources. But aren't avant-garde traditions and mainstream ones entirely different? Weren't avant-garde films made in opposition to mainstream fare?

Perhaps it is a mistake to think that avant-garde or experimental movements resist the mainstream. We take comfort in the knowledge that such movements resist 'the Man', but do they? In his elegantly written book *How A Film Theory Got Lost and Other Mysteries in Cultural Studies*, Robert Ray reminds us that 'to assume that increasingly rapid co-option will destroy the avant-garde ignores how much the avant-garde has, throughout its history, promoted its own acceptance' (2001: 75). His examples – cubism, abstract expressionism, pop art, the French new wave, punk rock, rap – show how these movements were not simply co-opted by the mainstream. Each, in its own way, actively sought out publicity and even acceptance. This happened through interviews, touring, promotion, notorious antics and the very process of making work and putting it before the public. The avant-garde's long, periodic journeys from the edges to the mainstream are in keeping with the way marginal movements operate, and shows how they in fact *depend* upon the mainstream for their very identity.

But what does it mean to call certain CGI sequences in certain movies surreal? At its heart, surrealism hates realism, even as it needs it as something to define itself against. Here is what André Breton said of realism in his 'Manifesto of Surrealism', published in 1924:

> The realistic attitude, inspired by positivism, from Saint Thomas Aquinas to Anatole France, clearly seems to me to be hostile to any intellectual or moral advancement. I loathe it, for it is made up of mediocrity, hate, and dull conceit. It is this attitude which today gives birth to these ridiculous books, these insulting plays. It constantly feeds on and derives strength from the newspapers and stultifies both science and art by assiduously flattering the lowest of tastes; clarity bordering on stupidity, a dog's life. (1972: 6)

Fyodor Dostoyevsky takes an especially good drubbing; Breton has no patience for his 'school-boy description' and doesn't understand why anyone would want to read about the 'empty moments' of anybody's life. 'Others' laziness or fatigue does not interest me', he writes (1972: 8). Breton's attacks on realism are both serious and seriously funny. His essay thrashes around in your mind. It's like trying to hold on with your bare hands to an enormous, angry fish just caught from a lake of oil. According to Breton, surrealism – by contrast – is alive to the absurd mysteries of life. For surrealism, he turns to dreams as a model, and considers 'waking life' to be a 'phenomenon of interference' that interrupts the 'dark night' of dreams:

I believe in the future resolution of these two states, dream and reality, which are seemingly so contradictory, into a kind of absolute reality, a *surreality*, if one may so speak … At this juncture, my intention [is] merely to mark a point by noting the *hate of the marvellous* which rages in certain men, this absurdity beneath which they try to bury it. Let us not mince words: the marvellous is always beautiful, anything marvellous is beautiful, in fact only the marvellous is beautiful. (1972: 14; emphasis in original)

It is significant that the one American Breton selects for his pantheon of surrealists is Edgar Allan Poe – 'Poe is surrealist in adventure' (1972: 27) he writes. Poe, who worked very clearly within emerging nineteenth-century genre conventions (adventure stories, tales of horror, the gothic mode) even as he subverted them. Poe, whose work – like the CGI blockbusters of today – could be read as fun and sheer Entertainment, yes, but also as Serious Art.

The most visually radical films of our era are not from the avant-garde, but from CGI blockbusters, where special effects tear asunder reality in ways that approach surrealism. In other words, often the most visually disjunctive and radical sequences in films today appear as often in CGI blockbusters as they do in the self-proclaimed avant-garde. Their 'art' is masked by the fact that we have no language to talk about them as art, buried in action sequences that we fail to see as aesthetic because we have no real tradition for appreciating blockbuster films as art. In this sense, the avant-garde dimension of mainstream Hollywood fare such as *Twister* and the *X-Men* and *Spider-Man* films is difficult to see; it represents a Path Not Taken. Clement Greenberg, in his 1939 essay, noted that the 'true and most important function of the avant-garde was not to "experiment" but to find a path along which it would be possible to keep culture moving in the midst of ideological confusion and violence' (2006: 3). Today, when the avant-garde has become an accredited and verifiable subject area in our universities, colleges and museums and an object of common, democratic knowledge on Wikipedia and YouTube, it is the task of writers to remind us that the avant-garde often emerges where we least expect it (for instance, in blockbuster multiplex movies) and not in the ironic, self-conscious realm of the world of self-proclaimed art.

But how are we to see and appreciate the avant-gardism of CGI in blockbuster films when it all happens so fast, when the speed and rush of images overwhelms us? The answer lies in slowing down – in actually stopping – the rush of images so that we can appreciate their acrobatic, surreal strangeness, and so that we can critique them. In Jonathan Lethem's short story 'Access Fantasy', the narrator thinks he sees, on a videotape, a murder in an apartment. There are shadows of what appear to be a woman being strangled. He wishes to slow down the tape, to investigate the scene in detail: 'If only he could watch it frame by frame – slow motion was disastrously fast now' (2005: 26). Therein lies a clue for how to harness the technologies of the digital era to foster a new form of theory, one that counteracts the speed of our age by slowing down images and temporarily removing them from the data stream.

The key to how to do this lies in an essay first published in 1970 – 'The Third Meaning: Research notes on some Eisenstein stills' – by Roland Barthes, who understood that in order to seize upon the radical, ambiguous beauty of film images, we need to learn to look at films in a radical, ambiguous way, one that frees us from the tyranny of interpretation imposed by critics and teachers. Barthes asked a simple but powerful question: what would we find if we treated individual frames from a film as still images? Would these images mean the same thing if we took them out of the speeding film and looked at them as if they were photographs? In part, this was motivated by Barthes' defiant streak: he wanted to disrupt the tyranny of images, to slow film down to its true and material level. What would happen if we looked at the source material of motion pictures, which is not motion, but stillness? What he found when he looked at stills from a film by Soviet director Sergei Eisenstein was not only a first meaning (an 'informational level' that tells us about the explicit message of the film), a second meaning (a 'symbolic level', the codes and signs that we pick up on when watching a film – how smoking cigarettes in a film sometimes suggests that lovemaking has just occurred), but also a *third meaning*, which refused to lay still for interpretation.

This third meaning – 'erratic, obstinate' – outstripped the intentions of the filmmaker, the will of the audience and the very world of the film from which it was taken. It was almost a form of anarchy. 'The filmic is that in the film which cannot be described', Barthes wrote (1977a: 64). And also: 'The still throws off the constraint of filmic time' (1977a: 67). In a sense, a film's stills – in revealing a third meaning – show us a secret history running parallel to the world that the film wants us to see. Of course, when Barthes published his essay on 'the third meaning' in 1970, it was very difficult – if not impossible – for the everyday film spectator to actually capture and contemplate a still image from a film. Apart from still reproductions in movie reviews or books about film, there was simply no way for viewers to seize upon the individual frames from a film. But this is not the case today. Despite the fact that DVDs – with all their behind-the-scenes, making-of bonus materials – have helped to demystify cinema, they also allow us unprecedented access to the hidden beauty of film. That is to say, our ability to pause films, to freeze them, to halt their motion, to ponder their *third meanings* and to look upon their pristine images is something that was practically impossible for the everyday moviegoer in the pre-digital era. The 'step-frame' button on your laptop DVD player, or on your remote control, freezes the images and captures them on your screen, so that you can in theory watch the film unfold before your eyes frame-by-frame, as a series of still images that are akin to photographs. This astounding yet everyday capability means that we can literally see movies today differently than we did before. Films are there for us in their frozen beauty, if we choose to look at them this way.

This suggests a revised paradigm for studying film images, one that relies not on the representative selection of film stills to illustrate a theoretical point, but rather on the sequential display of frames. The step-frame function on DVD player interfaces approximates – but does not exactly replicate – the 24 frames per second movement of film through a projector. 'Essentially', David Bordwell has noted, 'MPEG-2 technology encodes the film frame by frame … The result is that during freeze-frame viewing, a

DVD can yield the original film frames' (2007). Yet, as Bordwell and others have suggested, it is not so simple, as the frames on the DVD do not always match up to the film source. In some cases, what you see on a frame-by-frame movement through a DVD might correspond precisely to the frame count of the original film, while in other instances there might be missing, blended or repeated frames. This raises a few interesting questions, not the least of which is: does it matter? That may sound like a flippant question, but it is deadly serious. For certainly it matters if one considers the film (i.e., a 35mm print) to be the original, and the DVD version to be a reproduction. In that case, the DVD version is judged against the film version to be either a faithful, accurate reproduction, or else not. However, in an era when there are multiple versions and cuts of films (director's cut, extended cut, unrated cut, foreign market cut), with multiple restorations, with added or subtracted footage, with alternate endings, how can one legitimately claim that one film version is the 'original' against which all others are judged?

Perhaps what matters in a frame-by-frame analysis is not the correspondence of the analogue film frames (16mm or 35mm, and so forth) to the digital version, but rather the act itself of slowing down the film.

Virtual Humanism: Part 2
[Image Metrics, instantaneous celebrity, George W. S. Trow]

We do not recognise the avant-garde qualities of blockbuster films today because we get caught up in the stories they tell, no matter how worn-out and familiar they may be to us. We are distracted by plot. By the stars. By the music. And so moments of glorious, surreal mayhem come and go, often so fast that their physics-bending glory gets forgotten: the magic realism of the floating cows in *Twister*; the tidal wave hitting Manhattan in *The Day After Tomorrow*; Dr Otto Octavius/Doc Ock climbing up the side of a building grasping an old lady with a cane in one of his tentacles in *Spider-Man 2*; Magneto as he floats the Golden Gate Bridge across the water to Alcatraz Island in *X-Men: The Last Stand*; Dustin Hoffman's and Jason Schwartzman's faces breaking off into cubist pieces and floating around the screen in *I Heart Huckabees*; the entire black-and-white, avant-garde film within the film in *The Ring*. Consider the surrealism of the still from *The Day After Tomorrow*, absurd, logic-defying and – because of its embeddedness in a film that was critically panned – definitely not 'art'. But frozen and lifted out of the film, one could imagine walking up to this image in a museum and marvelling at its strange composition, its tightly controlled chaos: the man with the hat who could, in another context, be hailing a cab.

The pause function, and beyond that the ability of everyday users to capture movie stills and to print them or post them to the web, means that it is possible now to experience a film's images divorced from their location in the film's primary narrative.

In *The Harvard Black Rock Forest*, George W. S. Trow wrote: 'What joins the scientist and the entertainer is this: they create the modern world but do not live in it, while other people live in it without knowing much about how it has been made' (2004: 8). The trouble today is that we know entirely too much about how things are made. With the relentlessness of a scorched earth campaign, the postmodernists since the 1960s have deconstructed and exposed the secret workings of everything from novels to poems to television shows to movies. Nothing is off limits. Everything is game,

The Day After Tomorrow: the freeze-frame makes possible the appreciation of surrealist art disguised as mainstream cinema

and is a Game. Whereas once this cultural demystification was the province of cranky critics and professors – who at their best imbued it with a sort of radical chic and sly humour – today our art and our entertainment deconstruct themselves. As for movies, the bonus and supplementary material on DVDs only make it clearer that any given movie is not inevitable and mysterious, but is the product of planners and financers and writers and specialists and visionaries and sundry teams of people. In a strange way, DVDs are a form of practical Marxist theory: they show that ideas are made out of material things and the labour of human beings. No wonder so much art and entertainment today is self-reflexive: all of our digital technologies conspire to pull back the curtain, to reveal the making of everything. There are exceptions, of course. One thinks of the films of Alejandro Adams – especially *Canary* – that suggest a new wave of non-ironic, humanistic filmmaking in the digital era.

And so. Surely you have felt, even in the most terrible CGI movie, that there is something radical and beautiful lurking there in the images, beneath the surface, some image worth dwelling on, some moment of beauty undermined by the mundane dialogue, something flapping by, like silly pages and you want to say: wait, go back, show me that again. Yes, the movie itself comes up a little short on the 'please respect my intelligence' scale, but the sequence itself is beautiful, artistic, visually stunning. Despite the fact that the film is little more than *visual highlights* with *no particular interest in coherence* you find yourself wondering what would happen if you no longer judged the film by the usual, tired standards of the usual, tired critics, but rather by a new standard, one that took into account the crazy, incoherent tradition of innovation and experimentation that characterised early cinema. You find that there is an idea expressed in the CGI action sequence, the idea of a radical conflict between these avant-garde images in their commercial context. Spider-Man: a man in a bizarre tight suit flinging himself between skyscrapers on a sunny day above the mundane triviality of everyday life on the streets below – you know you are supposed to watch this as if it is just another Hollywood blockbuster, as nothing more than *visual highlights*, but part of you sees it as a form of cinematic art and innovation of the highest order.

Consider the tidal wave sequence in *The Day After Tomorrow*, for instance. Global Warming causes an enormous wave to crash into Manhattan. We actually see this happening. Death. Punishment. Followed by freezing. And more death. Surreal sequences involving wolves upon a ship frozen into the flooded passages between skyscrapers. Or the sequence in *X-Men: The Last Stand* when the boy suddenly sprouts huge white angel wings that carry him away to safety after his father tries to give him an antidote to cure his mutantism. If you freeze a single frame from that scene, you will find a surreal visual elegance and a screen composition that scrambles realism: the boy standing in the sterile lab, fists clenched, his wings outstretched in beautiful defiance. On the left side of the screen stands his father in a dull grey suit, his back to us. On the right a terrified nurse. The camera shoots from the ground up; even though he is in the background, the boy dominates the frame. The dull realism of the scene is shattered by the flagrantly realism-defying wings, and suddenly and momentarily we are in a film more visually radical than anything from Matthew Barney's *Cremaster* cycle or any other of today's so-called avant-garde filmmakers.

In fact, because new and marginal ideas are today absorbed so quickly into the mainstream, it is difficult to even imagine such a thing as the avant-garde. Back in 1955, the critic Lionel Trilling could openly and sincerely lament the difficulty men and women faced in preserving their identities in a society dominated by media and advertising: 'In a society like ours, which, despite some appearances to the contrary, tends to be seductive rather than coercive, the individual's old defences against the domination of the culture become weaker and weaker' (1965a: 98). The notion of life *outside* of culture or society seems quaint to us today, and perhaps nostalgic. Likewise for the avant-garde: how can an avant-garde exist when in popular culture the most extreme forms of artistic defiance result in almost instantaneous celebrity, and when today's art is so often steeped in familiar forms of camp and irony?

The CGI avant-gardists responsible for some of the most radical images, sequences and films today are probably not familiar to you by name. Unlike the stars of the auteur theory, popularised by the film critic Andrew Sarris in 1962, today's auteur experimentalists are not film directors. Instead, those most responsible for the relentless absurdity of images on the screen work for companies with names like Lola Visual Effects, Persistence of Vision, Double Negative, Asylum Visual Effects, and Animal Logic. And while it is the demands of conventional genre films – action, science fiction, fantasy, natural disaster – that give rise to these sequences, the sequences themselves frequently transcend these limits and enter the realm of Art. In all likelihood these names are not familiar: Zareh Nalbandian, Managing Director and co-founder of Animal Logic, or Chris Godfrey, Director of Visual Effects, or Andy Brown or Kirsty Millar, who were the Visual Effects Supervisors for *House of Flying Daggers*. Here – from the Animal Logic website – is a brief description of their work on *The Matrix Reloaded*: 'For *Reloaded* the team completed ten sequences, which included building entire 3D characters The Twins, who are able to fully interact with the live action stars when in their CG phasing states' (Anon. 1999b: 3). What is astounding is not that sentence, but rather that we no longer find sentences like that astounding. The invisible hand of the CGI avant-gardists is everywhere. Persistence of Vision – which has worked on *Star Wars Episode II: Attack of the Clones, Titan A. E.* and others – describes their work this way:

> P. O. V. works with the direction to conceive shots, solve storytelling problems, edit the sequence, and even add music, dialogue and sound effects. When complete, the animatic will communicate the composition, style, and elements of every frame in the sequence. It removes guesswork, aids in communication and budgeting, and, we've found, increases the morale of the crew before and during shooting. (Anon. 2008a)

But isn't 'guesswork' fundamental to the messy nature of the creative process? Lola Visual Effects: Digital Cosmetic Enhancements, a visual effects company based out of Santa Monica, California, specialises in making people look younger and fitter on the screen, digitally. This is not the 'soft focus' filmmaking of Alfred Hitchcock's era; this is digital lies using the cold binary logic of zeros and ones. If you happened to see the latest *X-Men* movie and wondered about the youthful Patrick Stewart – who looked younger and fresher than in movies he made when he actually was younger and fresher – it is because of companies like Lola VFX. Here is what they do: 'We remove scars, facial hair, pimples, wrinkles, dimples and blotches. We make bodies firmer, legs longer, faces younger, breasts fuller, cheekbones higher, eyes bluer and skin smoother. We achieve this while ensuring that all the effects are realistic and convincing' (Anon. 2007b). This is the image logic of the digital era, a form of re-enactment of ourselves. It is a system of radical filmmaking that goes largely unnoticed by scholars and theorists because film theory is still bound by a way of reading films that emerged in response to the classic era. There are deep and philosophical ramifications to statements like this: 'Our work has far-reaching implications, from extending an actor's career for one more sequel to overall success at the box office. We allow actors and studios to create one more blockbuster sequel (with the actor's fan base) by making the actor look as good (or better) than they did in their first movie' (ibid.).

What is there to say about such a brash and unapologetic thing as that statement? That statement was not written by Aldous Huxley, nor was it a darkly funny dystopian story by George Saunders. That was a real and true and sincere statement by a company that digitally alters the faces and bodies of the actors you see on the screen, a special effect so seamless, so natural that its very surrealism lies in the fact that it disguises itself as reality. It is the corporate executives of the new 'image realisation' companies who have become today's theorists of the image. Gareth Edwards, Founder and Chief Technical Officer at Image Metrics, has written that 'Human faces in games have rarely seemed "authentic". Authenticity is not just about the "realism" of the base mesh – it's certainly possible to present a single image of a 3D head which looks great, but expression is more about detailed, subtle movements and tiny nuances' (2006: 1). And what is it that Image Metrics does? According to Andy Wood, the company's CEO, 'Image Metrics' core technology automatically transfers a human being's facial performance onto a digitally-created character. We capture an actor's facial performance directly from a camera or an existing recording – there's no motion capture studio, no special equipment or metal markers. Whatever the actor does, the computer character does' (in Anon. 2006: 1).

What does it mean to be real in a movie in the digital era? What happens when we create a realism that outstrips the detail of reality itself, when we achieve and then go beyond a one-to-one correspondence with the real world? Jean Baudrillard has spoken and written about the pointlessness, the banality of art ever since it 'liberated' itself from its high status as 'art' and became coterminous with everyday reality: 'At the end of this history, the banality of art is mixed up with the banality of the real world' (2005: 90). In a cruel paradox, the deconstruction of art was completely successful: it no longer exists. Movies, too, have always depended on a boundary, however fluid, between natural reality and our manipulations of that reality. In fact, our entire taxonomy of cinematic genres – science fiction, historical epic, comedy, thriller, mystery, avant-garde – depended not only on these distinctions, but on a sort of base-line realism against which they were measured. After all, fantasy is a genre, but is realism? What happens in the digital age when the very conditions of the realism against which not only genre, but aesthetics, are measured no longer exist?

'We could put Marilyn Monroe alongside Jack Nicholson, or Jack Black or Jack White', says Andy Wood. 'If we want John Wayne to act alongside Angelina Jolie, we can do that. We can directly mimic the performance of a human being on a model. We can create new scenes for old films, or old scenes for new films' (in Waxman 2006: 2). What is different here is not that movies are devising new ways of compositing the real, but rather that the real itself is the product of this composition. What Andy Wood and others are doing is really an exercise in philosophy, forcing us to rethink not only our relationship to reality, but the fundamental nature of reality itself. And it seems – looking at these developments now, in the wake of postmodernism – perfectly natural that our cinematic technologies are finally fulfilling the promise and logic of deconstruction. Ironically, while the so-called postmodern rejection of Truth with a capital T and 'Reality' itself used to be associated with the radical chic professoriate, today its logic permeates popular culture and political discourse, even from the right. Ron Suskind recalls being told by a senior advisor to George Bush in 2002 that:

guys like me were 'in what we call the reality-based community', which he defined as people who 'believe that solutions emerge from your judicious study of discernable reality … That's not the way the world really works any more … We're an empire now, and when we act, we create our own reality. And while you're studying that reality – judiciously, as you will – we'll act again, creating other new realities, which you can study too, and that's how things will sort out.' (2004)

You can imagine this sort of thing being said in a graduate seminar in literary theory in 1988 and being understood as a statement of high theory: reality is not 'objective', out there waiting to be found, but rather something that is constructed, the product of social, economic, cultural and political forces.

When, in a *New York Times* article, Andy Wood uses the phrase 'soul transference' to describe the process of computer mapping an actor's face 'onto any character virtual or human, living or dead' (in Waxman 2006), and then goes on to say that 'the model has the actress's soul. It shows through', you know you have reached the point where Philip K. Dick's paranoid fictions of the 1960s and 1970s no longer serve as prescient harbingers of the future, but rather as bits of nostalgia for a time when such a future could be imagined. 'The Kalbfleisch simulacrum stopped', we read in Dick's 1964 novel *The Simulacra*, a story about a President of the United States who is a simulacrum. 'Its arms stuck out, rigid in their final gesture, the withered face vacuous. The simulacrum said nothing and automatically the TV cameras also shut off, one by one; there was no longer anything for them to transmit' (2002: 32).

In her pioneering book *How We Became Posthuman*, N. Katherine Hayles noted that 'one of the striking differences between researchers who work with flesh and those who work with computers is how nuanced the sense of the body's complexity is for those who are directly engaged with it' (1999: 244). It is precisely this human complexity that companies like Image Metrics (does this not sound like the name of a company out of a Philip K. Dick novel?) hope to capture for the screen. Under the sign of such companies, human beings become models for reality, mannequins upon which an even greater real is layered. 'When people see what we can do with this system – for example, making Marilyn Monroe say words she never spoke – they see how they can use it to make better games and films', Andy Wood has said. 'Our technology will ensure we achieve our goals … it can't fail to' (in Anon. 2006: 2). The place of human beings in digital cinema is not secure; technologies that were once used to create 'special effects' now create human beings *as* special effects. Companies like Image Metrics are not interested in creating realistic-looking explosions, tidal waves, fires, and so forth, but rather in creating human beings who look more real than us.

And so: we find ourselves as the subjects of our own vision machines, which we created to penetrate and capture reality. The reversal is nearly complete. In *Poltergeist*, a girl with blonde hair stares into the eerie static of the television, listening to ghosts. In *The Ring*, a girl with black hair – a ghost herself – crawls out of the television, across the floor and towards another screen, the one that separates us from her. The virus at the heart of the Koji Suzuki novels that include *Ring* is not really the videotape, but rather the screens that make the display of the tape possible.

Visible Language, Spring 1977
[blunders, Cleveland, digital binaries]

Consider an issue of the journal *Visible Language* ('The Journal of Research on the Visual Media of Language Expression'). Published out of Cleveland, one of the most economically distressed US cities at the time (besides Detroit), this issue, devoted to the topic 'At the Edge of Meaning', is as strange as a Talking Heads album, and as cryptically alluring as an essay by Jacques Derrida. Of special interest are two articles. The first is the lead essay, by Aaron Marcus: 'Insofar as the new media appear to have replaced the "book" as a source of communication, the glass screen has replaced the printed paper page. There has been a tendency, however, to overlook the full implications of that change. The screen of visible languages is being shattered' (1977: 7–8); the second is 'Observations Concerning Practical Visual Languages' by Herbert W. Franke, who writes that people

> are prepared for a new dimension of visible language by illustrated magazines, film, and television. Even in comic books one can find complex activities of visual communication which are by no means as simple as some theorists maintain. In a dozen frames of a cartoon series, occurrences are expressed whose narrative description might require a whole chapter of a novel … The use of quite general, easily understandable visual symbol languages should not be confined to comics. (1977: 32)

Before George Landow and Espen Aarseth (but after Marshall McLuhan, of course) this issue of *Visible Language* resolved to bridge the analogue/digital divide before it fully revealed itself. The rapid and rapidly transferable iconography that digital systems make possible (data as a series of discrete zeros and ones) helped usher in a new shorthand that would only become fully articulated in films like *The Blair Witch Project*, which understood more than any 'theory' that human beings – with all their mistakes

Observations Concerning
Practical Visual Languages
Herbert W. Franke

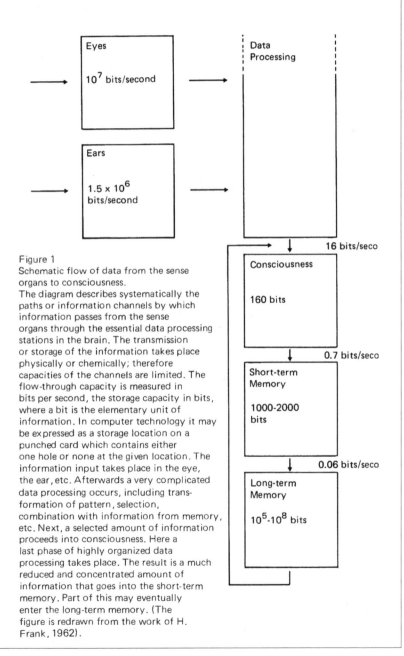

Figure 1
Schematic flow of data from the sense
organs to consciousness.
The diagram describes systematically the
paths or information channels by which
information passes from the sense
organs through the essential data processing
stations in the brain. The transmission
or storage of the information takes place
physically or chemically; therefore
capacities of the channels are limited. The
flow-through capacity is measured in
bits per second, the storage capacity in bits,
where a bit is the elementary unit of
information. In computer technology it may
be expressed as a storage location on a
punched card which contains either
one hole or none at the given location. The
information input takes place in the eye,
the ear, etc. Afterwards a very complicated
data processing occurs, including transformation of pattern, selection,
combination with information from memory,
etc. Next, a selected amount of information
proceeds into consciousness. Here a
last phase of highly organized data
processing takes place. The result is a much
reduced and concentrated amount of
information that goes into the short-term
memory. Part of this may eventually
enter the long-term memory. (The
figure is redrawn from the work of H.
Frank, 1962).

Illustration from the journal *Visible Language*, Spring 1977: The first stages of the digital era: information understood as bits, as patterns, as binary codes. Digital cinema disguises this information as narrative

and errors – are the only balance against the cold logic of the digital binary. Digital cinema both reveals and disguises the raw information of the binary code as narrative. We know all too well today that the images on our screens are nothing more than information. Information processing in the digital era is relentlessly imagistic and cinematic, and thus relentlessly, primally human, if for no other reason than we see each other before we talk to each other. A database logic that expresses itself in images is terrifying only insofar as the underlying code is expressed in a numerical language that is alien to most users.

The proliferation of images in the digital era is a confirmation of the basic human condition, not some postmodern rejection of humanism. All our technology conspires to replicate us, not replace us. In the digital era, we are everywhere, as never before. In the short-lived but influential fanzine *New Wave*, in 1977, Steven Seid wrote that 'During the past ten years or so there have been a handful of directors making films marked by the majesty of their blunders' (1977: 34). He referred to the imperfection of Orson Welles, John Cassavetes and Arthur Penn, who anticipated Thomas Vinterberg, Harmony Korine and Alejandro González Iñárritu. If it is always the same story repeated, then the digital code lays this out, cold and bare, for us. In the end, it is the mistakes, the errors that we assert in the face of the code that keeps it from consuming us with its purity. Mistakes must be our answer to the machines of perfection that we ourselves have built.

Filmography

21 Grams (Alejandro González Iñárritu, 2003, US)

24 (television series, various directors 2001–present, US)

28 Days Later (Danny Boyle, 2002, UK)

Adaptation (Spike Jonze, 2002, US)

A Face in the Crowd (Elia Kazan, 1957, US)

Amélie (Jean-Pierre Jeunet, 2001, France/Germany)

American Gangster (Ridley Scott, 2007, US)

Amores Perros (*Love's a Bitch*) (Alejandro González Iñárritu, 2000, Mexico)

Apocalypse Now (Francis Ford Coppola, 1979, US)

Around the Bay (Alejandro Adams, 2008, US)

A Scanner Darkly (Richard Linklater, 2006, US)

At Land (Maya Deren, 1944, US)

Babel (Alejandro González Iñárritu, 2006, France/US/Mexico)

Bamboozled (Spike Lee, 2000, US)

Batman (Tim Burton, 1989, US/UK)

Being John Malkovich (Spike Jonze, 1999, US)

Beetlejuice (Tim Burton, 1988, US)

Blair Witch Project, The (Daniel Myrick and Eduardo Sánchez, 1999, US)

Blue Velvet (David Lynch, 1986, US)

Boston Strangler, The (Richard Fleischer, 1968, US)

Brazil (Terry Gilliam, 1985, UK)

Breaking the Waves (Lars von Trier, 1996, Denmark/Sweden/France/Netherlands/
 Norway/Iceland)

Brothers Grimm, The (Terry Gilliam, 2005, UK/Czech Republic/US)

Bubble (Steven Soderbergh, 2006, US)

Canary (Alejandro Adams, 2008, US)

Catwoman (Pitof, 2004, US/Australia)

Chelovek s kino-apparatom (*Man with a Movie Camera*) (Dziga Vertov, 1929, Soviet Union)

Chelsea Girls (Andy Warhol and Paul Morrissey, 1966, US)

Chinatown (Roman Polanski, 1974, US)

Citizen Kane (Orson Welles, 1941, US)

Clerks II (Kevin Smith, 2006, US)

Confessions of a Dangerous Mind (George Clooney, 2002, US/UK/Germany)

Conversation, The (Francis Ford Coppola, 1974, US)

Cremaster Cycle, The (Matthew Barney, 1994–2002, US/France/UK)

Dancer in the Dark (Lars von Trier, 2000, Denmark/Germany/Netherlands/Italy/US/UK/ France/Sweden/Finland/Iceland/Norway)

Day After Tomorrow, The (Roland Emmerich, 2004, US)

Death Proof (Quentin Tarantino, 2007, US)

Direktøren for det hele (*The Boss of It All*) (Lars von Trier, 2006, Denmark/Sweden/ Iceland/Italy/France/Norway/Finland/Germany)

Dogville (Lars von Trier, 2003, Denmark/Sweden/Norway/Finland/UK/France/ Germany/Netherlands)

Dopperugengâ (*Doppelgänger*) (Kiyoshi Kurosawa, 2003, Japan)

Dressed to Kill (Brian De Palma, 1980, US)

Edward Scissorhands (Tim Burton, 1990, US)

Elephant (Gus Van Sant, 2003, US)

Empire (Andy Warhol, 1964, US)

Eternal Sunshine of the Spotless Mind (Michel Gondry, 2004, US)

L'Étoile de mer (Man Ray, 1928, France)

Faces (John Cassavetes, 1968, US)

Festen (*The Celebration*) (Thomas Vinterberg, 1998, Denmark/Sweden)

Fight Club (David Fincher, 1999, US/Germany)

Following (Christopher Nolan, 1998, UK)

Foreigner, The (Amos Poe, 1978, US)

Germania anno zero (*Germany Year Zero*) (Roberto Rossellini, 1948, Italy)

Go (Doug Liman, 1999, US)

Great Train Robbery, The (Edwin S. Porter, 1903, US)

Gummo (Harmony Korine, 1997, US)

Gun Crazy (Joseph H. Lewis, 1949, US)

Halloween (John Carpenter, 1978, US)

Head Trauma (Lance Weiler, 2006, US)

His Trust (D. W. Griffith, 1911, US)

Homicide: Life on the Streets (television series, various directors, 1993–99, US)

Human Nature (Michel Gondry, 2001, France/US)

Idiotern (*The Idiots*) (Lars von Trier, 1998, Denmark/Sweden/France/Netherlands/Italy)

I Heart Huckabees (David O. Russell, 2004, US/Germany)

Inland Empire (David Lynch, 2006, France/Poland/US)

In This World (Michael Winterbottom, 2002, UK)

julien donkey-boy (Harmony Korine, 1999, US)

Last Broadcast, The (Lance Weiler, 1998, US)

Lola rennt (*Run Lola Run*) (Tom Tykwer, 1998, Germany)

Lost Highway (David Lynch, 1997, France/US)

'Lucas with the Lid Off' (Michel Gondry, 1994, US)

Magnolia (Paul Thomas Anderson, 1999, US)

Master and Commander: The Far Side of the World (Peter Weir, 2003, US)

Matrix, The (Andy Wachowski and Larry Wachowski, 1999, US/Australia)

Matrix Reloaded, The (Andy Wachowski and Larry Wachowski, 2003, US/Australia)

Memento (Christopher Nolan, 2000, US)

Meshes of the Afternoon (Maya Deren and Alexander Hammid, 1943, US)

Minority Report (Steven Spielberg, 2002, US)

Mulholland Dr. (David Lynch, 2001, France/US)

Nines, The (John August, 2007, US)

Not Another Teen Movie (Joel Gallen, 2001, US)

Pink Flamingos (John Waters, 1972, US)

Planet Terror (Robert Rodriguez, 2007, US)

Poltergeist (Tobe Hooper, 1982, US)

Pulp Fiction (Quentin Tarantino, 1994, US)

Requiem for a Dream (Darren Aronofsky, 2000, US)

Retour à la raison, Le (Man Ray, 1923, France)

Riget (*The Kingdom*) (television series, Lars von Trier and Marten Arnfred, 1994–97, Denmark/France/Germany/Sweden)

Ring, The (Gore Verbinski, 2002, US/Japan)

Ringu (*Ring*) (Hideo Nakata, 1998, Japan)

Roma, città aperta (*Rome, Open City*) (Roberto Rossellini, 1945, Italy)

Rope (Alfred Hitchcock, 1948, US)

Russkiy kovcheg (*Russian Ark*) (Alexander Sokurov, 2002, Russia/Germany)

Science des rêves, La (*The Science of Sleep*) (Michel Gondry, 2006, France/Italy)

Scream (Wes Craven, 1996, US)

Screen Tests (Andy Warhol, 1966, US)

'Sentimental Journey' (Nagi Noda, 1994, Japan)

Serpico (Sidney Lumet, 1973, US/Italy)

sex, lies, and videotape (Steven Soderbergh, 1989, US)

Shi mian man fu (*House of Flying Daggers*) (Zhang Yimou, 2004, China/Hong Kong)

'Shining' (Robert Ryang, 2005)

Shining, The (Stanley Kubrick, 1980, UK/US)

Sopranos, The (television series, various directors, 1999–2007, US)

Spider-Man 2 (Sam Raimi, 2004, US)

Spider-Man 3 (Sam Raimi, 2007, US)

Star Wars Episode II: Attack of the Clones (George Lucas, 2002, US)

Stranger than Fiction (Marc Foster, 2006, US)

Sunset Blvd. (Billy Wilder, 1950, US)

Superman Returns (Bryan Singer, 2006, Australia/US)

Synecdoche, New York (Charlie Kaufman, 2008, US)

Tape (Richard Linklater, 2001, US)

Ten (Abbas Kiarostami, 2002, France/Iran/US)

Terminator 2: Judgment Day (James Cameron, 1991, US/France)

Thomas Crown Affair, The (Norman Jewison, 1968, US)

Time Bandits (Terry Gilliam, 1981, UK)

Timecode (Mike Figgis, 2000, US)

Titan A. E. (Dan Bluth, Gary Goldman and Art Vitello, 2000, US)

Twister (Jan de Bont, 1996, US)

Vertigo (Alfred Hitchcock, 1959, US)

X-Men (Bryan Singer, 2000, Canada/US)

X-Men: The Last Stand (Brett Ratner, 2006, Canada/US/UK)

Zodiac (David Fincher, 2007, US)

Bibliography

Aarseth, Espen J. (1997) *Cybertext: Perspectives on Ergodic Literature*. Baltimore: Johns Hopkins University Press.

Adams, Alejandro (2007) 'The Cult of Naturalism', *Post Identity*, 5, 1. Available at: http://hdl. handle.net/2027/spo.pid9999.0005.104. Accessed 14 February 2008.

Adorno, Theodor (1991a [1978]) 'Culture and Administration', in J. M. Bernstein (ed.) *The Culture Industry*. London: Routledge, 107–31.

_____ (1991b [1981]) 'Transparencies on Film', in J. M. Bernstein (ed.) *The Culture Industry*. London: Routledge, 178–86.

Albrecht, Katherine and Liz McIntyre (2006) *The Spychips Threat*. Nashville: Nelson Current.

Andersen, Thomas (1966) 'Eadweard Muybridge', *Film Culture*, 41, Summer, 16–24.

Anderson, Benedict (1983) *Imagined Communities: Reflections on the Origin and Spread of Nationalism*. London: Verso.

Andrew, Dudley (2005 [1967]) 'Foreword', in André Bazin *What is Cinema?*, Volume 1, trans. Hugh Gray. Berkeley: University of California Press, ix–xxiv.

Anon. (1913) 'A Cinematograph Hand Camera', *Scientific American*, 1 November, 112.

_____ (1917) 'A Motion-Picture Camera and a Projector for Home Use', *Scientific American*, 24 February, 206.

_____ (1926) 'Hundreds Now "Shoot" Movies of Their Own', *Washington Post*, 25 April, R14.

_____ (1927) 'The Amateur Cinema Movement', *Christian Science Monitor*, 15 July, 15.

_____ (1960) 'The Day of the Cinematologist', *Christian Science Monitor*, 6 December, 6.

_____ (1999a) '*The Blair Witch Project*', *Austin Chronicle*, 19 July. Available at: http://filmvault. com/filmvault/austin/b/blairwitchproject1.html. Accessed 6 April 2007.

_____ (1999b) 'Animal Logic: About Us', Animal Logic website. Available at: http://www.animal-logic.com/about/keypeople.html. Accessed 2 November 2007.

_____ (2003) 'Object Information Exchange: Smart Objects Manage Themselves'. Available at: http://www.accenture.com/accenturetechlabs. Accessed 23 September 2006.

_____ (2005a) 'The Point: Claiming the Future'. Available at: http://www.accenture.com/accenture/registration/PrintThis.aspx. Accessed 14 September 2007.

_____ (2005b) 'Today's Reality, Tomorrow's Promise', in *RFID Journal*. Available at: http://www.rfidjournal.com/article/articleview/487/1/79/. Accessed 14 September 2007.

_____ (2005c) 'The Man from Beyond: An Interview with David Thomas from Pere Ubu'. Available at http://www.leftofthedialmag.com/dthomas1.html. Accessed 21 March 2008.

_____ (2006) 'Andy Wood Goes to Hollywood: The MCV Interview', 7 July. Available at: http://www.image-metrics.com/news/im_news4_march24_2006.pdf. Accessed 19 February 2008.

_____ (2007a) 'Who We Are', Lola Visual Effects website. Available at: http://www.lolavfx.com/who.php. Accessed 18 April 2008.

_____ (2007b) 'What We Do', Lola Visual Effects website. Available at: http://www.lolavfx.com/what/php. Accessed 18 April 2008.

_____ (2008a) 'Pre-Visualisation', Persistence of Vision website. Available at: http://persistenceofvision.com. Accessed 3 March 2008.

_____ (2008b) 'Amazon.com Interview with David Lynch'. Available at: http://www.amazon.com/gp/mpd/perrmalink. Accessed 10 October 2008.

Anthony, James (2001) 'Following On: Interview with Christopher Nolan', *Memento and Following*. London: Faber and Faber, 56–63.

Atwood, Margaret (2004) *Oryx and Crake*. New York: Anchor Books.

Auden, W. H. (1989 [1929]) 'It was Easter as I walked in the public gardens', in *W. H. Auden: Selected Poems*, ed. Edward Mendelson. New York: Vintage International, 7–12.

Baker, Kenneth (1988) *Minimalism: Art of Circumstance*. New York: Abbeville Press.

Barthes, Roland (1975) *The Pleasure of the Text*, trans. Richard Miller. New York: Noonday Press.

_____ (1977a [1970]) 'The Third Meaning: Research notes on some Eisenstein stills', in *Image, Music, Text*, trans. Stephen Heath. New York: Hill and Wang, 52–68.

_____ (1977b [1972]) 'The Grain of the Voice', in *Image, Music, Text*, trans. Stephen Heath. New York: Hill and Wang, 179–89.

Baudrillard, Jean (1996) *The Perfect Crime*, trans. Chris Turner. London: Verso.

_____ (2001) *Impossible Exchange*, trans. Chris Turner. London: Verso.

_____ (2005) *The Conspiracy of Art*, ed. Sylvere Lotringer, trans. Ames Hodges. New York: Semiotext(e).

Baudry, Jean-Louis (1999 [1975]) 'The Apparatus: Metapsychological Approaches to the Impression of Reality in Cinema', in Leo Braudy and Marshall Cohen (eds) *Film Theory and Criticism*. New York: Oxford University Press, 760–77.

Bazin, André (2005a [1967]) *What is Cinema?*, Vol. 1, trans. Hugh Gray. Berkeley: University of California Press.

_____ (2005b [1948]) 'An Aesthetic of Reality: Neorealism', in *What is Cinema?*, Vol. 2, trans. Hugh Gray. Berkeley: University of California Press, 16–40.

Benjamin, Walter (1968 [1935]) 'The Work of Art in the Age of Mechanical Reproduction', in *Illuminations*, ed. Hannah Arendt. New York: Schocken, 217–54.

_____ (1999) *The Arcades Project*, trans. Howard Eiland and Kevin McLaughlin. Cambridge, MA: Belknap Press of Harvard University Press.

Bergson, Henri (1988) *Matter and Memory*, trans. Nancy Margaret Paul and W. Scott Palmer. New York: Zone Books.

Beville, Hugh M. (1977–78) 'Home Cassette Players and Audience Ratings', *Television Quarterly*, 14, 3, 75–84.

Birnbaum, Robert (2004) 'Birnbaum v. Brian Greene', *The Morning News*. Available at: http://www.themorningnews.org/archives/personalities/birnbaum_v_brian_greene.php. Accessed 2 November 2007.

Björkman, Stig (1999) 'Juggling in the Dark', *Sight and Sound*, 9, 12, 8–10.

Bolter, David Jay and Richard Grusin (2000) *Remediation: Understanding New Media*. Cambridge, MA: MIT Press.

Bordwell, David (2007) 'My name is David and I'm a frame-counter', 28 January. Available at: http://www.davidbordwell.net/blog. Accessed 28 February 2008.

Borges, Jorge Luis (1962 [1941]) 'The Circular Ruins', in *Ficciones*, trans. Anthony Bonner. New York: Grove Press, 57–63.

Born, Irene (2005) *The Born-Einstein Letters: Friendship, Politics and Physics in Uncertain Times*. New York: Macmillan.

Boyle, Danny (2002) 'Audio Commentary by Director Danny Boyle and Writer Alex Garland', *28 Days Later*. Fox Searchlight DVD.

Bradbury, Ray (1950) 'The Veldt', in *The Illustrated Man*. New York: Bantam, 7–19.

Breton, André (1972 [1924]) 'Manifesto of Surrealism', in *Manifestoes of Surrealism*, trans. Richard Seaver and Helen R. Lane. Ann Arbor: University of Michigan Press, 3–47.

Bulgakowa, Oksana (2001) *Sergei Eisenstein: A Biography*, trans. Anne Dwyer. San Francisco: Potemkinpress.

Carr, Roy (1976) 'Ramones review', *New Musical Express*, 18 September, 21.

Carter, Jimmy (1979) 'The "Crisis of Confidence" Speech'. Available at: http://www.pbs.org.wgbh/amex/carter/filmmore/ps_crisis.html. Accessed 10 October 2007.

Casciani, Dominic (2006) 'Crisis Threatened Nuclear Weapons', BBC News. Available at: http://newsvote.bbc.co.uk/go/pr/fr/-/2/uk_news/politics/6212557.stm. Accessed 30 March 2008.

Cheshire, Godfrey (1999) 'The Death of Film/The Decay of Cinema', *New York Press*, August. Available at: http://nypress.com. Accessed 13 June 2007.

Clover, Carol (1992) Men, Women and Chain Saws. Princeton: Princeton University Press.

Clowes, Daniel (1997) *Ghost World*. Seattle: Fantagraphics.

_____ (2000) *David Boring*. New York: Pantheon.

Cockburn, Alexander (1974) 'Press Clips', *Village Voice*, 15 August, 8.

Cubitt, Sean (2004) *The Cinema Effect*. Cambridge, MA: MIT Press.

Curry, Warren (2003) 'Basic: An Interview with *21 Grams* screenwriter Guillermo Arriaga'. Available at: http://www.cinemaspeak.com/Interviews/gaint.html. Accessed 19 December 2006.

Danielewski, Mark Z. (2000) *House of Leaves*. New York: Pantheon.

_____ (2006a) *Only Revolutions*. New York: Pantheon.

_____ (2006b) 'MZD answers the question "How did you write it?" (Columbia 3)'. Available at: http://www.youtube.com/watch?v=6DimPyoksy. Accessed 31 January 2008.

Davis, Zeinabu Irene (2001) '"Beautiful Ugly" Blackface: An Esthetic Appreciation of *Bamboozled*', *Cineaste*, 26, 2, 16–17.

Debord, Guy (1995) *The Society of the Spectacle*, trans. Donald Nicholson-Smith. New York: Zone Books.

Deleuze, Gilles (1986) *Cinema 1: The Movement-Image*, trans. Hugh Tomlinson and Barbara Habberjam. Minneapolis: University of Minnesota Press.

_____ (1989) *Cinema 2: The Time-Image*, trans. Hugh Tomlinson and Robert Galeta. London: Athlone Press.

DeLillo, Don (2001) *The Body Artist*. New York: Scribner.

Derrida, Jacques (1996) *Archive Fever: A Freudian Impression*, trans. Eric Prenowitz. Chicago: University of Chicago Press.

Dick, Philip K. (1993) *Now Wait for Last Year*. New York: Vintage Books.

_____ (2002) *The Simulacra*. New York: Vintage Books.

Doane, Mary Ann (2002) *The Emergence of Cinematic Time: Modernity, Contingency, the Archive*. Cambridge, MA: Harvard University Press.

Dornsife, Robert S. (2006) 'Coming to (Digital) Terms: The Work of Art in the Age of Non-Mechanical Reproduction', *Radical Pedagogy*, 8, 1, 1–4.

Edwards, Gareth (2006) 'Next-gen games need to face facts', 7 July. Available at: http://www.image-metrics.com/news/im_news4_march24_2006.pdf. Accessed 21 July 2008.

Eggers, Dave (2001) *A Heartbreaking Work of Staggering Genius*. New York: Vintage Books.

Eisenstein, Sergei (1977a [1929]) 'The Filmic Fourth Dimension', in *Film Form: Essays in Film Theory*, ed. Jay Leyda. New York: Harvest, 64–71.

_____ (1977b [1944]) 'Dickens, Griffith, and the Film Today', in *Film Form: Essays in Film Theory*, ed. Jay Leyda. New York: Harvest, 195–255.

Ellis, Bret Easton (2005) *Lunar Park*. New York: Alfred A. Knopf.

Enticknap, Leo (2005) *Moving Image Technology: From Zoetrope to Digital*. London: Wallflower Press.

Faber, Michael (2005) 'The Eyes of the Soul', in *Vanilla Bright Like Eminem*. New York: Harcourt, 37–48.

Feeny, Catherine (2004) '*Master and Commander*: Interview with Nathan McGuinness'. Available at: http://www.uemedia.net/CPC/vfxpro/printer_6368.shtml. Accessed 23 September 2007.

Feyerabend, Paul (1988) *Against Method*. London: Verso.

Figgis, Mike (2000) 'Director's Commentary, version 15', *Timecode*. Lion's Gate.

Foucault, Michel (1984 [1969]) 'What is An Author?', in *The Foucault Reader*, ed. Paul Rainbow. New York Pantheon, 101–20.

Frampton, Daniel (2006) *Filmosophy*. London: Wallflower Press.

Franke, Herbert W. (1977) 'Observations Concerning Practical Visual Languages', *Visible Language*, 11, 2, 22–32.

Friedberg, Anne (1993) *Window Shopping: Cinema and the Postmodern*. Berkeley: University of California Press.

Frith, Simon (1981) *Sound Effects: Youth, Leisure, and the Politics of Rock 'n' Roll*. New York: Pantheon Books.

Gaggi, Silvio (1997) *From Text to Hypertext: Decentering the Subject in Fiction, Film, the Visual Arts, and Electronic Media*. Philadelphia, PA: University of Pennsylvania Press.

Gere, Charlie (2002) *Digital Culture*. London: Reaktion Books.

Geuens, Jean-Pierre (2002) 'The Digital World Picture', *Film Quarterly*, 55, 2.

Gibson, William (1999) 'William Gibson's Filmless Festival', Wired.com, October. Available at: http://www.wired.com/wired/archive/7.10/gibson_pr.html. Accessed 4 April 2007.

_____ (2007) *Spook Country*. New York: Putnam's.

Goldman, Michael (2006) 'Going Tapeless'. Available at: http://digitalcontentproducer,com/ videosys/revfeat. Accessed 10 December 2007.

Goleman, Daniel (2006) 'Talk of the Nation', 23 October. Available at: http://www.npr.org. Accessed 29 January 2008.

Gould, Jack (1967) 'Soon You'll Collect TV Reels, Like LP's', *New York Times*, 3 September, D13.

_____ (1970) 'Renting a Movie Or a Professor To Take Home', *New York Times*, 5 April, 4.

Greenberg, Clement (2006 [1939]) 'Avant-Garde and Kitsch'. Available at: http:www.sharecom. ca/Greenberg/kitsch/html. Accessed 15 June 2007.

Greene, Brian (2004) *The Fabric of the Cosmos: Space, Time, and the Texture of Reality*. New York: Vintage Books.

Greenfield, Adam (2006) *Everyware: The Dawning Age of Ubiquitous Computing*. Berkeley: New Riders.

Griffiths, Keith (2001) 'The Manipulated Image'. Available at: http://www.animateonline.org/ editorial/article002a.html. Accessed 8 May 2007.

Gunning, Tom (1990) 'The Cinema of Attractions: The Early Film, Its Spectator, and The Avant-Garde', in Thomas Elsaesser (ed.) *Early Cinema: Space, Frame, Narrative*. London: British Film Institute, 56–62.

_____ (1991) *D. W. Griffith and the Origins of American Narrative Film*. Urbana: University of Illinois Press.

_____ (2005) 'Introduction: The Diva, the Tiger, and the Three-Legged Spider', in Luigi Pirandello *Shoot!*, trans. C. K. Scott Moncrieff. Chicago: University of Chicago Press, vii–xiv.

Hall, Steven (2007) *The Raw Shark Texts*. New York: Canongate.

Hampton, Howard (2007 [2003]) 'Let Us Now Kill White Elephants', in *Termite Dreams, Dialectical Fairy Tales, and Pop Apocalypses*. Cambridge, MA: Harvard University Press, 167–82.

Hand, Elizabeth (2007) *Generation Loss*. Northhampton, MA: Small Beer Press.

Haridas, B. (2002) '*Ten*: It is the Journey'. Available at: http://www.chaosmag.net/tenstudy. html. Accessed 7 February 2008.

Harper, Graeme (2001) 'DVD: The Shift to Film's New Modernity', *Cineaction*, 56, 20–5.

_____ (2005) 'DVD and the New Cinema of Complexity', in Nicholas Rombes (ed.) *New Punk Cinema*. Edinburgh: Edinburgh University Press, 89–101.

Havel, Václav (1986 [1978]) 'The Power of the Powerless', trans. P. Wilson, in *Living in Truth*, ed. Jan Vladislav. London: Faber and Faber, 36–122.

Hayles, N. Katherine (1999) *How We Became Posthuman: Virtual Bodies in Cybernetics, Literature, and Informatics*. Chicago: University of Chicago Press.

Hebdige, Dick (1979) *Subculture: The Meaning of Style*. New York: Verso.

Heffernan, Virginia (2003) 'Camera Down the Hole, and the World Follows It', *New York Times*, 16 December. Available at: http://nytimes.com/2003/12/16/arts/television/16NOTE.html. Accessed 2 July 2006.

Hillis, Aaron (2007) 'Internet Killed the Video Star', *Village Voice*, 24 July. Available at: http://www.villagevoice.com. Accessed 3 March 2008.

Holcomb, Brian (2007) 'The Head Trauma of Independent Filmmaking', *PopMatters*. Available at: http://www.popmatters.com/pm/features/article42623/the-head-trauma. Accessed 11 January 2008.

Hoyt, Clark (2007) 'When Bad News Follows You', *New York Times*, 26 August, A17.

Hunter, Sandy (2005) 'RES 10', *RES Magazine*, 8, 2, 42–5.

Iser, Wolfgang (1974) *The Implied Reader: Patterns of Communication in Prose Fiction from Bunyan to Beckett*. Baltimore: Johns Hopkins University Press.

Ishiguro, Kazuo (2005) *Never Let Me Go*. New York: Alfred A. Knopf.

Itzkoff, Dave (2007) 'A Brave New World for TV? Virtually', *New York Times*, 24 June, Section 2, 28.

Iversen, Ebbe (2003 [1998]) 'Tracing the Inner Idiot', in Jan Lumholdt (ed.) *Lars von Trier Interviews*. Jackson: University Press of Mississippi, 125–9.

James, Nick (2001) 'Digital Deluge', *Sight and Sound*, 11, 10, 20–4.

Jameson, Fredric (1991) *Postmodernism, or, The Cultural Logic of Late Capitalism*. Durham, NC: Duke University Press.

Jardin, Xeni (2006) 'Thinking outside the box office'. Available at: http://www.wired.com/wired/archive/13.12/soderbergh_pr.html. Accessed 8 May 2007.

Jewison, Norman (2005) 'Director's Commentary', *The Thomas Crown Affair*. MGM DVD.

Johnson, Steven (2005) *Everything Bad is Good for You: How Today's Popular Culture is Actually Making us Smarter*. New York: Riverhead Books.

Kael, Pauline (1970 [1969]) 'Trash, Art, and the Movies', in *Going Steady*. Boston: Little, Brown, 87–129.

_____ (1994 [1965]) 'Is there a cure for film criticism?', in *I Lost it at the Movies*. New York: Marion Boyars, 279–85.

Kaku, Michio (2005) *Parallel Worlds*. New York: Anchor Books.

Kaufman, Anthony (2001) 'Mindgames: Christopher Nolan Remembers *Memento*', *Indiewire*. 16 March. Available at: http://www.indiewire.com/people/int_Nolan_Christoph_010316.html. Accessed 16 June 2006.

Kaufman, Charlie (2002) *Adaptation: The Shooting Script*. New York: New Market Press.

Kaufman, Debra (2003) 'Metadata's Impact on "Artistic Intent"', *American Cinematographer*, December. Available at: http://www.thesc.com/magazine/dec03/sub/index.html. Accessed 10 October 2006.

Kern, Stephen (1983) *The Culture of Time and Space: 1880–1918*. Cambridge, MA: Harvard University Press.

Kevles, Barbara L. (1965) 'Slavko Vorkapich on Film as a Visual Language and as a Form of Art', *Film Culture*, 38, Fall, 42–8.

Kiarostami, Abbas (2002) 'Commentary from "10 on Ten"', *Ten*. Zeitgeist.

Kirby, Lynne (1997) *Parallel Tracks: The Railroad and Silent Cinema*. Durham, NC: Duke University Press.

Korine, Harmony (2001) 'A comprehensive and forthright guide to mistakist cinema', in Shari Roman (ed.) *Digital Babylon*. Hollywood: IFILM Publishing, vii–ix.

Kracauer, Siegfried (1997) *Theory of Film: The Redemption of Physical Reality*. Princeton: Princeton University Press.

_____ (2004) *From Caligari to Hitler: A Psychological History of the German Film*, ed. Leonardo Quaresima. Princeton: Princeton University Press.

Kroker, Arthur (2007) 'The Spirit of Jean Baudrillard. In Memoriam: 1929–2007'. Available at: http://www.ctheory.net/articles.aspx?id+573. Accessed 29 August 2007.

Leacock, Richard (2000 [1961]) 'For an Uncontrolled Cinema', in P. Adams Sitney (ed.) *The Film Culture Reader*. New York: Cooper Square Press, 76–8.

Le Grice, Malcolm (2001) *Experimental Cinema in the Digital Age*. London: British Film Institute.

Lessard, Bruno (2005) 'Digital Technologies and the Poetics of Performance', in Nicholas Rombes (ed.) *New Punk Cinema*. Edinburgh: Edinburgh University Press, 102–12.

Lethem, Jonathan (2005) 'Access Fantasy', in *Men and Cartoons: Stories by Jonathan Lethem*. New York: Vintage Books, 23–45.

Lias, Godfrey (1933) 'Added Leisure Gives Spurt to Making Amateur Movies', *Christian Science Monitor*, 30 October, 5.

Ling, Van (2005) 'Interview with Ian Failes'. Available at: http://www.fxguide.com/fxblog1640.html. Accessed 23 September 2006.

Linklater, Richard (2001) 'Production Commentary', *Tape*. Lions Gate Home Entertainment.

Louchheim, Aline B. (1952) 'The Case for Abstract Art Films', *New York Times*, 20 January, X9.

Macaulay, Scott (1999) 'Against the Grain: Interview with Anthony Dod Mantle', *Filmmaker*, Spring. Available at: http:www.filmmakermagazine.com/spring1999. Accessed 8 May 2007.

MacDonald, Scott (1993) *Avant-Garde Film: Motion Studies*. New York: Cambridge University Press.

Macnab, Geoffrey (2006) 'I'm a control freak – but I was not in control', *The Guardian* online, 22 September. Available at: http://arts.guardian.co.uk/filmandmusic/story/0,1877511,00.html. Accessed 25 January 2008.

Magid, Ron (2002) 'Exploring a New Universe: Interview with George Lucas', *American Cinematographer*, September. Available at: http://www.thease.com/magazine/sep02/exploring. Accessed 6 April 2007.

Manovich, Lev (1998) 'Database as a Genre of New Media'. Available at: http://vv.arts.ucla.edu/AI_Society/manovich.html. Accessed 17 January 2007.

_____ (2001) *The Language of New Media*. Cambridge, MA: MIT Press.

Manovich, Lev and Andreas Kratky (2005) *Soft Cinema: Navigating the Database*. Cambridge, MA: MIT Press.

Marcus, Aaron (1977) 'At the Edge of Meaning', *Visible Language*, 11, 2, 4–20.

Marcus, Greil (2006) *The Shape of Things to Come: Prophecy and the American Voice*. New York: Farrar, Straus and Giroux.

Marinetti, F. T., Bruno Corra, Emilio Settimelli, Arnaldo Ginna, Giacomo Balla and Remo Chiti (1916) 'The Futurist Cinema'. Available at: http://www.unknown.nu/futurism/cinema.html. Accessed 3 March 2008.

Markland, John (1936) 'Film Hobby Ranks Grow', *New York Times*, 23 January, C3.

McCaffery, Larry (1993) 'An Interview with David Foster Wallace', in *Review of Contemporary Fiction*, 13, 2, 127–50.

McCarthy, Cormac (2006) *The Road*. New York: Alfred A. Knopf.

McCarthy, Tom (2007) *Remainder*. New York: Vintage.

McCormick, Carlo (2004) 'Notes on the Underground', in Kirsten Anderson (ed.) *Pop Surrealism: The Rise of Underground Art*. San Francisco: Last Gasp and Ignition Publishing, 2–13.

McGrath, Charles (2004) 'Not Funnies', *New York Times Magazine*, 11 July, 24–35.

McLean, Greg (1979) 'The Dils: Victory on the Eastern Front!', *New York Rocker*, August, 19–20.

McLuhan, Marshall (1995 [1966]) 'A McLuhan Sourcebook', in *Essential McLuhan*, eds Eric McLuhan and Frank Zingrone. New York: Basic Books, 270–97.

Meadows, Mark Stephen (2003) *Pause & Effect: The Art of Interactive Narrative*. Indianapolis: New Riders.

Mekas, Jonas (2000 [1962]) 'Notes on the New American Cinema', in P. Adams Sitney (ed.) *Film Culture Reader*. New York: Cooper Square Press, 87–107.

Meltzer, Richard (1972) *Gulcher: Post-Rock Cultural Pluralism in America (1649–1980)*. San Francisco: Straight Arrow Books.

Melville, Herman (1996) *Pierre; or, The Ambiguities*. New York: Penguin.

Menasche, Louis (2003) 'Filming Sokurov's *Russian Ark*: An Interview with Tilman Büttner', *Cineaste*, 28, 3, 21–3.

Mendelsohn, Jane (2000) *Innocence*. New York: Riverhead Books.

Miller, Paul D. aka DJ Spooky (2004) *Rhythm Science*. Cambridge, MA: MIT Press.

Milutis, Joe (2006) *Ether: The Nothing that Connects Everything*. Minneapolis: University of Minnesota Press.

Mitchell, W. J. T. (1994) *Picture Theory: Essays on Verbal and Visual Representation*. Chicago: University of Chicago Press.

Mittell, Jason (2006) 'Narrative Complexity in Contemporary American Television', *Velvet Light Trap*, 58, 29–40.

Moerk, Christian (2005) 'The Powers Behind the Home-Video Throne', *New York Times*, 3 April, 2.

Moran, James M. (2002) *There's No Place Like Home Video*. Minneapolis: University of Minnesota Press.

Mulvey, Laura (1975) 'Visual Pleasure and Narrative Cinema', *Screen*, 16, 3, 6–18.

____ (2006) *Death 24x a Second*. London: Reaktion Books.

Musser, Charles (1990) *The Emergence of Cinema: The American Screen to 1907*. Berkeley: University of California Press.

Norris, Clive and Gary Armstrong (1999) *The Maximum Surveillance Society: The Rise of CCTV*. Oxford: Berg.

O'Gorman, Marcel (2006) *E-Crit: Digital Media, Critical Theory, and the Humanities*. Toronto: University of Toronto Press.

Palahniuk, Chuck (1996) *Fight Club*. New York: W. W. Norton.

_____ (2001) *Choke*. New York: Doubleday.

_____ (2002) *Lullaby*. New York: Doubleday.

_____ (2007) *Rant: An Oral Biography of Buster Casey*. New York: Doubleday.

Pirandello, Luigi (2005) *Shoot!*, trans. C. K. Scott Moncrieff. Chicago: University of Chicago Press.

Poniewozik, James (2007) 'The End of Fairy Tales?', *Time Magazine*, 21 May, 83–5.

Raeburn, Daniel (2004) *Chris Ware*. New Haven: Yale University Press.

Ray, Robert (1985) *A Certain Tendency of the Hollywood Cinema, 1930–1980*. Princeton: Princeton University Press.

_____ (2001) *How a Film Theory Got Lost and Other Mysteries in Cultural Studies*. Bloomington: Indiana University Press.

Rees, Joseph (1980) 'Items: Target Video', *Damage*, 4, January, 34–45.

_____ (2008) 'At that time in the 1970s', e-mail to the author, 8 February.

Robbe-Grillet, Alain (1965) *For a New Novel: Essays on Fiction*, trans. Richard Howard. Evanston: Northwestern University Press.

Roberts, Martin (2003) 'Decoding D-Day: Multi-Channel Television at the Millennium', in Mette Hjort and Scott MacKenzie (eds) *Purity and Provocation: Dogma 95*. London: British Film Institute, 158–70.

Robinson, Richard (1973) 'Media Energies: The Japanese', *Creem*, January, 82.

Roman, Shari (2001) 'Interview with John Bailey', in Shari Roman (ed.) *Digital Babylon*. Hollywood: IFILM Publishing, 112–25.

Rosner, Richard (1976) 'It's More Fun Than Crayons', *Byte: The Small Systems Journal*, November, 26–7.

Rubin, Michael (1991) *Nonlinear: A Guide to Electronic Film and Video Editing*. Gainesville: Triad Publishing.

Rushdie, Salman (1989) *The Satanic Verses*. New York: Viking.

Said, S. F. (2004) 'Shock Corridors', *Sight and Sound*, 14, 2, 16–18.

Sanneh, Kelefa (2007) 'Outrageous farce from R. Kelly: He's in on the joke, right?', *New York Times*, 20 August, C3, 2.

Sarris, Andrew (2000 [1962]) 'Notes on the Auteur Theory in 1962', in P. Adams Sitney (ed.) *The Film Culture Reader*. New York: Cooper Square Press, 121–35.

Scott, A. O. (2006) '*Pirates of the Caribbean*: Eat My Jetsam, Davy Jones', *New York Times*, 7 July, D1.

Sculatti, Gene (1976) 'Ramones', *Creem*, August, 66.

Seid, Steven (1977) 'Enter the Avant-Garde Surfers', *New Wave*, August, 33–4.

Siepmann, Charles A. (1950) *Radio, Television, and Society*. New York: Oxford University Press.

Silverman, Jason (2006) 'Short Films from a Long Life', 19 December. Available at: http://www.wired.com/news/culture/1,72318-0.html. Accessed 3 March 2007.

Smith, Gavin (2003 [2000]) 'Dance in the Dark', in Jan Lumholdt (ed.) *Lars von Trier Interviews*. Jackson: University Press of Mississippi, 144–52.

Soderbergh, Steven (2005) 'Director's DVD Commentary', *Bubble*. Magnolia.

Solanas, Valerie (1968) *SCUM Manifesto*. Available at: http://www.womynkind.org/scum.htm. Accessed 27 June 2007.

Sontag, Susan (1966a [1965]) 'On Style', in *Against Interpretation and Other Essays*. New York: Picador, 15–36.

____ (1966b [1964]) 'Notes on "Camp"', in *Against Interpretation and Other Essays*. New York: Picador, 275–92.

Spengemann, William C. (1996) 'Introduction', in Herman Melville *Pierre; or, The Ambiguities*. New York: Penguin, vii–xx.

Stephenson, Neal (1992) *Snow Crash*. New York: Spectra.

Sterling, Philip (1937) 'Sowing the 16mm Field: Hays Office Cultivation May Produce a Harvest for the Amateur Experts', *New York Times*, 25 July, C7, 3.

Suskind, Ron (2004) 'Without a Doubt', *New York Times Magazine*, 17 October. Available at: http://cscs.umich.edu/~crshalizi/sloth/2004-10-16b.html. Accessed 10 October 2007.

Suzuki, Koji (2003) *Ring*, trans. Robert B. Rohmer and Glynne Walley. New York: Vertical.

____ (2006a) *Spiral*, trans. Glynne Walley. New York: Vertical.

____ (2006b) *Loop*, trans. Glynne Walley. New York: Vertical.

Swenson, John (1974) 'Campus Video: Portapak Backing', *Crawdaddy*, November, 32.

Taubin, Amy (2007) 'The Big Rupture: David Lynch, Richard Kelly, and the New Cinematic Gestalt', *Film Comment*, January/February, 54–9.

Thill, Scott (2006) 'David Lynch Interviews – Uncut', Wired.com, 10 March. Available at: http://www.wired.com/print/culture/lifestyle/news/2007/01/72391. Accessed 17 April 2008.

Trilling, Lionel (1965a [1955]) 'Freud: Within and Beyond Culture', in *Beyond Culture: Essays in Literature and Learning*. New York: Harcourt, Brace, Jovanovich, 77–102.

____ (1965b [1962]) 'The Leavis-Snow Controversy', in *Beyond Culture: Essays on Literature and Learning*. New York: Harcourt, Brace, Jovanovich, 126–54.

Trow, George W. S. (1972) 'Editorial', *National Lampoon*, September, 4–5.

____ (1981) *Within the Context of No Context*. New York: Atlantic Monthly Press.

____ (2004) *The Harvard Black Rock Forest*. Iowa City: University of Iowa Press.

Van Dijck, José (2007) 'Memory Matters in the Digital Age', *Configurations: A Journal of Literature, Science, and Technology*, 12, 3, 349–73.

Van Ness, Elizabeth (2005) 'Is a Cinema Studies Degree Becoming the New M. B. A.?', *New York Times*, 6 March. Available at: http://www.nytimes.com/2005/03/06/movies/0o6vann.html. Accessed 14 September 2007.

Vaux, Rob (2007) 'Grindhouse', *Flipside Movie Emporium*, April. Available at: http://www.flipsidemovies.com/grindhouse.html. Accessed 15 December 2007.

Virilio, Paul (1989) *War and Cinema: The Logistics of Perception*, trans. Patrick Camiller. New York: Verso.

____ (1994) *The Vision Machine*, trans. Julie Rose. London: British Film Institute.

Vollmann, William T. (2003) *Rising Up and Rising Down*, Vol. 1. San Francisco: McSweeney's Books.

Wallace, David Foster (1996) *Infinite Jest*. Boston: Little, Brown.

____ (1997 [1993]) 'E Unibus Pluram: Television and US Fiction', in *A Supposedly Fun Thing I'll Never Do Again*. New York: Little, Brown, 21–82.

Walters, Tim (2004) 'Reconsidering *The Idiots*: Dogma 95, Lars von Trier, and the Cinema of Subversion?', *Velvet Light Trap*, 53, 40–54.

Ware, Chris (1995) *Quimby the Mouse*. Seattle: Fantagraphics Books.

_____ (2000) *Jimmy Corrigan*. New York: Pantheon.

Wasser, Frederick (2001) *Veni, Vidi, Video: The Hollywood Empire and the VCR*. Austin: University of Texas Press.

Waxman, Sharon (2006) 'Cyberface: New Technology that Captures the Soul', *New York Times*, 15 October. Available at: http://www.nytimes.com/2006/10/15/movies/15waxm.html. Accessed 19 December 2007.

Weibel, Peter (2003) 'The Intelligent Image: Neurocinema or Quantum Cinema?', in Jeffrey Shaw and Peter Weibel (eds) *Future Cinema: The Cinematic Imaginary After Film*. Cambridge, MA: MIT Press, 594–601.

Weiberg, Birk (2002) 'Beyond Interactive Cinema'. Available at: http://www.keyframe.org/txt/interact. Accessed 31 January 2008.

Weschler, Lawrence (2006) *Everything that Rises: A Book of Convergences*. San Francisco: McSweeney's.

Williams, I. A. (1923) 'The Importance of Doing Things Badly', *The Living Age*, 671–3.

Williams, Raymond (1976) *Keywords*. London: Fontana Communications Series.

_____ (2001 [1973]) 'Base and Superstructure in Marxist Cultural Theory', *The Raymond Williams Reader*, ed. John Higgins. Oxford: Blackwell, 158–78.

Winslow, Ken (1979) 'Welcome to the Age of Video', *The Video Programs Index*. Syosset: The National Video Clearinghouse, i–v.

Wolk, Douglas (2007) *Reading Comics: How Graphic Novels Work and What They Mean*. Cambridge, MA: Da Capo Press.

Youngblood, Gene (2003) 'Cinema and the Code', in Jeffrey Shaw and Peter Weibel (eds) *Future Cinema: The Cinematic Imaginary After Film*. Cambridge, MA: MIT Press, 156–61.

Zielinski, Siegfried (2006) *Deep Time of the Media: Toward an Archaeology of Hearing and Seeing by Technical Means*, trans. Gloria Custance. Cambridge, MA: MIT Press.

1794